REVIEWS

Beautifully written, freshly conceived, and immensely literate while getting its many (multi-layered and integrated) points across with practically poetic economy.

Michael Tucker D. Litt.
Professor of Poetics
University of Brighton

This will be an important 'seminal' text for all those interested in communicating contemporary meanings through group improvisation and the means it offers the human experience of community. Reflective, energising and informed, Rod Paton argues for the innovative thesis that *Lifemusic* is actually the continual creation and recreation process by which people orient themselves through group improvisation. This book offers a rich tapestry of theoretical discussions and practical approaches for uncovering and describing the phenomena of *Lifemusic*; which is not just for those who compose and perform music for a living but for us all to constitute living more meaningful lives through engagement in group improvisation.

Dr. Pamela Burnard
University of Cambridge
UK.

A quick look at *Lifemusic*...

Rod Paton has been a tireless force for the cause of music-making for decades, concentrating on the kind of music-making that contributes to the health and well-being of both the individual and of society. His work in community music is a perfect example of this, one that goes against the grain of the way most academic music curricula are set up: dividing up everything in separate (read: isolated) divisions, emphasizing immaculate recitation of music from the Great Composers at the expense of expression and communication, music-making for the few rather than music for all. His new book *Lifemusic*: Connecting People to Time weaves a rich tapestry of description of the complex current state of music. The narrative demands time and thought to absorb the many layers of detail, but the effort is well-rewarded. The author's primary aim is, in the end, not political, but to open new "paths of musical renewal through which communities might find new and beneficial forms of self-expression, well-being, collective identity and creative energy." Dr. Paton is keenly aware of how modern life leaves everyone plugged in but isolated. He examines in considerable detail the state of music(s) today in our modern world and the challenges they present to a return to a healthy, healing, active kind of music-making in which all can take part. Paton is interested in prescribing ways for people to engage again in making music and reconnecting with time itself and thus to each other. His answer is a kind of music that anyone can learn, but few do right now, including and especially classical musicians, i.e. (free) improvisation. He discusses the theory behind improvisation and also gives practical suggestions on how to go about it. The depth and breadth of *Lifemusic*'s discussions are tremendous, making it very challenging to a reviewer to more than give the barest outline of the scope of the content. Suffice it to say here that this volume is an absolute must-read for anyone interested in the subject of improvisation. I heartily agree with Paton's definition of improvisation as the primary musical act, and, as such is something that everyone – not just every musician – should be not only interested in, but actively engaged in. The subject is as powerful as it is elusive. By its very nature, improvisation resists both description and method. *Lifemusic* is a landmark volume that conquers those twin challenges and takes its place as a peer of such exalted books as Derek Bailey's *Improvisation: Its Nature and Practice in Music* and Stephen Nachmanovitch's *Free Play: Improvisation in Life and Art*, complementing their message and going beyond in its own way. *Lifemusic* should be required reading for every performer, music educator, music therapist, and everybody else.

Jeffrey Agrell
Professor of Music
University of Iowa

Rod Paton, one of the world's foremost authorities on improvisation, has provided us, in his latest book *Lifemusic*, with a significant addition to the research. *Lifemusic* is a fresh look at improvisation and our involvement with it whether we are musicians or not. Many classically trained musicians will feel challenged by the book but if the reader is open to the exploration of new musical territory they may find huge reward in its pages.

Lifemusic, in essence, is a book about our relationship to the creativity offered by our ability to make sound together. It addresses the impact of the recent development of cultural imbalances which have created, in our time, a sense, for many, of musical impotence. Consumer-oriented imperatives have led to a disconnect of musical experience. Rod describes how most musical experience is now often once-removed from our ability to enjoy the direct expression of soul. Rod's *Lifemusic* project, a series of teachings and experiential workshops, is successfully re-dressing this yawning gap. Much of the meat of this latest book is drawn directly from the project. The book points to ways of reclaiming our ownership, whatever our level of musical ability, of musical creativity and performance.

This book is for everyone who wants to rediscover their inner musical magic.

Andrew Hodges
Violinist & Community Director
www.soundtravelsforum.com

THE AUTHOR

A native of the county of Pembrokeshire in West Wales, Rod's deep, personal interest in music has been part of his make-up since he was a young child. After completing his education in the UK, he spent several years in Eastern Europe, studying composition, horn playing and the music of the Moravian composer Leos Janacek. Since that time, he has worked as a jazz horn player, composer and university teacher, specialising in the social meanings of music and the therapeutic properties of improvisation. In 1995, he completed his doctorate at Sussex University on the theme of musical renewal and since that time has been active in developing community projects which demonstrate the wider accessibility and social functions of creative music. His largest composition, the "Ascension Jazzmass" was described as "a moving testament to the human spirit" (Jazz Journal International) and his book "Living Music" as "a goldmine" (Sounding Board Magazine). He is currently directing a series of music projects along the south coast of England together with a training programme in the *Lifemusic* method.

Photograph by Melanie Durkin

LIFEMUSIC
Connecting People to Time

The Wisdom of the Transpersonal

Journey in Depth: A Transpersonal Perspective
The Fires of Alchemy: A Transpersonal Viewpoint
The Raincloud of Knowable Things: Transpersonal Psychology
Symptom as Symbol: A Transpersonal Handbook

For a full list and details of all our titles
please see our website:

transpersonalbooks.com

LIFEMUSIC
Connecting People to Time

Rod Paton

ARCHIVE publishing

2012

First published in Great Britain by
Archive Publishing
Dorset, England

Designed at Archive Publishing by Ian Thorp

© 2011 Archive Publishing
Text © Dr Rod Paton, 2011

Dr Rod Paton asserts the moral right to be identified
as the author of this work

A CIP Record for this book is available from
The British Cataloguing in Publication data office

ISBN 978-1-906289-14-0
(Sewn Paperback)

All rights reserved. No part of this publication may be reproduced,
stored in a retrieval system, or transmitted at any time or by any means
electronic, mechanical, photocopying, recording or otherwise,
without the prior permission of the publisher.

Printed and bound by
Short Run Press
Exeter England

DEDICATION

To the memory of
Doreen Gwendoline Paton,
songbird and soulbird.
1918 – 2004

ACKNOWLEDGEMENTS

I wish to thank all those who have allowed fair usage of quotations, whether formally granted or by default. All are gratefully acknowledged through references in the footnotes and in the bibliography.

Grateful thanks to Nicki Norris for her photography and providing an excellent image of the Creation tapestry, by the late Jean Lurçat, which is in the Bishop Otter Art Collection, University of Chichester and owned by the Bishop Otter Trust..

I am deeply grateful for the use of this image for the book cover, permission for which has been sought from the Jean Lurçat Estate.

FOREWORD

In *The Magic Mountain* (1924), his multi-layered investigation of the dialectics of illness and health, Thomas Mann observed that music "quickens time, she quickens us to the sharpest enjoyment of time". Like many before me, I've long felt that Mann's central insight into the mystery of this art and its relation to time, and vice versa, merited at least another book's worth of further such insight and congruent elaboration. Finally, such a book has appeared. With *Lifemusic: Connecting People To Time* Rod Paton has given us a quite magnificent meditation on the theme of music and time.

Superbly researched, its wide-ranging social and historical literacy and many musical, philosophical and mytho-poetic insights are presented in the sort of lucid, reader-friendly text which should ensure that *Lifemusic* assumes its natural place alongside the published reflections of, for example, George Russell and Sir Michael Tippett, Joseph Campbell, Christopher Small and Peter Michael Hamel.

Rod Paton is both an accomplished, jazz-loving musician, very much aware of the value of improvisation, and a striking composer, of diverse scale and compass. Employing shaman-like overtone singing as well as bebop-fired jazz improvisation, his Ascension Jazzmass (recorded live at the Turner Sims Concert Hall at the University of Southampton in 2000) was scored for female vocalist, 4-part choir, 9-part jazz ensemble and organ, plus 21 marimba-style xylophones. In the sleeve-note for the recording, issued on Cornucopia/*Lifemusic*, Rod explained that the idea of using the xylophones came to him in a dream, "…in which I was surrounded by xylophone music. When I asked a villager what the piece was about he explained that it was the 'Music of Life' and, should it stop, the world would come to an end".

In today's world, where music – especially recorded music – is ever present, the prospect of such a cataclysmic fate might seem 'simply' the stuff of which dreams (or rather, nightmares) are made. But Rod Paton is not just a musician and a composer with a capacity to dream. Blessed with a 'journeying' soul, he is also a most unusual academic: a university lecturer endowed in equal measure with an open-minded critical intelligence and a discriminating appetite for both the visible sociopolitical detail of history and the power of the psychological archetype which may underlie (and perhaps help us challenge and transform) such detail.

As someone who has thought long and hard about the condition of music today, and who has both the intellectual means and the poetic sensibility to penetrate deeply – creatively – into its many mysteries, Rod is critically aware of how much the presence of what one might call so much pre-packaged music today may signify, not so much any increase in our sense of being, or 'world', but rather a diminishing of the same.

As an educator and an enabler who, through his many *Lifemusic* workshops, has worked tirelessly to help people from all walks of life come to appreciate the creative extent of their own (perhaps previously unsuspected) musicality, Rod Paton has long been concerned to help us sense how much we may be able to reclaim, or revision, the truly creative, even transformative, potentialities of the medium which has fascinated him all his life.

Hence this excellent book, as practical in import as it is both poetic and philosophical in its freshly cast investigative verve. Enjoy!

Michael Tucker D. Litt.
Professor of Poetics
University of Brighton

TABLE OF CONTENTS

Prelude   14
Introduction: Connecting to Time   21

Part 1   The Concept of Lifemusic

Chapter 1   The Kairos of Transition   33
Chapter 2   Orphic States   61
Chapter 3   Unforeseen Magic   109
Chapter 4   Pathways to Healing   133

Part 2   The Practice of Lifemusic

Chapter 5   Defining *Lifemusic*   169
Chapter 6   The Uses of *Lifemusic*   195
Chapter 7   General Principles of Group Improvisation   219
Chapter 8   Patterns, Projects and Pieces   241

Postlude   *Lifemusic* in Action (CD)   275
Bibliography   277
Index   282

PRELUDE

This book offers both a perspective on the contemporary condition of music and some practical ideas for enrichment and expansion. In doing so, it casts a somewhat critical eye on many aspects of current musical activity which most people take for granted, such as the ubiquity of recorded music, the classical concert, the hegemony of the music industry and graded examinations. However, whilst advocating a renewal of our personal, social and cultural relationship to music it is not my intention to argue for the dismantling of *any* musical practice. It would be impossible as well as futile to attempt to sweep away cultural habits which are, for whatever reasons, embedded in the fabric of society. As I argue at the beginning of Chapter 6, the word 'culture' has many meanings, one of which is connected to the ways in which forms of art-making reflect prevailing social conditions, political structures and the collective intentionality of populations. The current state of musical affairs, the diverse ways in which we collectively use music, can therefore be understood as an inevitable result of the particular aspirations of our cultural history, a kind of sonic barometer which measures the myth[1] of that history. Thus, the multi-layered and complex political economy of music which drives contemporary practice might be regarded as an accurate reflection of the diverse ways in which our culture thrives and organises itself. Yet, it seems to me that it is equally important to acknowledge what is inevitably lost when we accept without question the prevailing cultural patterns which resonate through our musical practices and to address those aspects of musical experience which are neglected, by-passed or eclipsed by the overwhelmingly consumer-driven model to which most of us subscribe. The primary motivation for writing this book is then not to bemoan the condition of music but to enrich it, opening up paths of musical renewal through which communities might find new and beneficial forms of self- expression, well-being, collective identity and creative energy.

Some years ago, the composer and writer Maxwell Steer organised a series of conferences labelled *Music and Psyche*. Initially, these gatherings were primarily academic, connected to the publication of two editions of

---

[1] I use this term to denote a communal belief system which is reflected in cultural patterns many of which are accepted without question by the population at large.

Contemporary Music Review devoted to the subject of Music and Mysticism[2]. Yet in these volumes and the gatherings which grew from the writings, we encounter a quest, if not a longing, to re-connect with musical experience as an *expression of soul*, a need to renew musical culture in such a way that the capacity of music to take us not merely into the interiority of self but beyond the self into a transpersonal space is acknowledged and nurtured. For the conferences, Steer brought together an impressive range of figures including composers such as Jonathan Harvey and John Tavener, visionary writers such as Michael Tucker and musicians such as Frank Perry and Paul Robertson all of whom, in a variety of ways, seemed to be seeking a renewal of music's inner qualities. Following these ground-breaking conferences and recognising that re-introducing soul into contemporary musical practice might require something of a paradigm shift, a small group, which included myself, Maxwell Steer, composers Peter Wiegold, Jenni Roditi and Clement Jewitt, music therapists Sarah Verney-Caird and Susan Nares plus several specially invited musical guests, began a series of gatherings on Holy Island in Anglesey where we began to explore, mainly through group improvisation, new musical forms infused with the spirit of place, the rise and fall of the tides, time, dreams, the seasons, the landscape and, most of all perhaps, the flowing structures of the relationships of those making the music which, needless to say, were not without inevitable tensions and conflicts as well as purposive attunement. Spending even short periods of time isolated from the constant flow of mediated sound, recorded and notated forms, commercial imperatives and fixed genres, the *Music and Psyche* project began to develop a glimpse of what music could offer to the soul when stripped down and recast in its primary forms.

At around the same time, under the inspirational leadership of psychotherapist and writer Dr. Marie Angelo, the University of Chichester was developing a unique Masters programme in Transpersonal Arts and Practice to which I was invited to contribute a course based around the Music and Psyche project. For five years, groups of mainly mature students, only some of whom were trained musicians but all of whom were focused on re-imagining the world through arts and therapy, gathered for study days, improvising, communing, toning, attuning and reflecting, exploring the power of music to connect us to time and memory, place and persona, spirit and soul. I owe a great debt to these

---

2   Contemporary Music Review, Music & Mysticism Vol. 14, 1/2 1996. Routledge, London.

students and their enthusiasm for a project which deepened my own understanding of music's transpersonal qualities and which led in part to the decision to write this book.

Alongside these developments and in a more visible and public arena the practice of community music has been slowly but steadily developing. There has been and continues to be plenty of discussion around the term 'community music' but however we choose to label it, there appears to be a significant upsurge amongst people of all ages to reclaim the ownership of musical creation and performance, something which for so long has been the domain of composers, producers, impresarios and the music industry and to explore new ways through which people might participate directly in music-making. From the pioneering work of the late John Stevens and the radical writings of Christopher Small to the expanded educational visions of academics such as Pamela Burnard and Lee Higgins and the inspirational work of animateurs such as Phil Mullen, Bruce Cole, Pete Moser and Richard McNicol, and assisted by organisations such as Sound Sense under the tireless leadership of Kathryn Deane, community music is forging a steady path, providing an increasing number of alternative social contexts and cultural paradigms for music and music-making. The formation of Sound Sense in 1990, the UK professional association for community musicians, as well as organisations such as Youth Music and Music Leader, point towards new horizons beyond which the creativity present in every human might be granted space and time to thrive and sound out. Through the numerous initiatives, activities and projects generated by these organisations some of which connect up with traditional centres of musical excellence such as symphony orchestras, opera companies and recording companies, more and more people are beginning to appreciate the vast benefits – personal, social, emotional, mental and spiritual, which are to be derived from participatory music-making.

So whilst some of the ideas outlined in these pages appear as radical alternatives to contemporary practice they are offered within this framework of social and musical renewal, complementing what is already available or providing practical ideas which could be usefully woven into current forms of music-making. However, thinking outside of the box in this way inevitably leads to some notions which may seem challenging or even to some minds, unrealistic. There are already numerous examples of group music-making in contexts such as schools, health-care environments, arts centres and other workshop venues. But what would happen, for example, if improvised music was to be introduced, even in small doses, directly into places where people work, a modern equivalent of the work-song perhaps, but not in fields of cotton or rice paddies but in the office, the computer room and in employees' rest rooms and staff clubs? What if the boardroom itself was to be enhanced by managers and company directors devoting small amounts of time engaging in group improvisation? At the very least, this would prevent it becoming a bored room! What would be the effects on major decisions made by civil servants, politicians, police or even the military should discussions begin and end with a short session of group drumming? So, whilst asking questions about the *soul* functions of music, this book simultaneously examines the *social* functions of music. In discussing how music affects us, why we need it and how it works, I am also suggesting that these primary functions are in many ways absent, narrowed down, weakened or even blocked by contemporary forms of production, mediation and education. I am considering therefore how desirable it might be to expand ownership, participation and autonomy in its creation and in its social uses and how enriching it might be to bring the soul functions and the social functions of music into closer proximity.

If people, many of whom would not readily describe themselves as musicians, are to be able to engage in creative musical activity, then perhaps it is necessary both to expand our definitions of music and simultaneously to provide the means by which anyone can participate. One of the primary precepts of *Lifemusic*, as defined at the beginning of part 2 of the book, is 'everybody is musical', a proposition which is borne out by my own experience of working with groups over a long period of time. I have not yet met anyone who was incapable of engaging in musical activity, not just as a listener or audience member, but as a lively and creative participant. The ingredient of *Lifemusic*, as a method, which makes this possible is *improvisation* and therefore discussion of this fundamental (though insufficiently acknowledged) musical practice forms a significant part of the book, both theoretically, in chapters 3 and 4 and practically in part 2. In the modern world, the practice of improvisation is largely absent from classical musical training and performance, virtually ignored in popular forms and only significantly employed in jazz and jazz-related musics. 'Free' improvisation, meaning spontaneous music-making which is not wedded to any specific style, idiom or genre, despite having some strong advocates, is almost entirely ignored except within small arenas[3] and within the contained world of music therapy where it is actually a core activity. So this book presents both a theory of improvisation, based on the notion of the 'holding form' plus a set of practical guidelines which grow from the same principle which it is hoped people will use in whichever ways they wish, to discover for themselves the surprising joys and profound benefits which can come from improvising music together. Examples of improvisations based upon selected holding forms can be heard on the accompanying CD.

A book such as this does not emerge from an isolated pocket of ideas but is the sum of experiences and activities involving many other people. I owe a debt to those who have, over many years, shared in various ways the musical journey which led to the development of the *Lifemusic* concept and method. First and foremost, the many students from what is now the University of Chichester who, over the years, have been willing to expand their musical horizons through often experimental improvisatory workshops as well as engaging in lively and challenging discussion. Former students who have since become fellow improvisers and longstanding friends include the versatile musician Nigel Rippon, creative keyboardist Laurence Burrow (aka Monty OxyMoron), jazz musician and teacher Nick Reynolds and bassoon player Alison Gall who can be heard playing alongside the inspirational Suzie Shrubb on the CD which accompanies this book. For many years, groups of students such as these would meet regularly on Thursday evenings to improvise with breadth and freedom and to no other purpose than to explore the capacity of music to emerge spontaneously from the moment. Students would often comment on how each evening was unique and would often bemoan the absence of recording equipment which would have preserved these sessions for posterity. Yet how would it ever have been possible to record the *experience* of these events or the deep satisfaction and sense of community which was often so palpable at the close of a session? The magic would get lost in translation and despite a general wish to hold onto the special feelings which emerged from each session, it is unlikely that the recordings (and some do still exist) would be listened to again except for academic purposes. And is an audio recording really the best way of achieving posterity? Better by far, as I often remarked, to believe that the next live event would result in equally rich and unique music-

---

3 The late Steve Harris, drummer and community musician, established his "safe house" concept to provide spaces where people could improvise freely and without any fixed adherence to genre or style. But such instances are relatively rare.

making. And it always did.

I must also acknowledge the influence and inspiration of colleagues from the same institution, especially those from the period when the inspirational Related Arts degree programme (now sadly no longer running) gave us the opportunity to collaborate creatively across different disciplines – dance, fine art, music, film, drama and creative writing combining in surprising and enlightening ways to open up original perspectives on art and life. I thank in particular Dr. John Saunders, (who was able to demonstrate the riches and significance of modernism to generations of students through his revelatory teaching style) and my wonderful late friend and colleague Dr. Hugo Donnelly whose improvisational manner of lecturing belied a deeply informed understanding of philosophy and literature and with whom conversation so often touched on the mysterious properties of soul.

Over a long period of time I have also been fortunate to play alongside numerous jazz musicians whose improvisational skills and dedication to the art of jazz have been revealing as well as inspiring. I owe a debt to friends such as Bruce McGavin, Nick Sorensen and Julian Nicolas and to the indefatigable pianist Ray d'Inverno who has been so tirelessly supportive not only to myself but to so many other musicians, young and old. Not least, I thank Tony Woods as much for his passionate and remarkable saxophone playing as for his modest and generous heart.

Some years ago I was assisted in running longer *Lifemusic* workshops, extending to whole weekends, by singer/songwriter Philip Milburn and the violinist and life coach Andrew Hodges who has also been tireless in developing the excellent online Sound Travels forum[4]. More recently I have been inspired by the opportunity to improvise alongside people from various walks of life who have undertaken the *Lifemusic* training, many of whom have had no previous formal musical instruction. In particular, the energetic and enthusiastic Chris North, who has been able to demonstrate how the simplest of musical means can be used to bring joy directly into the lives of families and children and Mike Fry, who combines exceptional musical gifts with the selfless ability to communicate with and to inspire people with varying levels of ability to make music.

I need to express my sincere gratitude to 'lifemusician' Alison Mawdsley and her daughter Hannah for their invaluable assistance in preparing the text. Finally, this book might never have been completed

---

4 www.soundtravels.co.uk

were it not for the warm support and encouragement of Jitka Vanyskova whose idyllic hideaway in the Moravian woods provided the perfect space in which to write.

Lifemusic is then presented both as philosophy and method, a set of reflections on the nature of music and time and a practical pathway towards musical renewal, a means through which people from all walks of life can connect to time, since, as I argue in the introduction, music could be defined, perhaps simply as the *intentional time*. However, such a definition also recognises time and space as a continuum so that, in connecting to time, through music, we are also connecting profoundly to the space in which we are present at precisely that moment and equally profoundly to whoever happens to be present with us in that space at that precise moment. To be truly present is to be aware: of time, of space, of self, of others and, perhaps also beyond the self, of the transpersonal. *Improvisation creates presence*: the moment in which music is created represents a unique coalescence of time, space and circumstance and the structure of music will inevitably represent this synchronicity, imbuing the event with significance. Those who share the moment, who come together at precisely this point in time to create such music for themselves will surely find the experience enriching, revelatory, healing and above all, *numinous*. What else is music for?

INTRODUCTION

Connecting to Time

Time is one of the great archetypal experiences of man, and has eluded all our attempts towards a completely rational explanation.[5]

The universe was created with time and not in time.(St. Augustine)

This book is about time and how we connect to it, though it is not, as some readers may (or may not) be glad to discover, about quantum theory or particle physics but about music. Time is the autonomous, unconditional, inevitable and ultimately, mysterious process through which life grows and decays and music not only measures time, delineating in a purely abstract but palpable way its passage but it also infuses time with emotional significance and therefore, with meaning: in this sense, it creates out of time a hermeneutic canvas. So the connection to time, through music, becomes also a connection to ourselves, to our senses and how we make sense of ourselves in relation to the world. Music therefore connects us both to the rhythmic quality of our inner lives and feelings, and to those external events and rituals which measure our passage through life and determine our cultural understanding: music not only makes us conscious of time but it simultaneously deepens our awareness of time's significance. We therefore use music not merely as an accompaniment to life (although we may sometimes think that that is all it is doing) but as a barometer of the inner and outer patterns which make life more than a set of random events that somehow take place between birth and death. Music connects us to time and in so doing, it deepens our connection to life itself. The concept and the practice of *Lifemusic* grow out of this epistemology.

Throughout this book, I will be focusing on the degree to which the way we use music, culturally and socially, acknowledges (or fails to acknowledge) its capacity to articulate time and thus to express the significance of the moment. This places music more in the domain of "Kairos" than "Kronos". In Greek, "kairos" means not simply time but the appropriate moment for an event to take place or the significance lent

---

5 Von Franz, Marie-Louise (1978).

to an event through the moment in which it happens. It means "felt time" as distinct from delineated time, qualitative as opposed to quantitative. It is about our capacity to understand the import of where we are in time and then to act accordingly. If, through lack of awareness, lack of courage or simply bad luck, we fail to appreciate the fateful quality of the moment and "miss the boat", then difficulties, if not tragedy can follow. The yellow lemon butterfly hatches at the precise moment when the lemon blossom, the source of its nourishment, appears; if it emerges too early or too late it flies around in vain and eventually dies[6]. Its survival therefore depends upon its alignment with "kairos". "Kronos" on the other hand, regulates time with clocks, bells and timetables. The "old man of time" keeps the trains running and ensures that we turn up on time for our lessons but he may be insensitive to those inner needs which often require the timetable to be suspended or the carefully laid out plan to be abandoned or the journey to be more leisurely. I shall return to this theme in more detail in Chapter 1.

Defining music

As a teacher, I have often asked my students the simple question "what is music?" Answers to this question are inevitably variable in both length and content. Some will argue that music is essentially an expressive tool, their answers emphasising what music does. For example, "it uses sounds to express joy or passion" or, 'it helps me to relax". Others, of a more scientific frame of mind, will home in on the physical properties of music, focusing on what music is. For example, "patterns of sound and vibration in the air". Unsurprisingly, many students, "schooled" musicians with perhaps many years of conventional and theoretical musical training behind them, will talk of melody, harmony, musical instruments or even scales or notated scores as the basis of their definitions. (Indeed, in English, since "music" also means the written texts which represent the sound music makes, a sentence such as, 'did you remember to bring your music with you?' could appear nonsensical.) Usually the discussion will develop in a reductive direction, searching for an axiomatic definition that will be true under all conditions and for all cultures. Is music simply "wiggling air molecules" (Zappa) or "organised sound" (Varese)? Is it capable of expressing "a whole world" (Mahler) or is it "incapable of expressing anything at all" (Stravinsky)? Is it a "portal to the soul of the world" (Kepler)? Is music

---

[6] There is a beautiful poem by Eduard Morike called *Zitronenfalter in April*, set to music by Hugo Wolf, which expresses this microcosmic tragedy.

"the form of our feelings" (Langer), expression or form, or both (Meyer)?

Quite often, at some point in the discussion, someone will mention John Cage's notorious or celebrated (depending on your point of view) composition, originally published for solo piano in 1946, titled *4'33"*. It would be fair to say, that, over the years, in my own experience, this little piece has generated more discussion or, frequently, heated debate, than almost any other work I can think of. Why should this be so, when each of its three variable length movements is simply marked "tacet", i.e. *silent*, requiring no physical intervention whatsoever from the performer apart from some indication that the piece has begun and when it ends. Some feel outraged or simply baffled that a work such as this should have achieved published status in the first place. "Who collects the royalties?" is an often asked question. Occasionally, when for example the work was recorded on CD or, more recently, when an orchestral version was performed at London's prestigious Barbican Centre, the debate spills out into the media with the inevitable resulting discussion and punditry. Opinions vary widely, often revealing much more about the attitudes and feelings of the commentators towards the phenomenon of music than about the piece itself. Almost invariably, it is the lack of any concrete, objectified reality in *4'33"* which causes the most problems. People, it seems, require music, a) to make some sounds, b) to be entertaining, c) to stir the emotions, d) to demonstrate effort and skill on the part of the composer and the performer. In other words, people want music to be an identifiable object which has a cause (clever vibrations) and an effect (good feelings). An often heard argument in favour of the piece is that the sounds of the environment which occur by chance within the allotted time span actually become the music. Whilst I am sure this reflects the composer's own interest in *aleatory*, that is, in the significance of chance events, it does not entirely convince. Indeed, during the recording sessions in the Royal Albert Hall some years ago, the production team decided on a re-take because of a background rumbling which turned out to be a distant tube train!

If, however, we shift our thinking towards the *experience* of the piece, as opposed to its existence as an *object*, if we can strip away the concrete nature of our expectations and expose the fluctuating qualities of our emotions, it becomes clear that the work provides an experience which rests, simply and uniquely, in time. After all, this property of the piece is neatly contained in its title: it does what it says on the label, it lasts 4'33" but, more than that, it divides this time into three 'movements' each of different duration, a fact often ignored. So by stripping music down to its one essential ingredient, time, and then not requiring any further intervention in the process, Cage presents the listener with a satisfying, somewhat mysterious, even mystical realisation, that music is, quite simply, *intentional time*; periodicity with purpose; precisely measured, significant moments set aside in order to be mindful of time as it passes.

It often feels to me as if Cage's genius in conceiving this work and then his courage in publishing it rests in his realisation that we, (in the developed world at any rate) needed to somehow 'zero out' before starting again: the *principle of renewal*. Music within the European tradition had become so complex, so composed, so clever and so self-conscious that it became necessary to reduce it to next to nothing in order to remind ourselves of its mystery. So if the answer to our question 'what is music?' is *intentional time* we might begin to see that this provides us with a starting point both for a fresh understanding of what music is and what music does. Moreover, it reveals the deep connection between music and life itself, at the heart of which stands the mystery of time. It might also point the way to how we might all be able to participate in its creation. These three pillars – renewal, connection and creativity – provide support for the discussion and ideas contained here.

Arnold Schoenberg, who would not accept Cage as a student due to his lack of skill in harmony, is quoted as saying "one always goes back", yet even he was unwilling to take this radical step into the obvious but culturally neutral zone of pure time. He was, in a sense, ensnared by his own genius, having a comprehensive grasp of the great European tradition in his extraordinary musical mind which would not let him go. A 'reluctant revolutionary' he was in this sense, like so many other musicians working within the confines of the European canon, imprisoned in the cage of tradition and it needed somebody who was, ironically, called 'Cage' to discover how to open the gates, and fly free.

So what of time?

Time is a prayer
And time is a spirit,
And time is a shadow
And time is the wind.

These words of writer and lyricist John Mash[7] express poetically something of the mystery, meaning and magic of time. It seems to me that the essence of both life and music rests in the fluctuating quality of our relationship with time and the passing of time. We spend endless time talking and writing about the past, trying to make sense of history; we spend even more time perhaps planning and fretting about the future; we are in danger of losing contact with the present. *Lifemusic*, both as theory and as practice, aims to connect people to time past, time future but, most importantly, to time present and in the process to articulate and deepen our relationship with ourselves, with others and with this ultimately mysterious essence of life. Throughout the book I shall be exploring the notion that Music is the universal language which makes our connection to time real, audible, coherent, sensate and therefore meaningful.

It was a musician, a mathematician and a seer, Pythagoras, who first demonstrated the natural properties as well as the inherent rationality of musical sound and, following his lead, we can safely say that the laws of music are deeply embedded in the autonomous laws of nature. More recently, Joachim Berendt (1985) in his radio broadcasts and books based on the Hindu principle of *Nada Brahma – the World as Sound* attempted to demonstrate how these fundamental properties of music are relevant for the contemporary world. As musical consumers living in the developed world, with its emphasis on music as a commodity, such notions might appear a little far-fetched but that only serves to demonstrate how narrow our definition of music has become. After all, it was not so long ago that music was considered to be our principal point of access to the mysteries of the cosmos, the *harmony of the spheres*. I hope therefore that this book will demonstrate how much more broadly music can be defined and applied in our own time and how its inherent but often forgotten properties may be accessed at a level where it can enhance our lives in a surprising number of ways. This esoteric function of music is at the heart of Peter Michael Hamel's (1978) book "Through Music to the Self" where he writes of virtually ignored contemporary pioneers developing musical practices only now in their infancy. Following Hamel's lead I aim to explore not merely the many ways in which music develops and expands the sense of "Self" but also how it takes us beyond the Self. This connection between music and life is what gives the book its title.

---

7 Mash is a writer who lives in Salisbury. These words form the refrain of a song called 'Chichester's Children' from his 2008 play of the same title.

The transpersonal quality of music

Although music may be considered a language, (and it is certainly governed by many of the prerequisites by means of which we define language) it is in reality an entirely unique phenomenon through which our connection to time is equally uniquely articulated. Time may be encountered most immediately through music since, unlike other means we use to delineate temporal experience sound itself is abstract and immaterial: after all, as Frank Zappa (1989) expressed it, music is no more than 'wiggling air molecules'. Human beings have generally used moving objects to represent, measure or regulate the passing of time, whether these be celestial, (such as the sun, the moon and the stars), or human inventions which reflect the celestial, such as clocks, calendars and time tables, all of which give us some sense of control over time's passage. More recently, time has been explored through the modern physics which emanates from Einstein's theories in forms of mathematics accessible only to relatively (sic) few people. Yet, the theory of relativity only serves to reinforce the notion of time as a mystery which cannot be understood or explained by simple observation. But we do not need to be mathematical geniuses to experience music and it is only through music perhaps that we can *all*, regardless of background or ability, experience time, not merely as an objective phenomenon but also as an affective encounter, *felt time*. Only, it seems to me, do dance, theatre and film come anywhere near this special condition of music, since they are also time-dependent art forms. Yet even these media work with moving objects and images or else with the literal and logical properties of speech and thought. Somehow, music suspends thought, continues where speech ends, extends gesture, enables us to experience images with peculiar emotional force and, whilst it may move the body as well as the emotions, it is in no way dependent on either.

This seems to place music within the *transpersonal* domain: the autonomous laws which govern music may be ultimately beyond human intervention and however far musical theorists attempt to measure and quantify its laws, they inevitably fall short, often missing the most vital point which is that, when composers compose or improvisers improvise they are simply following a trail, or, as Stravinsky famously remarked after creating the Rite of Spring, "merely vessels" through which the music passes. Both creating music and listening to music puts us in touch therefore with a reality which is beyond the self and in the process this enables us to encounter the self at a different, enhanced level of consciousness. We have all experienced this, for example, in films where an otherwise perfectly innocent image or action is totally transformed by the addition of as little as a single held tone or the beating of a drum.

The transpersonal quality of music is also demonstrated by the term we most commonly use to describe the function of music in the contemporary world, "entertainment". That this term has come to mean something which is peripheral to the real business of living reveals much about the way in which a culture centred on, indeed obsessed with, material objects, orders its priorities. Yet, 'entertainment' in essence means something which, far from being at the margins of life, is at the heart of things, literally holding us together, integrating soul and body. In this sense, "entertainment" makes it possible to experience life with greater integrity, in greater depth and with enhanced awareness. By entertaining us, music shifts our consciousness of things into a deeper space, a domain which is, literally, integral to our being. Music turns life into soul.

Participating in music

But *Lifemusic* is not just a concept and this book therefore also has a practical application, presenting a model for musical participation through which people and communities may readily connect to time. So whilst the first part of the book explores the nature and functions of music itself – *Lifemusic* as a concept – the second part demonstrates some of the ways in which music might be readily integrated into everyday life, including a range of activities and projects primarily designed for group music-making – *Lifemusic* as a method. The foundation for these projects is the practice of improvisation since, as I will argue, it is through improvised music that we can become instantly and intimately connected to music and thus to time, to each other and to life as a whole. We improvise constantly, whilst conversing or cooking, for example, but also from moment to moment as we plan our futures and create the narratives of our lives and we might also presume that natural life is also a form of improvisation in its creative unpredictability (think of the weather). From the arcane world of particle physics there is also some evidence to suggest that the basis of living matter provides an analogy for, if not replicates and depends upon improvisation, or working with probabilities. But improvised music, literally the *unforeseen* but felt immediacy of the next moment in time, provides a means, the only means perhaps, through which we can readily, from instant to instant, encounter time and its felt properties: time as motion and emotion.

However, human life, at least in the developed (minority) world has generated a strong belief in the primacy of planning and control (think of weather forecasts) and our general attitude towards music reflects this need for *predictable outcomes*. Composed music, which, together with recorded music, has become a cultural norm in the west and increasingly globally, both perpetuates this myth[8] and keeps us at a distance from time since, by definition, it removes us from the immediate moment in which the music came into being: in other words, it dislocates us from time. In the case of music of the classical tradition this often means that we are experiencing music which was originally improvised and composed in some cases many centuries ago and in the case of recorded music the living process which gave the music life has been re-routed through digital electronics and speaker cones so that it comes to us essentially via a sophisticated system of numbers. Very often this re-routing means that we often listen to it in the most unlikely or inappropriate contexts, a dislocation of both space and time[9].

Furthermore, composed and recorded music leaves us dependent on the expertise of highly trained individuals with specialist skills – composers, musicians and recording engineers mainly, who create and mediate the music for us, reducing many people to the role of passive consumers as opposed to active creators. This is not to pour scorn on any of the great (art) music which exists within these embedded cultural frameworks but the notion of *Lifemusic* aims to bring musical activity, creativity and mediation back to people, regardless of background, age, ability or training so that the music becomes a direct representation not only of the time and the place to which it belongs but also of the people who are making it happen. This restores to music a quality of action and creates a verb, to musick, out of the noun, *music*[10]. And perhaps NOW is precisely the historical moment when this renewal of our relationship to music and to time is not merely desirable but, perhaps inevitable.

---

8 I use the word "myth" here to describe a collectively held set of beliefs which are accepted, though often unconsciously, as social and cultural norms.
9 My favourite example of this is of hearing Gregorian chant on the car radio whilst stuck in a traffic jam on the M25!
10 The re-introduction of this verb into the English language has been advocated by Christopher Small in various writings, most recently in Musicking (1998). Wesleyan University Press.

About this book

This book is intended to be of use and interest to a wide variety of people: academics, musical and cultural historians, musicologists, professional musicians, music teachers and music therapists. It is also aimed at the rapidly growing numbers of musicians from all types of background and training (or none) who are seeking alternative ways of sharing their musical skills precisely at a time when people from many walks of life are looking for ways in which they can participate creatively in music-making themselves and use music directly to enhance and enrich their own lives. It aims to contribute and seeks to support a growing area of cultural activity, now generally termed *community music*, through which, in the words of Chris Small it will be possible to "give back to people the music that belongs to them." Since the primary precept of *Lifemusic* is "everyone is musical" this book is offered to absolutely anybody who wishes to discover how to use music directly and creatively in their lives and in their work.

Part 1 of the book – *The Concept of Lifemusic* – deals with the philosophical, historical and cultural background whilst Part 2 – *The Practice of Lifemusic* – outlines the method, suggesting where, how and with whom it can be used. This part ends with a set of guidelines for participatory music-making and a CD which demonstrates some of the work in action.

The first chapter takes its title, *The Kairos of Transition* from an essay by James Hillman (1967/1979) in which he outlines the unique characteristics of the current historical period, a time of transition, polarities and conflict, warning of the dangers of the failure to acknowledge and respond to the special challenges which our time presents. If music has the capacity to connect people to time, then it might also be expected to play a primary role in our response to the contemporary world though not perhaps, as I argue here, in its currently available forms. This chapter therefore provides a context for *Lifemusic*, outlining what purpose there might be in making music in a way which, in many respects runs counter to prevailing notions of mediation, conditions which have in many ways objectified music and turned it into an inflated currency. The chapter concludes therefore, with an attempt to relocate music in the mind, perceptions and imagination of the whole person, underlining the importance of music as experience as distinct from object: something we create rather than something we consume.

Chapter 2 titled *Orphic States* then examines musical experience from an archetypal perspective. The notion that music flows with the underlying rhythms and energy of life itself is central to the *Lifemusic* concept and thus, archetypal imagery can be revelatory and invaluable in re-imagining the art of music. The archetypes are employed to demonstrate what are regarded as the four primary properties or functions of music – form, ritual, narrative and affect. This entails exploring musical meaning through some of the images and myths which exist at the roots of European culture and at the heart of musical experience, inevitably focusing on the Orphic tragedy which underlines music's narrative function but equally involving Apollo (representing the archetypes of structure, form and spirit), Dionysus, (the archetypes of transformation, feeling and ritual) and Psyche (the archetypes of affect and soul). It is argued that through relocating musical practice in its archetypal roots, musical renewal becomes more achievable.

The title of Chapter 3, *Unforeseen Magic*, reflects the nature of its subject – improvisation, which means, literally, "unforeseen". The chapter defines improvisation, examining its cultural positioning and briefly charts its curious history in European culture, where, like magic, it came to be regarded with suspicion. From this standpoint, we can begin to understand some of the negativity which still surrounds what is in effect, the primary musical act and more generally, the art of living.

Chapter 4, *Pathways to Healing*, examines the therapeutic qualities of music and considers what the practice of improvisation offers to the soul. It looks more closely at the nature of improvisation itself, how its structures provide a bridge between conscious and unconscious worlds, how it dances in this transitional space – a dance which transforms the dancer. The chapter presents a theory of improvisation, based around the notion of the *Holding Form*, which is intended both to explain something about the structure of the musical imagination as well as providing the basis for a practical and creative tool, something which facilitators, music therapists, teachers and community musicians may well find useful and which therefore leads directly into the second part of the book.

Chapter 5, the first chapter dealing specifically with the practice of *Lifemusic*, outlines the method, introducing four precepts, four ingredients and four levels of musical perception defined as hearing, listening, sensing and feeling. Chapter 6 then directly addresses how *Lifemusic* might be used in the contemporary world beginning by examining the ways in which we define musical culture and suggesting how the notion of *carnival* provides a model for imaginative renewal, both psychologically and socially. The chapter then focuses upon a variety of contexts in which participatory music might have a significant effect, some of which may seem surprising. For example, how might creative music-making be of benefit to civil servants, politicians, corporate management or even to the police and the military? It is only our tendency to separate the creative imagination from rational decision-making which makes this seem a strange idea. The chapter concludes by suggesting how one of the largely lost functions of music might be restored, its potential to measure people's progression of experience through the annual cycle; how it can articulate those rituals which connect us to time in a form which is both practical and natural, renewing the capacity of music to mark the seasons and express the underlying rhythms and meanings of life.

Chapter 7 provides a practical set of guidelines for improvisation. The holding form approach is now reintroduced as a facilitating tool, providing creative frameworks through which improvisations can emerge and around which musicking can build and grow. This chapter also includes the '*Lifemusic*ian's Toolkit', an outline of the most useful instruments currently available and some ideas as to how they may be best employed.

The final chapter presents the method itself, through exercises, games, projects and themes, a practical and useable but hopefully never over-prescriptive raft of ideas for people to use as they will. Each exercise and game is an access point into the deeper and more maze-like *Holding Form*. Even ten minutes of improvising a day can make a world of difference to a person's mood, energy levels, sense of well-being, attitude to self and therefore relationship to others. If *Lifemusic* really is about connecting people to time then some kind of regular practice might be both revealing and life enhancing.

The book is accompanied by a CD – a demonstration of how some of these forms can result in flowing, surprising, even startling improvisations. All the tracks are based upon games and exercises included in the final chapter.

How to use this book

Although this book sets out the concept before the method it is not intended in any way to be read from cover to cover. So if your interest is mainly theoretical, read on. But if you want to get straight into the 'musicking' turn now to Part 2 to start using some of the forms immediately. You may then wish to dip in and out of the theoretical ideas contained in Part 1 according to what interests you. The core of the practice suggested here revolves around improvisation so, in using the book, please, *improvise*.

PART ONE

The Concept of *Lifemusic*

CHAPTER 1

THE KAIROS OF TRANSITION

In dance and music we express the rhythmicity of our whole structure – these are the arts through which we relate to time and give it meaning.[11]

Diversity and Polarity

The concept of *Lifemusic* is built on the notion that music has the capacity to connect people to time so I begin by taking a closer look at the time in which we live, the contemporary world, its special characteristics and qualities, considering how the music which is available to us, which has been created in this time, reflects these conditions. Nobody would doubt that we live in a period of extraordinary change, diversity, contrasts and polarities. James Hillman (1979) has commented upon how such conditions are often to be experienced towards the end of long periods of history, echoing Jung's (1959) notion that we are in transition between the Piscean and Aquarian ages and that the new aeon "will constellate the problem of the union of opposites".[12] Such periods as ours present peculiar and far-reaching challenges both physically and psychically: we respect and honour tradition and often cling to the old ways of doing things, yet, simultaneously, we seek renewal and therefore we constantly try to find ways to reinvent ourselves. We can look back over 2 millennia to the birth of Christ (which provides us with our *common era* calendar as well as our historical religious beliefs), or 3 thousand years to the stirrings of Hellenism (which

---

11 Marie-Louise von Franz, op.cit.
12 Jung, C.G. (1959) Page 87.

provides us with so many of our basic tools of thinking as well as our utopian politics) and in doing so we are prompted to record, evaluate and celebrate the past in a wide variety of social and cultural activities. At the same time, we have a sharpened appetite for the new in the knowledge that traditional methods are fast becoming obsolete and inevitably prone to failure – their time is past. So whilst the paintings of the old masters still carry enormous price tags and the music of Bach, Beethoven and Mozart continues to fascinate, the Turner prize celebrates (most recently for example) the transitional, the ephemeral and the conceptual whilst much contemporary music appears to be reinventing itself on an almost daily basis.[13]

We might list some of the polarities which colour and define the contemporary world: in social economy, the enormous divide between rich and poor; in global economy, the gap between developed (minority) and developing (majority) countries; in political economy the contrast between democratic systems and authoritarian regimes; in religion, the yawning chasm between atheism and fundamentalism; in social demography, the division of dwelling places between old and young; in musical culture, the often uneasy divide between popular forms and the classical tradition, pop and art music; the division of media channels into programming for the masses and programmes for the cultural elite. In archetypal psychology, this is expressed as a conflict between *Senex*, the fixed, traditional and sober traditions of the old and *Puer*, the idealistic, inspirational, though often reckless, challenge to tradition presented by the young: in everyday life, we might experience this as the divide between the establishment status quo and youth culture: "ageing leaders and systems attempting to maintain law and order and the rebellions of youth in the name of rights and freedom." (Hillman, op.cit. p. 5)[14] Hillman has described this contemporary world in terms of the Greek concept of 'kairos' – moments in time, transitional periods, which prepare the social, cultural and political ground for major transformations and he emphasises how important it is to acknowledge the significance of such periods.

> *To have no real contact with the forces that are shaping the future would be to fail the kairos of transition. To come to terms with*

---

13 Richard Wright, the artist who won the 2009 Turner prize paints much of his work directly onto the walls of galleries so that when the exhibition closes the work is painted over and disappears for good.
14 This conflict is nowhere better expressed perhaps than in Philip Roth's masterpiece, American Pastoral (1997) where he charts the tragedy of what happened when the utopian and seemingly secure ideals of white American culture were challenged and shattered by the events of the sixties and the rebellions of the dispossessed.

this kairos would mean discovering a connection between past and future. For us, individuals, makeweights that may tip the scales of history, our task is to discover the psychic *connection between past and future, otherwise, the unconscious man within us who is as well the primitive past will shape the historical future perhaps disastrously. Thus the* kairos, *this unique moment of transition in world history, becomes a transition within the microcosm, man, within us each individually as we struggle with the psychological connections between past and future, old and new, expressed archetypally as the polarity of senex and puer.* (Hillman, op.cit. page 4)

So if music is about time and how we connect to it then, far from failing this 'kairos of transition', we might expect music to be capable of harnessing precisely those forces and patterns of renewal which the current period demands. Music has the potential to achieve this because each time a musical act occurs it quite literally connects the past with the future, moving from its starting point in time to its conclusion: in this sense it can be said to provide both remembrance and prophecy, drawing upon the past yet projecting into the future. So in these pages I am asking what kind of musical acts might best serve this process of renewal and what kind of music-making connects us authentically to the time in which we live?

Music education

Some will argue that the major arena for musical renewal is that of music education and there is, currently, plenty of investment here, both in the formal and the non-formal sectors. Yet, the very polarisation which is under discussion here has resulted in a seemingly permanent divide between school music, with its curricula, its graduated approaches to learning and its prescribed outcomes and music beyond the school gates, the music of communities, with its freedom to explore and create, its auto didactic, even haphazard learning shapes and its direct access to cultural roots. If music education is ever going to serve the true demands our time is making on it, then a major paradigm shift is required. Recent initiatives in the field of community music are attempting to bridge this divide[15] but perhaps, as some have argued, music needs to be taken out of schools

---

15 In the UK, the Music Manifesto provides a well-meaning and enlightened statement of intent and an ongoing series of projects, not least the "Sing Up" programme designed to rekindle singing amongst young people, though I fear its potential has been largely misunderstood or ignored by the general public. See www.musicmanifesto.co.uk.

altogether in order to preserve its vitality and its health![16]

The ideas outlined in these pages do not necessarily advocate alternative teaching methods but rather suggest how new forms of music-making might find their way, potentially, into almost any currently existing cultural patterns, projects, initiatives, institutions or social groupings. One of the underlying principles behind the concept of *Lifemusic*, is that musical renewal stems from an inner space, from the realm of the imagination which connects to the individual self and to the collective unconscious and is therefore partly hidden and not easily accessed by most prevailing learning styles.[17] This emphasis on inner process contrasts with much formal musical learning, which is often based upon patterns and styles presented to the young musician from an existing tradition, whether these belong to the historical canon, the music of often long dead composers fixed in its forms and modes of performance or to the equally rigid, though imaginative conventions of blues, jazz and pop music. All of these represent "norms" which have hardened into traditions and therefore run (logically) counter to *renewal*.

There is, of course, nothing intrinsically wrong with such norms or the traditions which they represent and much great music stems from them; a problem arises, however when, as so easily happens, they become 'fetishized' as theory (the case with the classical tradition) or over worked in cultural practice (the case with popular styles) which causes the process of renewal to atrophy. Musical learning has for so long been dogged by theory which is nothing more than a means of fixing common practice at a specific point in its development. Significantly, the theory of music, in as far as it explains how musical structures work, is almost exclusively centred on the European tradition of art music, the theory of harmony and tonality, of pitch relationships and notated forms. Yet, the musical act is, in essence, a primary form of knowledge, an a priori, archetypal reality, which does not need theory any more than the ability to dance depends upon a knowledge of anatomy or the facility of speech requires an understanding of grammar. A true theory of music would be a theory of soul. Throughout this book I attempt to demonstrate that the primary properties of music can be intuitively and imaginatively accessed and employed by all. When allowed to take shape in this inner space, in people's hearts and souls and in the dynamic spaces which exist between

---

16 Andrew Peggie, writing in *Sounding Board*, the journal of Sound Sense, the community music association, in 2001.
17 Attempts to provide kinds of learning environments which acknowledge the primacy of the imagination do exist but tend to be marginalised, e.g. Steiner, Waldorf and Krishnamurti schools.

people in relationships, then renewal – musical, social and cultural – becomes ever more possible. So what stands in the way? Where are the barriers to musical renewal?

Modernism

Part of the problem may simply be fear: fear of the unknown, the unfamiliar, the untested or the unexplored. Such diversity, contrast and conflict as we experience in the current time is indeed frightening and we might often despair at the seemingly impossible task of reconciling people and nation states who represent extreme ends of the spectrum. The crisis of faith and the relative absence of a secure, collectively shared belief system leave us with the choice either to cling ever more strongly to tradition or to work ever harder towards renewal.

C.G. Jung described the dilemma of modern man as *loss of soul*.

> *Modern man has lost all the metaphysical certainties of his medieval brother, and set up in their place the ideals of material security, general welfare and humaneness. But it takes more than an ordinary dose of optimism to make it appear that these ideals are still unshaken. Material security, even, has gone by the board, for modern man begins to see that every step in material progress adds just so much force to the threat of a more stupendous catastrophe. (Jung, 1933 page 235)*

Loss of soul is in fact, etched into the history of music, via the Orphic myth which I will be discussing in greater depth in chapter 2. But the date on which Jung published these words is significant, falling as it does exactly within the modernist period of the last century. In music and the other arts, modernism had responded to the expansion of materialism by plunging into the often nightmarish world of the unconscious, expressing the fear of catastrophe; or else it had embraced materialism itself, creating scenarios which also often appear similarly nightmarish. Examples of the former can be found in the paintings of Kandinsky where the expression seems to flow from a deep unconscious source: spontaneous, highly charged with nervous energy and spiked with half-remembered images which become more abstract as they move closer to their archetypal source. The free atonal music of Schoenberg, most of which was composed in the first decade of the 20th century, carries a similar vein of dream-like expressionism. The closing lines of *Pierrot Lunaire*, for example, "oh ancient scent from the time of fairy tales", perfectly describe the vein of memory and nostalgia which seems to flow in the half-conscious, fragile world of the collective imagination: Pierrot is cast here as a helpless victim of the harsh reality of progress.

In their dynamic, flowing intensity, Kandinsky's paintings come very close to music: they resonate with colour and they draw our eyes into patterns of movement which feel close at times to the dance. Many of them are actually titled "compositions" or "improvisations" and they leap from their canvasses with the startling immediacy of instant creations. The dynamic energy of a painting such as Improvisation 28 (see plate section) from the year 1912, seems to draw directly from the unconscious yet at the same time it presents images in a half-remembered, dream-like world of shape and feeling. According to Nancy Spector[18], this painting also represents polarised extremes between "cataclysmic events on one side of the canvas and the paradise of spiritual salvation on the other".

The free atonality of Schoenberg in turn, seems to move closer to the world of painting, replacing the dynamic structures of tonal resolutions, the grand narratives of the symphony, with almost static, framed events. This is particularly true of a piece such as the almost stationary third composition from his *Five Pieces for Orchestra* Op. 16 (composed in the same year as the Kandinsky example and titled in the published score "Farben" – colours) but also evident in the more restlessly flowing pieces from the same set which, in the virtually total absence of tonal expectation and resolution seem to arrive constantly at the point where they began[19]. In these and other similar works from the modernist period, Schoenberg seems to be re-mapping our relationship to time, taking us up and down but not from A to B. Roberto Gerhard[20] described this tendency in Schoenberg's music as "stalling": it is almost as if the weight of expression makes forward movement all but impossible, as if whatever goals may have existed keep disappearing in the mists and the music falls back into a pool of self-reflection. *Pierrot Lunaire* floats in a sea of dreams, a far remove from the dynamic narratives of the music of the first Viennese School (Haydn, Mozart, Beethoven) and far less comfortable than the rich and heroic narratives of Romanticism. Schoenberg's music perfectly encapsulates the sense of foreboding felt in the first decade of the twentieth century with the imminent collapse of

---

18 www.guggenheimcollection.org accessed in May 2009.
19 See Anthony Payne's (1970) book *Schoenberg* (op. cit.) for a revealing discussion of Schoenberg's atonal music.
20 In his analytical essay on Schoenberg's Orchestral Variations.

long held belief systems, the "death of God" and the erosion of hegemonic social and political structures. These works are significant since they appear at precisely the moment in time when the "kairos of transition" is most keenly felt, when the thin veneer of civilisation had become almost transparent and the masks of society, particularly in Schoenberg's (and Freud's) Vienna, were slipping away to reveal a dark and unsettling interiority[21].

If Schoenberg's atonal music is prophetic then this is equally true of Stravinsky's *Rite of Spring*, a key work of Modernism which sounds as fresh and challenging today as it did at its first performance in Paris in 1913 when, as is well documented, it created a riot. Here we find another relationship to time created in a very different manner to that of Schoenberg. Where the Viennese composer creates a static world out of continuous motivic development and what can be termed pan-tonality,[22] Stravinsky creates an almost vertical structure by employing the opposite means, repetition within a modal framework. By piling chords on top of one another (often a semitone removed) and by repeating fragments of melody with a circularity of design, Stravinsky maintains a series of static tensions, full of colour and energy but with no unfolding temporal narrative. Furthermore, part of the enduring appeal and interest in *The Rite* stems from its relative simplicity of structure: despite the extraordinary skill and ingenuity of the work, the basic framework, with its short, folk-like melodic ideas and constantly repeated pulsating chords, is actually quite easy to replicate making it an ideal model for imitation. This amazing work represents an almost complete departure from almost anything that preceded it and in this sense it embodies exactly the time in which it appeared whilst simultaneously, in its structural properties, re-casting how time is articulated.[23]

For anything similar from the same period, it is necessary to cross the Atlantic to the United States where, at exactly the same time, the first decade of the 20th Century, the Blues, arguably the most influential musical invention of the new century was beginning to emerge, significantly from the area around the swamps of the Mississippi delta. It is only necessary to listen to a handful of classics such as Robert Johnson's *Me and the Devil Blues* or John Lee Hooker's *Hobo Blues* to instantly understand that the basic musical building blocks of the Blues

---

21 This was perfectly captured in Michael Frayn's 1977 television documentary titled *Vienna: Mask of Gold.*
22 It is as if the music is in all keys all of the time. This then creates the illusion of being in no key at all and this is what makes the music sound so static.
23 I shall be returning to these modernist works in Chapter 2 in relation to Dionysus.

idiom bear a strong resemblance to many of the motivic ideas out of which the *Rite of Spring* is formed. The *Dances of the Adolescent Girls* for example uses a repeated three note idea which is also a prototypical Blues motive. But where the music of the two great European modernists grew out of the European tradition of art music, the Blues emerged from a very different cultural source, mixing African and European religious and musical traditions and inflected with a very different form of expressionism born of deprivation, slavery and genocide. As such, the music of the Blues grows from a kind of expressive imperative which is deeply rooted in the underbelly of life and thus in some respects more authentic than the tradition of European concert halls and drawing rooms. The Blues speaks the truth with unerring immediacy.

If we pause to consider the history of just one aspect of Blues, the lineage of the African-American spiritual, we discover a tradition of extraordinary resilience based around musical patterns deeply encoded with the spiritual messages of West African communities. This music grows from a totally different cultural space and a completely different aesthetic to that of European music, one based not on the notion of beauty but more on a principle of functionality.[24] In other words it is more important for the music to be socially useful than please the ear or satisfy the mind. And in some respects this is what connects the Blues with the Schoenberg and Stravinsky examples which in so many ways overthrew at a stroke the Romantic obsession with beauty, replacing it with what Kandinsky termed "inner necessity".[25]

There are four major features of these musical examples which are relevant to the unfolding idea of this book. The first is connected to the improvisational manner in which they were created. When inventing something as new and startling as *The Rite* or the *Five Pieces* or indeed the Blues, there are, initially, no existing templates within which the works can be formed: no sonata form, no fugal structure, no tonal dialectic, no ready-made tradition. Indeed it is in the nature of renewal that such music springs from an *unconscious*, archetypal source which somehow bypasses the existing cultural framework, the collective conscious. Stravinsky originally conceived of *The Rite* in a dream which further underlines its archetypal source and therefore its link to the collective *unconscious*. He also reflects that initially, though he was able to improvise the *Sacrificial Dance* at the piano, he had no idea how it

---

24 See John Miller Chernoff (1979), *African Rhythm African Sensibility: Aesthetics and Social Action in African Musical Idioms*. Chicago University Press.
25 Wassily Kandinsky (1910): *Concerning the Spiritual in Art.*

might be notated.[26] This improvisational method is also apparent in Schoenberg's free atonality, music composed at great speed, directly notated into the orchestral score. The composer also remarked once that improvising and composing are, to all extents and purposes the same. Improvisation will be discussed in detail in later chapters but its significance here rests in the fact that two essentially mainstream composers found themselves possessed by such force of expression that the music appears to have emerged from its own volition, its own dynamic, its own life. The sense of urgency which accompanies the genesis of these works seems to be strongly related therefore to a *zeitgeist* which demands firstly that the work is created as far as possible in the moment and secondly that the outcomes are unpredictable: both of these are parts of the definition of improvisation.

Next, we discover in this music a redrawing of the relationship to the audience. The riot which attended the first performance of *The Rite* may well have been at least partly due to the fact that the audience simply had no idea how to react to music of such force and immediacy. Schoenberg's music was similarly baffling for audiences, dividing them, polarising them, between those who clearly understood the reason such music had to be written and performed (those who understood its inner drives) and those who would prefer to have been listening to waltzes by the Strauss family (those for whom music is a means of *masking* inner drives). In the case of the Blues, the original "audience" would have comprised local communities, small groups linked, socially, to the performers. Audiences are therefore either challenged or split, as in the case of Stravinsky and Schoenberg, or else, as with the Blues, much closer to the music and more intimately involved in the event, almost certainly participating in its creation. *The Rite of Spring* is especially interesting in that it depicts an imagined tribal custom, a ritual attended by the transformational and ecstatic energy of Dionysus, yet one in which the audience is invited not to participate but merely to witness. There is a mismatch in this sense between the social event (an exotic performance by the *Ballet Russes*) and the actual quality and function of the music itself which seems to demand participation.[27]

This brings me to the third feature, the relative accessibility of each of these pieces: they are ideal templates for imitation and participation. In each case, whether the free atonalism of Schoenberg, the primal

---

26 Stravinsky and Robert Craft (1981), *Memories and Commentaries*. California University Press.
27 Though it is perfectly conceivable that the seated audience, inspired by the spectacle, might leave their seats to join in, social convention does not permit this.

modality of Stravinsky or the archetypal directness of the Blues, we are invited to take part. Despite the apparent complexities of Schoenberg's music, by abandoning tonal centres, embracing all twelve notes and dissolving the harmonic rhythms of chord progressions and the hierarchy of key centres, we create extraordinary freedom – *if all notes are possible, none are false*. And if we strip away the evident sophistication of The Rite, we are left with a series of structural templates which can very quickly be assimilated and put into practice by almost anybody. It is as if the composer had returned to a chthonic, primal substrate of rhythm and energy, modality and tone colour which is available to the entire tribe. The social conventions which created a clear demarcation between audiences and performers and a hierarchal structure which keeps audiences in their seats and elevates the conductor to a podium seem more than ready to break open something which is reflected in the structure of the music itself which dissolves the hierarchies and narratives of tonality, replacing them with the equal distribution of 12 notes and the primal qualities of rhythm. The Blues, in turn, either hovers around a single chord onto which is superimposed a basically pentatonic (five-note) scale, where the absence of semi-tones also dissolves the hierarchy of pitch represented by the diatonic scale or, at a later stage of development (so-called Chicago blues), settles for a cyclic 12 bar structure which simply repeats the same progression of chords over and again with improvised variations. Thus, at a stroke, the notion of musical structure as a specialised arena reserved for composers with listeners left largely in the dark as to how it all actually works, is replaced, potentially at least, by a new aesthetic which keeps no secrets – *anyone can do this*.

The final feature which connects this music with the theme of this book is the way in which the music grows directly out of its own time. In the modernist period we witness a sudden, even violent shedding of tradition which makes it possible to experience time with an immediacy and energy which is at once refreshing and unnerving. When Kandinsky[28] wrote that "every work of art is a child of its time" he expresses how the spirit of modernism embodies a need to return to a primary mode of expression where the concern is less for the preservation of tradition and external appearance and more for the breaking open of tradition in order to expose an internal truth. In other words, the artist, whether musician, painter or architect, needs to be in tune with the "kairos of transition" – in touch with the pulse of the moment – in order to create authentic art.

---

28 Op. Cit.

Beyond Modernism

I shall return to these works in Chapter 2, when discussing musical archetypes in more detail, but we find the reverse of the modernist coin as it flips over in the years after the first European conflict. In music, the neo-classicism of Stravinsky and the formalism of Schoenberg's 12-note compositions appear to thrive on a more taut and objectified world view where the structures of the compositions seem to grow out of a kind of *joie de vivre* which contrasts with the darkening clouds which were gathering over the continent and beyond. Although the basic vocabulary of European modernism remains, it somehow seems tamer, less raw and more controlled than when it first emerged. This might have had something to do with the fact that the original composers were simply growing older but it applies equally to the new generation who seemed more prepared to embrace the new age and celebrate it. The Blues (12 bars, as contrasted with 12 notes) is quickly assimilated into the mainstream of jazz, colouring if not dominating the increasingly accessible music of the 1930s. In a sense, music, both within the continuing traditions of European classicism and in the popular forms which grow from the jazz of the swing era, seems to act as a counter-balance to the terrors and traumas of the European experience, the holocaust and eventually the birth of the nuclear age.

Immediately after the Second World War, the formalism of art music becomes even more intense while the growth of the recording industry creates an ever more widely accessible popular musical culture. The latter in particular maintains the general optimism, even perhaps hedonism which rode on the waves of euphoria following the armistice. The birth of rock and roll and the development of a new primitivism in popular culture are ever more starkly contrasted with the complex structures which characterised the music of the European avant-garde, though the two paths occasionally crossed. Media channels quickly divided into those which catered for the masses (such as Radio Luxembourg and the pirate station Radio Caroline) and those which represented established tradition and authority (the BBC's Third Programme for example).[29] The dividing lines between tradition and the forces of renewal seem to become increasingly demarcated.[30]

As we moved from modernism into the current 'postmodern' period

---

29 Until the 1960s the Third Programme, which existed primarily for intellectual stimulation, might as well have been called the 'Heavy' programme, balanced as it was by the splendidly named 'Light' Programme, a channel devoted to mass entertainment.

30 The university music curriculum which I followed as an undergraduate in the mid-1960s for example, ran its innocent course as if jazz, blues, rock and roll, the Broadway musical and popular song were simply non-existent or else simply did not count as music worthy of serious study.

we find another form of solution to the problems and contradictions of polarisation through an acceptance of cultural pluralism, the validity of popular culture and a radical juxtaposition of seemingly unrelated phenomena. Many conservative academics and educationalists are dismayed by this embrace of popular culture, fearing that it supports a form of relativism, equating the genius of Shakespeare with the transient pleasures of soap opera. But postmodern thinking reminds us perhaps, that many of the uncertainties of which Jung wrote stem from the realisation that everything is indeed in flux and that traditions which we might, at one time, have held sacred, are in reality merely cultural constructs built around the arbitrariness of linguistic expression. Postmodern theory is but the inevitable response to a globalised and commercialised world where the previously revered objects of diverse cultures are tossed into a vast consumerist cauldron. Nothing is sacred.

And yet we crave the sacred! Alongside (and in opposition to) our expanded and highly sophisticated materialism there runs a deep longing for transpersonal experience, expressed popularly through so-called 'new age' culture but more seriously perhaps through the diverse and sophisticated explorations of the Self which stem from the psychotherapeutic community and which have found their way into all of our lives whether or not we choose to be in therapy. If music is seriously capable of meeting the dilemmas and demands of our time then perhaps it needs to find a medium of expression which bypasses the complex and diverse cultural and artistic industries which, despite the often extraordinary breadth and depth of their products have been maintained through structures of political economy which have not changed radically since the 1600s.

Musical Inflation and Musical Roots

According to Jacques Attali,[31] we are approaching a new phase in a long historical process which has its roots in pre-history, whilst its tentacles reach out into an uncertain but potentially creative future. According to Attali we can trace this history through four stages. In the deep past, music functions as *ritual*, a role in which it is used by communities to accompany the stations of the sun as well as the celebrations of bonding, childbirth and death. He also ascribes to music in this context, the power to channel violence, to carry in its "noise" the conflicts and resolutions of the personal and collective psyche. Then

---

31 Attali, Jacques (1987). *Noise: The Political Economy of Music*. Manchester University Press.

comes music as *representation* in which the power of music is harnessed and musicians become virtually enslaved by political and religious institutions, (noblemen, kings, popes, archbishops and municipalities) to re-present, in musical form, the hegemony and potency of their rule. When, through the course of the nineteenth century, the public sphere emerged to challenge and in some instances even replace the old order, it might have been expected that control over the art of music would devolve to people more generally. However, as Attali describes it, we moved from an era of representation into an era of *repetition* in which mechanical reproduction made it possible for a music industry to emerge, a political economy which ensured that musical output remained generally safe, standardised and predictable as any commodity needs to be.

> *Fetishized as a commodity, music is illustrative of the evolution of our entire society: deritualize a social form, repress an activity of the body, specialize its practice, sell it as a spectacle, generalize its consumption, then see to it that it is stockpiled until it loses its meaning. Today, music heralds the establishment of a society of repetition in which nothing will happen anymore. But at the same time, it heralds the emergence of a radically new organization never yet theorized, of which self-management is but a distant echo.*[32]

Attali therefore looks to a newly emerging phase which he calls composition in which the production of musical texts is devolved to people, where individuals take back ownership and where the true value of music is no longer related to its status as a commodity but relocated in the experience of the music itself.

However we choose to view Attali's analysis there seems little doubt that the dilemmas of uncertainty and the polarisations and fragmentations which characterise the postmodern period are now firmly and inevitably mapped onto our musical culture. We have a fixed tradition of 'art music' embedded in the trusted canon of European culture, notated, endlessly recorded, played ceaselessly as entertainment through the air waves and sufficiently hallowed to be preserved through public subsidies, a museum culture in many senses. Alongside this comes the vast and inflated popular music industry with its cult of celebrity and major icons of worship, most of whom emerged during the fifties, sixties and seventies of the last century though many more continue to emerge from the social

---

32 Ibid. P. 5

cauldron like so much alphabet soup – Abba, The Beatles, Chuck Berry, Diana Ross, Elvis Presley, Franz Ferdinand, Gary Glitter, Hayley Mills, Iggy Pop, Janet Jackson, Katy Perry, Lady Gaga, Motorhead, Noddy Holder, Mike Oldfield, Pentangle, Queen, Rolling Stones, Santana, Talking Heads, U2, Van Halen, Wizzard, Xiu Xiu, The Yardbirds, Frank Zappa, - an endless list of performers shedding a comet trail of golden discs, endlessly re-issued CDs and an infinity of imitators. The popular music industry is fuelled by the musical appetites of a population hungry for the constant feed of this materialistic yet non-material medium, its metaphysical values exploited endlessly by those with good business sense. Surrounding this classical/pop divide is an almost infinite number of musical genres to connect with every possible sub-culture, every brand of musical taste and every type of social function.

Moreover, music follows us around everywhere we go. It follows us into lifts, into restaurants and pubs, it follows us down the street and across the parks and, if it is not available in a particular place we can easily carry it with us through, most recently, mp3 players, devices which can pour noise into our heads 24 hours a day. As John Sloboda (1996) has demonstrated, we mostly listen to music as an accompaniment to "maintenance tasks" such as driving, ironing, jogging and washing the dishes. Some of this output, this 'noise', is of high quality. Yet much of it, most of it perhaps, is simply just that...noise! On hearing yet another vocalist 'belting' through the speaker cones of the local pub or in a shopping precinct or at the airport it becomes easy to forget that this was once a real person, in another place, at another time, singing their heart out. The outcome, which applies to any inflated currency, is that the medium of music itself then becomes devalued and the greater the pace of devaluation the faster the political economy races to catch up. In other words, the more music we hear, the more it is taken for granted, the less potent it becomes and more of it then needs to be consumed to produce the desired effect: a recipe for inflation as well as a form of addiction.

Yet, within this cultural dilemma, there exist clues as to the direction the political economy of music might take in the very near future. One of these is the catch-all and problematically labelled 'genre' World Music. To many, this might suggest anything that is popular, pluralist and patchworked. But the rise in interest and the popularity of this musical domain, which opens up localised, indigenous traditions to a global market perhaps leads potentially to new pathways of renewal. On the one hand, World Music is an inevitable product of postmodernism and globalisation. Yet, much of the music which has emerged under this banner stems from rooted and often sacred traditions of different cultures. Encoded in these patterns of rhythm and modality we often hear not merely exotic 'otherness' or simply attractive alternative counter weights to the musical cultures of Europe, but perhaps a deeper, more soulful, even shamanic sense of purpose[33]. To listen for example to Jan Garbarek joining forces with, at one moment, the Siberian shamanic voice of Sainkho Namchylak, and the next moment the voices of the Hilliard Ensemble is to enter the sacred spaces which emanate from two utterly opposing traditions and then to make deep connections between them. The genius of Garbarek rests in his ability to dissolve or unite polarities simply by opening his musical mind, his ears and his creative senses to the inner qualities of musical tone regardless of cultural background and traditions. The increasing popularity of the music of different cultures may be related to the recognition of the spiritual purpose which is often encoded into the rhythms and modal flavours which we hear and which are both accessible and fresh to our ears. Such music comes to us from a source which is close to its roots and therefore more in touch perhaps with its functions as a transformational medium, more equipped to play an important role in expressing the kairos of transition.

Throughout this book, I will be suggesting alternative ways of encountering and experiencing music, attempting to restore some of these root qualities and, in the process, bypassing not just the great composers of the past (and present) who, in their individual narratives somehow became the guardians of collective expression, or the music industry, which has exploited endlessly the mechanical means of musical production but even those fixed styles and genres in which music is located and defined. Is it possible to conceive of a kind of music which grows spontaneously and organically from the moment, a process of renewal propelled by ordinary people doing something extraordinary and magical - making music together with no help from composers and no recourse to stereo systems? Thinking outside the box, imagine what it would be like to live in a world without orchestras, without conductors, without CD players, without MP3 systems, without MIDI, without amplifiers, without specialists, pop groups, managers, musicologists or music critics. What would a major music festival like Glastonbury feel like if all were involved not as consumers but as creators? Yet this is not

---

33 I refer to Michael Tucker's rich essay on the shamanic elements in contemporary music *The Body Electric* published in Contemporary Music Review (ed. Maxwell Steer) Music and Mysticism (1) P. 67-85. See also Tucker's (1998) book *Deep Song*, a study of the music of Jan Garbarek. East Note: Hull studies in Jazz.

a utopian or idealistic notion, simply an image which, if we follow through the consequences, might just lead to an exciting alternative musical culture. In reality, as I hope to demonstrate in due course, this process has already begun.

Recorded Music

Perhaps the greatest musical challenge in a material culture such as ours is how to resist rendering music itself into a material object. When we examine contemporary music it becomes rapidly clear that it is not only musical theory which feeds this process: the whole mediation of music creates a climate of objectification which makes it difficult if not impossible to experience the depth meanings which much of the music originally carried. This applies as equally to Beethoven symphonies as it does to rock anthems. So what happens to music when it is turned into an object and how different might the map of the political economy of music look if we were to shift the emphasis from music as object to music as experience? I shall examine a number of examples of musical objects but I start with the most obvious and ubiquitous which is music as a recorded medium.

Today, recorded music is still largely dominated by Compact Discs, though these are rapidly being supplanted by MP3 players, downloadable music files and mobile phones. Before CDs of course, we had gramophone records; and, in between and alongside the transition, we had the now virtually obsolete cassette tape. The ease with which it became possible to reproduce cassettes ensured that they multiplied in exponential patterns, resulting in bucket loads of often neglected and unmarked C60s and C90s – small, compact, handy and ultimately unloved they were yet often imprinted with some of the most profound music ever created. Whole orchestras, vast symphonies, legendary jazz performances, supergroups in some far-distant rock stadium or festival arena, all reduced to something you could hold in the palm of your hand. To begin with, this seemed like a great idea but the history and demise of the music cassette demonstrates how easily the object can replace the experience in such a way that, as the object itself becomes ubiquitous, inflated and devalued, so also does the potential experience it contains. The ease with which that little casket, with all its magical, golden contents, could be slipped into the dashboard of your car as you negotiated the traffic jams on the homeward drive, ensured that, however much enjoyment it offered to begin with, when it was still novelty, ultimately, the gold itself became worthless.

The music cassette also became a convenient tool for both recording the past and simultaneously, dislocating ourselves from the experience of the past. The attraction of recording a musical event rests in how it apparently captures a significant moment in time, an event, an experience in such a way that we can revisit it whenever we wish. We all loved our cassette recorders since they made this process so easy and so accessible. And yet, this is doomed to disappoint: removed from the moment in which it was created, the magic is lost, the original event loses its sheen and we feel cheated. The experience gets lost in translation. The demise of the music cassette was no doubt further exacerbated since, despite its relative cheapness and ease of use and despite technical wizardry such as noise reduction (the ubiquitous Dolby stamp) the musical quality was inconsistent. Yet, it stands as an instructive example of the dangers inherent in the objectification inherent in recorded music. What happened to the music cassette is ultimately what happens in every case where the experience of music is transplanted from its live source to a "dead" medium, taken out of its original time frame and context, uprooted, re-routed, recast, beamed across some chasm of space and time to be re-constituted or resuscitated in living room, car, restaurant or shopping mall. In every case, the experience is weakened and the soul quality is diluted.

The issues surrounding recorded music have been debated frequently and most famously perhaps by Theodore Adorno[34] who identified dangers in the standardisation which had come to permeate popular musical culture, unfavourably comparing this with the richness of development which characterised high musical art, particularly that represented by the European tradition. To some extent I agree with his analysis, especially to the degree that he describes as 'fetishisation' the process which occurs when culture is commodified and sold as a standard product to basically passive consumers. However, we might substitute for 'standardisation' the term 'convention' considering that there exist numerous examples of highly imaginative and expressive music which work within standardised conventional forms: the 32-bar standard song format for example became a vehicle for innumerable and imaginative jazz improvisations. Adorno may argue that music needs to be complex in order to qualify as art, yet

---

34 See Adorno, Theodore, (1938) On the Fetish Character in Music and the Regression in Listening. In *The Essential Frankfurt School Reader.* Blackwell

the very complexity which inhabits much contemporary art music and which emerged in central Europe through the 20th Century becomes itself a victim of conventions which are both over-complex and elitist, resulting in music which is often too baffling or downright dissonant for the majority of people to understand or appreciate let alone pay for. The musical avant-garde then too easily disappears up a cul-de-sac of specialism, usually coming to rest in a university music department where 'modern' composers can make a living from teaching and researching and where notated scores can be pored over by musicologists devising ever more ingenious ways of explaining and analysing what is happening. This seems to me to be exactly the kind of 'fetishism' which Adorno warned against and about as far removed from what music is meant to do as can possibly be imagined, an almost entirely pointless activity, akin to Sudoku and what Hans Keller[35] no doubt would have referred to as a 'phoney profession.' Nothing kills musical experience more quickly or more effectively than musical analysis, yet musical analysis is highly regarded in the academic world, earning precious research points for those who indulge in this particular form of alchemy.

Notation

And so to another instance of musical objectification which predates the recorded medium, the notated score. Let me be clear before this discussion begins that I regard notation in Western music as a remarkable and ingenious invention and an invaluable communication tool, examples of which will be found later in this book. Most musical cultures have developed ways of notating music though most of these have been approximations which allow for the actual performance to reflect more closely the context and time in which the performance takes place. What I am discussing here therefore is not whether notation is a *good thing* but rather to cite it as an example of how easily a useful invention can become an objectified phenomenon, something which weakens the experience of music by shifting the focus from ear to eye, from right brain to left brain, from body to mind, a process which can so easily rob music of its soul qualities and upon which trained musicians so easily become utterly dependent.

In the European tradition we have come to take for granted an invention which allows for the detailed re-creation and repetition of music in some cases hundreds of years distant from the time in which it was

---

35 See Keller, Hans (1986) *Music, Closed Societies and Football*. Toccata Press, London.

created. In a global context this is highly anomalous. When music is notated and published it becomes, to a greater or lesser degree, fixed and isolated in the time of its creation leading to the situation where a single and unchanging musical text, authenticated by 'the composer' comes to be regarded as sacrosanct: in other words the written text takes on significance as a cultural icon. In ancient Greece and in Arabic and Indian cultures, notation was only ever used as the lightest guide for musical performance. Improvisation was and still is central to the practice of, for example, Indian classical music. In the west this holds true also for blues, jazz and associated popular forms where the basis of the structure is often sketched out with melody and chords whilst the rest is left to the imagination of the musicians during the live performance. This was also the case with much sixteenth and seventeenth century European music where the tradition of basso continuo allowed for improvisation at least on the part of the keyboard player. So what happened to European classical music? Somehow, the musical score becomes so central, so iconic within the culture that the word 'music' itself, in English at least, equates with the written text.

From the early days, around the 9th century, the purpose of the written score seems to have been to provide a means whereby sacred music, such as Gregorian chant, could be recorded for continued use. This provided continuity and, more importantly perhaps, control over what was being sung and, furthermore it allows this control to be exportable, all of which was no doubt very attractive to the authoritarian mindset of the Church or to the controlling instincts of noblemen such as Frederick the Great.[36] The notion that there is but one authenticated version of a musical text was therefore embedded in European musical culture at an early stage and these texts were sufficiently prized to have been reasonably well preserved. A whole industry of so-called authentic performance has built up around the notion that, if the secrets of the earlier scores can be decoded, along with historical research into performance practice then we can somehow experience the *music as it is meant to be heard*. Initially, this approach was applied mainly to early music, meaning music written before 1600. But increasingly, the drive towards authentic performance has come to embrace music up to the end of the 19th Century as well. Yet, since we can never be really sure what the music sounded like when first performed we do not know whether the re-creation is accurate; and since we all experience music in different ways there is no reason to

---

36 See Blanning, T.C.W. (2002), *The Culture of Power and the Power of Culture*. Oxford. P. 92-94.

believe that a historical performance is in any sense more valid than one which re-arranges the notes to suit modern sensibilities; and since we live in any case in a different period, so-called "authentic" performance means, in effect, merely the pursuit of a myth of performance which elevates the past over the present. And can a performance recorded onto a CD ever be called truly authentic?

One effect of the tradition of notation has been to sanctify the musical text to such an extent that it almost becomes heretical or taboo to improvise through a performance of, say, a Mozart piano sonata even though this is something Mozart himself almost certainly did. So why not do it now? The canonisation of European classical music which only began in Germany in the 1830s creates a cultural imperative which was, and still is only made possible through the existence of printed musical scores. After all, without these objects, the re-creation of the works of the 'great tradition' becomes impossible. Moreover, as we move through the 19th Century, notation becomes ever more precise and prescriptive with composers leaving little, if any scope for any individual input on the part of the performer. Thus, the training of musicians has become largely concerned with how to interpret a score according to the conventions of the time and classically trained musicians, by and large, become not only incapable of improvisation, but extremely resistant even to the idea of attempting it. We can say that the practice of music has then become objectified at a number of levels: through the notated score – relocation from sound to vision; through performance in a manner which belongs to a previous era – dislocation in time; through the performance of music which has been imported from another country or context – dislocation of place; through an attitude to performance which limits the creativity of the performer – dislocation of affect; and through performance by highly trained musicians who can read music, to largely untrained audiences, most of whom cannot – social dislocation. Finally, since this music is largely designed to be listened to whilst seated, it dislocates mind from body, thus reinforcing the classic dualistic split which lies at the heart of Platonic philosophy.

Whilst great interpretations of notated scores undoubtedly exist and whilst the experience of a great musical work can be a life-enhancing event, this is at the expense of the countless middle class children whose parents, subscribing to a cultural norm which goes unquestioned, put their offspring through the rigours of graduated training in musical instruments (in the UK this is dominated by Associated Board examinations) which, assuming they do not drop out (as many do), is crowned by the coveted Grade VIII certificate. Once this is achieved, once they have become members of the *Grade VIII club*, they then rapidly discover that this achievement has very limited social, personal or musical usefulness and they then equally rapidly become *Grade VIII survivors*, musically literate but often strangely isolated in their skills. After all, except at the highest level, there is little social or cultural demand for someone who can perform a Mozart piano sonata or a Bach Prelude and Fugue, however competently. This is not to deny the intrinsic or knock-on effects or indeed the personal satisfaction which derives from the learning of such skills as are needed to achieve this award. Self-discipline, commitment and determination are certainly required and the motor skills and undeniably valuable 'brain-gym' results of musical study will also be evident. Yet, at the end of the day, countless young musicians, having reached this point will also get the feeling that, as fully paid up members of the *Grade VIII Club* they are all dressed up with nowhere to go!

If we pause to consider for a moment the dualism which is reinforced by the objectification of music, we might find pointers towards ways in which we can reclaim music as *unified experience* and thus regain some kind of balance if not heal the dualistic split altogether. As far as music is concerned, it appears that the use of notation, which is a much more cognitively based activity than improvisation, assumes a dominant function, rendering the player less able and less willing to create music spontaneously. John Sloboda (1987) has recorded how learning to read music increases reliance on left brain activity and this has the result of both creating over-reliance on the notated score and reducing the sense of ownership of the musical act. The performer then somehow moves further away from the internal experience of the music whilst the performance itself runs the danger of becoming affectively sterile. In the course of my own research, I came across a young musician who had become virtually unconscious of the music as she was performing it until brought back into awareness by applause from the audience. Most of the performance time was spent fighting with nerves, a fairly typical response to playing in public. In another case study a young musician had initially improvised a simple melody and was able to perform it fluently and expressively. Yet, the following day, this fluency completely disappeared when she attempted to play it back from the 'score' she had herself (proudly) written down overnight.

It takes a long period of musical training for most to master the art of playing from a notated score; yet, the experience of music can often be eclipsed by the musical training itself which so often places emphasis on the mental and cognitive aspect whilst suppressing emotional and physical qualities. As students of music in the 1960s it was almost taboo to use the piano whilst composing: all 'harmony and counterpoint' had to be notated without recourse to any physical source of sound resulting, for most, in purely mechanical and utterly meaningless music, since for most, the link between the inner ear and the written score is not sufficiently developed. This results in a form of mental activity more absurd and pointless even than Sudoku. This would not be such a tragedy were it not for the fact that many of those same students, having achieved some kind of success in this artificial domain by dutifully passing their exams, yet ill-equipped to create and perform *real music*, then went on to become music teachers, continuing the pointlessness through a kind of self-perpetuating oligarchy.

The notated score also makes it easier to write about music, as opposed to thinking directly in the medium of music. As Frank Zappa famously remarked, "writing about music is like dancing about architecture", singularly absurd, though dancing to music, of course, makes good sense. There are many other examples of activities peripheral to music-making but very much part of contemporary musical culture which are much more about ideas than feelings, privileging the object over the experience. The concert programme note or CD insert is a prime example, where people feel that somehow they need the written word as explanation in order to more fully appreciate the musical text itself. Yet, as Hans Keller once remarked, "nobody needs to be told that a related theme is a related theme". To witness an audience member with their head stuck in the programme whilst the performance is in full flow is akin to the not uncommon practice of visiting an exhibition of paintings and spending more time reading the titles of the paintings than contemplating the canvasses themselves.

I have already referred to musicology, but what would happen to that other 'phoney professional' the record reviewer, if the experience of music was to be properly reclaimed. When we think about it, it soon becomes obvious that the quality of the experience need not be at all dependent on either the quality of the object (in this case, the recorded medium) or the opinion of an expert: it is the subjective state of the listener, the context and mood of the moment which most likely determines the quality of the experience and this cannot be either adequately preserved or safely predicted.

When notation becomes impotent (a digression)

A few weeks before writing this I played in a pub gig with an old friend. We chose a variety of bits and pieces culled from our joint memories including some songs from Ghana and the Central African Republic, a Czech folk song, some Scandinavian-style 'yoiking', some Mongolian-style throat singing and also two jazz standards, 'Summertime' and 'How Deep is the Ocean'. Now here is an interesting thing. Had we chosen to perform these jazz pieces from photocopies of notated scores, we most certainly would have been in breach of copyright and could well have been fined. However, since we were performing from memory (the brain as photocopier?) we were probably in the clear. If a musician simply memorizes a work having listened to it a few times (or, in the case of a Mozart, once) and then performs it in public, is she in breach of copyright? Music is a slippery medium. The rights of Gershwin and his successors might be protected in law but what about the African songs? Who is going to channel funds back to Ghana for a song we chose to perform in a pub in Winchester, UK?

In the early 1970s, a group of jazz musicians based at the famous Berklee School of Music in Boston decided to notate what jazz musicians had been memorizing for many years, to wit, jazz standards.[37] Countless performances of standard tunes (plus improvisation of course) had long been common practice among jazz musicians. Copyright of these tunes rested of course with the composer or with the publisher of the sheet music, but most jazz musicians play intuitively, performing standards by heart. Why buy the sheet music which represents in any case only one, maybe rather starched version of the original? Nevertheless, the Berklee musicians decided to write out by hand the tunes and chords of around 500 standards as 'lead sheets'. This roughly sketched and roughly bound collection was then printed and sold as an aide memoire for jazz musicians. Thus, *The Real Book* was born, quickly becoming popular and virtually indispensible for jazz musicians, young and old. Subsequently, musicians the world over began making photocopies of selected songs from this entirely illegal publication, compounding its

---

37 Bassist Steve Swallow and pianist Paul Bley are sometimes mistakenly implicated in the production of the original Real Book.

illegality. Today, peek into any jazz musician's gigging bag and you will surely find numerous dog eared photocopies of their favourite jazz standards from *The Real Book* vying for space with discarded reeds, chocolate bar wrappers and old CDs which have lost their cases.

My own copy of *The Real Book* was a reduced, "funsized" version with four pages of the original condensed onto each page, giving both me and my optician a headache. This was all entirely illegal of course, and most copies (including mine) were sold under the counter. But so ubiquitous was the presence and use of *The Real Book* that sustained legal action would have been futile. More recently, music publisher Hal Leonard bought the rights to all of the songs contained in the original and *The Legal Real Book* then appeared. Yet, for whatever reason, almost every jazz musician I have spoken to prefers to use the original, handwritten version which seems somehow more authentic – more 'real'. But why call it the "real" book? Perhaps because playing from notated charts was traditionally called "faking it" and the notations themselves were then termed "fake books". Yet, had the Berklee people focussed on memory training, all those musicians who rely on *The Real Book* would have the material imprinted in their musical minds. The result would be the same in practice but who can copyright a person's brain cells?

The Cult of Celebrity

The objectification of music is further reinforced by the cult of celebrity, in particular the lionisation of pop stars onto whom people readily and willingly project their own unconscious (heroic) selves. Being an adoring music fan means giving up responsibility for one's own creative genie. Not that great artists do not deserve the acclaim or that the high value attached to their performances is out of proportion to their worth. But the immense gap which exists between the celebrity artist and the fan is yet another example of the polarisation which exists in contemporary music and which represents the wider culture. It is surprisingly easy for people to reclaim ownership of the production of music, yet difficult to find contexts which allow or encourage them to do this since the investment in the music industry and in the pop artist as a money-making machine is very high and usually tightly controlled by managers or entrepreneurs. Many people simply suppress the creative musician inside them and live their musical lives through the voices and performances of others. This is now so commonly accepted that we take it for granted, in the same way that soap opera television creates an imaginal screen onto which people can project their unconscious selves, rendering the mundane business of life more meaningful and extraordinary.

None of this is, in any sense, 'wrong', rather, it seems culturally inevitable. But, for the purposes of this book, I am simply asking what happens to the experience of music when it becomes channelled in this way? It is possible that its true meaning, or some of its fundamental qualities and functions, become displaced by an object that stands in place of the experience. The foot is an erotically appealing part of the body and may contribute to the erotic success of a relationship; but a fetishist may become so engrossed with the foot itself that the relationship is weakened: he (or she) ends up having a relationship with the foot instead of with the person! Idolising a musical celebrity may be very similar: a pop "idol" is exactly that, the image has become the main attractor whilst the musical experience itself has been relegated to second place. In recent years, the world of classical music has also become more concerned with image and presentation as economic realities have begun to bite. Marketing has become an essential component in preserving the viability of much classical music with images of glamorous young cellists and groups with names like "Sax Appeal" becoming commonplace, whilst others such as "All Angels" are "designer groups" created by recording companies and aimed at specific markets.

Music in the Head

In his book *The Triumph of Music*, Tim Blanning[38] provides a less weighted, more optimistic reading of musical history of the past 300 years than Attali (see above). For Blanning, the explosion of access to musical culture which resulted from the liberation of artists and composers from patronage and the empowerment of the public sphere, reaches its apogee in the current time, a period of unprecedented musical creation and reception. In many ways, Blanning's perspective is borne out by the apparent optimism of a culture which believes in its own utopian destiny (although he does not put it like this). In other words, whilst viewing the social and political history of Europe through the lens of the parallel history of the musical development of the period (1700 to the present), Blanning is describing a musical tradition which resonates with liberty, social justice, freedom of thought and the emancipation of the artist. As

---

38 Blanning, Tim (2008) *The Triumph of Music*. Penguin books, London.

a cultural historian, Blanning is fairly blasé when he talks about 'listening to noise'.[39] He is similarly neutral about the 'disembodiment' of musical experience which recording technology promotes as well as the relativisation of aesthetic values which inevitably attends the commercialisation of music. First opera houses, then concert halls, recording studios and finally internet technology become shrines of liberty, freeing the musical arts from control and giving musical artists unprecedented exposure.

> *Every time that the death of the music industry is announced, music wriggles around the apparent blockage and resumes its inexorable progress. [...] What can be said with confidence based on the knowledge of what has happened during the past two or three centuries, is that, whatever technological advances are made in the future, the art form most likely to benefit is music.*[40]

As I argued in the prelude, such musical "benefits" are a fairly accurate representation of social development which is then reflected in the demands of the market and music is such a precious commodity that it is bound to feed upon whatever is available to increase its dissemination and, like flood waters, to find its way into every aspect of life. Who would argue with that? Yet it is impossible not to feel when viewing someone sitting on the tube or on the beach piping music directly into their heads from a tiny square of polished aluminium, that some vital aspect of participation and physical engagement has been lost.

As for the average classical concert, it has to be asked what percentage of the audience actually follows the music from beginning to end without frequently wandering off into personal reveries or gradually dozing off until awakened by an unexpected fortissimo? Haydn famously catered for this eventuality in his "Surprise" Symphony but the phenomenon must be equally common in today's concert halls. There are many subtleties in a classical piece often to do with key structures and contrapuntal procedures, which are in any case difficult to follow and may not be critical to an overall appreciation of the music. But simply as a matter of endurance, it seems highly unlikely that the average audience member stays fully aware of the experience of a piece throughout its length. This interrupts their connection to time and with the articulation of the relation to time which the musical event represents.

---

39 Blanning, Tim (2008) *The Triumph of Music*. Penguin books, London. P. 218
40 Ibid, P. 229-230

The most powerful kind of musical experience is surely that which comes through *participation* both in the creation and the performance of the work. In order to truly connect to time, people may need this total involvement, a kind of focus which cannot be achieved simply by being a listener. The concept of *Lifemusic*, of connection not merely to the length of time it takes to perform a musical act but to the special quality of the moment in which the piece is being both created and performed, is based on the idea that, in order for the kairos of transition to be met, acknowledged and expressed, people may need to be encouraged to make the music themselves. This would entail a radical restructuring of the political economy of music; it might mean a whole new way of training musicians; and it might involve abandoning some of the musical myths which we cling to, often with passion. Most of all it might mean *consuming less and creating more*. The *experience* of music is of primary importance and perhaps it is only through direct participation that this experience can be fully lived. In order to reconcile the split represented by these opposing dualisms of object and experience, in order to open up creative access to music, in order to connect to time with the kind of immediacy which our time demands, in order to set in progress this process of renewal, it may be necessary to return to music's archetypal roots.

CHAPTER 2

ORPHIC STATES -

MUSIC AND THE ARCHETYPES

"...art should enrich the soul; it should teach spirituality by showing a person a portion of the self that they would not discover otherwise."[41]

"The abstract nature of music allows it to become symbolic of archetypal content without the need for precise image."[42]

What is the source of music's power? From where comes the capacity of music to move us to laughter or tears, to change our feelings about a situation or an image in an instant, to imbue even the most ordinary moment with special significance, yet also to provide precisely the right holding frame for important events and rituals? How can "wiggling air molecules"[43] achieve such transformational effects on body and soul and condition so readily a person's capacity to respond to the world?

The Force that through the Green Fuse Drives the Flower

The German idealist philosopher, Arthur Schopenhauer (1788-1860), as is well-known, separated music from the other arts, arguing that whilst architecture, sculpture, painting and poetry are representations of life, creating images which strive to provide ideal forms of objects, music reflects the dynamic forms of the living world itself, a direct expression of the underlying force which gives life its creative energy and which he termed *The Will*.[44] The Welsh poet Dylan Thomas was inspired to describe it as "the force that through the green fuse drives the flower" a root principle of life which, according to Schopenhauer, music replicates. The emotional force of music, according to this notion, derives from the fact that its formal properties, its rhythms, tones and textures, are

---
41 Bill Evans, jazz pianist, quoted in the *Jazz Aids Handbook* by Jamey Aebersold, New Albany.
42 Marie-Louise von Franz (op. cit.).
43 Frank Zappa's (1989) concise definition of music.
44 Schopenhauer, Arthur (1818) *The World as will and Representation*. Translated by E.F.J. Payne, Dover Publications, New York (1969).

themselves identical in shape to both natural processes and the forms in which our feelings are cast, an idea which was taken up and developed considerably by the 20th Century philosopher Suzanne Langer (1947).

Schopenhauer's ideas were extremely influential in the late 19th and early 20th Centuries, when thinkers, writers, scientists and musicians alike were attempting to come to terms with the breakdown of old certainties and understand more about the unconscious and instinctual drives which appeared to be eating away the fabric of European social, political and cultural life. We can find strong echoes of Schopenhauer's *Will* in Henri Bergson's (1896/1994) concept of "prime reality" connected in this case to the musical qualities of duration and memory. Freud's theory of the unconscious and the objective significance of dreams seem to emerge from Schopenhauer's insistence that the instinctual forces which make the world essentially irrational are nonetheless critically important since they have such a powerful guiding influence on human behaviour.

Schopenhauer's writings also influenced the depth psychology of C.G. Jung and we can draw strong parallels between the philosopher's concept of an underpinning universal principle (the aforementioned Will) and Jung's concept of the collective unconscious, a universal driver which lies at the heart of both physical and psychic reality. For Jung, the structure of the psyche is complex and layered. The outer crust is the ego self, conscious, active, visible and defended. Beneath this outer layer we have an expanding series of unconscious layers, personal, group, cultural, intercultural. Then, underlying everything, like a deep primordial well, we have the collective unconscious containing the underlying patterns of life or *archetypes* which cannot be directly explained but which find expression through the images and narratives found in myths, fables, folk tales and dreams, thus making the imagination the primary human faculty. The archetypes, according to Jung and his followers, therefore strongly condition much of our behaviour as well as providing a sense of significance to things, rendering experience *numinous*. In this model, archetypal content is one of the primary motivations for all kinds of action and it is what draws us into our deepest relationships. For Jung, as for Schopenhauer, it is above all, music which provides a direct representation of these archetypal patterns. Music is ultimately abstract: it does not depend upon images to represent its narratives, it simply moves us and makes sense because it resonates with our deepest instincts, the primordial patterns that underpin not merely our collectively shared inner lives, but the dynamic of life itself – not merely the individual soul but the world soul.

Dionysic stirrings

Between Schopenhauer and Jung, it is Nietzsche who provides the strongest argument for music's archetypal power and its necessary presence in our lives. For him, music represented the crucial link with the underlying life force which is essentially non-dualistic and irrational. This 'prime reality', according to Nietzsche had become overlaid with the heavy rationalism of European culture with its predominantly Christian mythology and this had also created a condition of music which was in some senses safe and comfortable. Despite the extraordinary ability of composers such as Beethoven, Berlioz, Liszt, Chopin and Wagner to override the inbuilt restrictions of tonality and equal temperament, musical practice maintained and encouraged a split between a largely passive public and active creators supplying the goods. The ritual aspects of music which would place emphasis on its participatory and transformational properties had all but disappeared. The cult of Apollo which Nietzsche believed had come to dominate the modern scientific life needed to be balanced with a more cthonic energy, the ordered harmonies and elegant grace of Apollo required what Nietzsche called Dionysian music which grew from the energy of the dance. In *The Birth of Tragedy*, he argues that where the Apollonian sphere was "myth-destroying" the Dionysian domain was capable of re-connection with the primal energy of life and the deep feminine.

> *The music of Apollo was Doric architecture expressed in sound, but only in intimate tones characteristic of the cithara. (The Lyre) It kept at a careful distance, as something un-Apollonian, the particular element which constitutes the character of Dionysian music and, along with that, of music generally, the emotionally disturbing tonal power, the unified stream of melody, and the totally incomparable world of harmony. In the Dionysian dithyramb man is aroused to the highest intensity of all his symbolic capabilities; something never felt forces itself into expression, the destruction of the veil of Maja, the sense of oneness as the presiding genius of form, in fact, of nature itself. Now the*

essence of nature is to express itself symbolically; a new world of symbols is necessary, the entire symbolism of the body, not just the symbolism of the mouth, of the face, and of the words, but the full gestures of the dance, all the limbs moving to the rhythm. And then the other symbolic powers grow, those of the music, in rhythm, dynamics, and harmony – with sudden violence.[45]

In this passage we encounter the unstoppable and relentless energy which drives human experience and which leads towards renewal. In Nietzsche's world view, renewal only becomes possible when we are able to access the primal energy which runs at the source of human life and connects us, in one flowing stream, to the rest of the living world.

Under the mystical joyous cries of Dionysus, the spell of individuation shatters and the way lies open to the maternal source of being, the innermost core of things.[46]

This understanding of the inner process and the importance of connecting with it is at the core of Nietzsche's philosophy and it is what the true experience of music offers. Music connects us directly with life.

The World as Sound

It is therefore possible to explore musical universals by referring to those archetypal images and narratives which have been a constant, if not always obvious, presence throughout the history of musical experience. In examining music from this archetypal perspective we discover a series of reference points from which we can explore the primary functions of music, the foundation stones which underpin and support the process of renewal which *Lifemusic* seeks to stimulate. In order to extend our understanding of how music connects people to time it may be necessary to peer into the mists of time itself, to take a journey into our deep past, the 'once upon a time' of myth and fable. Through the encounter with these ancient images and narratives we might learn more about the nature of musical experience. What do these myths, and the archetypal messages which they carry, tell us about the fundamental properties of music and their functions? Furthermore, such elemental patterns are present in each and every one of us: it is what makes us ALL musicians.

According to Jung, we unconsciously encounter the archetypes, which

---

45 Nietzsche, Friedrich (1871), *The Birth of Tragedy*. Trans. Ian C. Johnston (2000) Malaspina University-College, Nanaimo, BC.
46 Ibid.

carry our deepest collective narratives, as projections on to the deep laws of nature (the archetypes themselves are unknowable except when cast as projections) and music seems to directly represent these projections, connecting us to the universal shapes and myriad patterns of the collective unconscious, the drivers behind the whole 'wondrous machine.' So by examining the archetypes as they appear in musical experience we are reminded that the laws of music are analogous to the natural processes of life: the slow swing of the seasons, the rotation of the planets, the whirling of atoms and, most of all, the passage of time. In this sense, the archetypes therefore reveal the *transpersonal qualities* of music and its *transcendent functions*; they remind us of music's *autonomy* so that when we create it we are in fact working with natural laws which might appear to lie beyond us, but are in reality, part of us. As Joachim Berendt (1984) puts it "before we make music, the music makes us". And if this notion corresponds neatly with Schopenhauer then that is no accident since he was very familiar with the same oriental doctrines which inspired Berendt's own investigation of *Nada Brahma*, the world as sound: how the structure of the universe itself is musical. Thus, the creative principle which underpins all matter (Brahma) finds its realisation in individual consciousness (Atman) as music.

Plato, Pythagoras and Pirsig

The fox knows many things but the hedgehog knows one big thing.[47]

In European thought, the notion of an underpinning reality can be traced back to Plato, who, in making a distinction between corporeal forms and ideal forms, separated out physical experience from what we might term soul awareness. As many have observed, this distinction between two types of reality, between the fox's view of the world as made up of many different examples of something and the hedgehog's capacity to unify everything into a grand vision, has coloured European thinking ever since. We find it, for example in Kant's distinction between *numen* and *phenomenon* as well as more recently in Robert Pirsig's (1976)[48] distinction between subject and object. Pirsig uses a third term, *quality* to describe the archetypal source of subjects and objects, leading towards a philosophy of unity. We suffer as modern human beings, from a split

---
47 This quote is attributed to Greek poet Archilocus (7th Century b.c.e.) though it is best known from its use by Isiah Berlin in his celebrated essay on Tolstoy.
48 Pirsig, Robert (1976) *Zen and the Art of Motorcycle Maintenance*. New York.

between a 'romantic' attitude, which is exemplified in Pirsig's book by riding a motorcycle, and a 'classic' attitude, exemplified by maintaining the motorcycle. He sees this split as both artificial and a cause of dissatisfaction and unhappiness suggesting that in fact the two attitudes can be unified, that we can, in Seymour Papert's words, 'fall in love with gears'.[49]

If we apply this to music we immediately see that there is no distinction between the mechanics of music and its expressive power – the one is dependent on the other. This suggests deeper, pre-socratic roots which go back further than Plato, to Pythagoras certainly, of whom much is written but little is actually known. Yet, whatever their historical accuracy, the links between the philosophy of unity and the musical theories attributed to Pythagoras have maintained a strong hold on the imagination, providing a model of the universe as a harmonious structure. For the Pythagoreans, both the unity of the physical universe and the integrity of the soul can be measured in arithmetical proportions which are perfectly replicated in musical sound.

The best bond is the one that effects the closest unity between itself and the terms it is combining; and this is best done by a continued geometrical proportion.[50]

Thus, vibrating within a single tone is a range of sympathetic tones which combine in arithmetical proportions: 2:1, 3:2, 4:3 and so on. If we then sound these together as new tones we immediately discover them to be 'harmonious'. So, in modern terms, the proportion 2:1 gives us an octave, 3:2 the perfect fifth, 4:3 the perfect fourth, 5:4 the major third, 6:5 the minor third.[51] When combined, this set of primary vibrations, the fundamental plus the first five harmonics, result in a major triad such as we hear in the first bar of the first Prelude of Bach's 48 Preludes and Fugues and at the beginning and end of almost every work of European classicism thereafter – the alpha and omega of music.[52]

Later, this set of proportions was also mapped onto the cosmos,

---

49 See the introduction in Papert, Seymour (1984), *Mindstorms*.
50 Plato, *The Timaeus*.
51 A simple experiment on a grand piano will instantly demonstrate this property of sound. Choose a low note (one which employs only a single string.) Then, play the note repeatedly on the keyboard with the left hand whilst running the middle finger of the right hand slowly and lightly along the length of the string in both directions. This will isolate the various harmonics which can be heard clearly as "fluted" or veiled tones.
52 One of my favourite examples is the opening of Bruckner's 7th Symphony which presents the triad of E major almost exactly as it is ordered in the harmonic series.

resulting in the well-known concept of the *harmony of the spheres*.[53] For Plato, this proportionality is also connected to the concept of soul and for later cosmologists, such as Kepler, this leads to the notion of a "world soul" which provides a kind of cosmic template for the music which we, as mortals, imitate each time we sing or play. For Pythagoreans (who believed, amongst other precepts, in the transmigration of souls), there was no dividing line between the rational and the magical and therefore, the proportionality found in musical tones becomes automatically linked to their transformational and healing powers. For Plato, the soul itself was defined in terms of a kind of entrainment or dynamic flow between *divine essence* and *physical reality* and this 'flow' is also arithmetical and therefore, in ideal terms, harmonious. In his Republic, he recounts the *Myth of Er* in which the soul of a soldier killed in battle rises to the cosmos and experiences a heavenly music created from these cosmic proportions.

It is this series of links connecting living matter (constantly in flux), universal patterns (unchanging or ideal) and human emotions which provide the basis for arguing (see the definitions in chapter 5) that music turns life into soul. The qualities of music in this sense combine rational structure with affective responses and further reinforce Suzanne Langer's (op.cit.) argument that the forms in which music is cast replicate the forms of feelings which we, as humans experience. It also suggests that music somehow provides us with an *understanding* of soul, indeed it may be the principal medium for 'soul-making' since it connects personal experience with transpersonal reality. When we make music, we are both foxes and hedgehogs.

The Archetypal Potential of Music

Whether we turn to Schopenhauer, Nietzsche, Plato or Pythagoras, it is surely unequivocal that when we experience music we undergo a shift in consciousness, we experience things differently. Wherever we might be or whatever we are doing, *the sound of music*[54] appears to connect us to different dimensions of the self or, at the very least, it alters our perceptive and affective state in such a way that we feel differently about the world. This can be classed as an archetypal experience in the sense

---

53 For an excellent modern perspective on the significance of this concept and its relationship to modern thinking see James, Jamie (1993), *The Music of the Spheres: Music, Science and the Natural Order of the Universe*. New York.

54 The universal appeal of this musical undoubtedly rests in its exploration of the archetypal properties of music. "The hills are alive with the sound of music" is a direct reference to Orpheus, whose singing apparently, could even cause stones to move.

that something deeply embedded in our senses awakens, and we experience the world afresh. This capacity of music to transform experience is fundamental to the concept and to the practice of *Lifemusic* which aims to connect us to life in new and revealing ways. The moment we hear music, we connect to that particular moment in time, unique and unrepeatable, and made numinous by the sonic event. Our need for music is then related to this transformational property and the way in which it opens us up to hidden parts of ourselves, enhancing our sense of meaning and direction.

How can we therefore access music, not as consumers but as creators? Is it possible to reclaim the deep, esoteric functions of this intangible and invisible art, uncovering its hidden potential and drawing out the properties which lie deep within the recesses of our own imaginations? Is it possible to re-connect with those (archetypal) functions of music which lie beyond the reach of the consumerist jungle with its emphasis on music as entertainment? Can we restore more fully to music its felt reality, its transformative function, its healing qualities, its revelatory properties and its prophetic powers? Such qualities and such powers, if we can access them, have profound implications for the way we encounter the world, relate to others and treat the environment. Viewing music from the perspective of its archetypal roots may well aid us in developing an understanding of the deep and powerful connections between the practice of music and the process of life.

The Four Musical Functions

I want to begin by dividing the experience of music into four functions, outlining the four fundamental properties which emerge, often in the company of gods and heroes the significance of whose stories increase as we become more familiar with their domains. It is slightly dangerous perhaps to delineate these four functions separately since they are all present in varying proportions in all music. However, different musical acts will inevitably place emphasis on different functions so with this in mind we can suggest these four underlying functions:

FORM – RITUAL – NARRATIVE – AFFECT

The first of these, the *formal function*, connects music to mathematics as well as to the Platonic theory of Ideals, since music always seeks to arrive at a perfect integration of its formal elements, abstract and precise. In fact, unless music works at a formal or structural level, however simple or complex, surprising or predictable, it fails to connect with us at all. Even randomly produced sounds can seem structured due to the mind's inevitable tendency to rationalise chaos.[55] The structural properties of music engage us even when they are not understood or are difficult to explain: most people can respond to music without having the slightest idea of how it is put together or how it maintains coherence, even at its most complex. The elegant craftsmanship which we find in Bach's F sharp minor fugue from book 2 of the '48' can be appreciated as a thing of beauty whether or not we perceive that it is a cleverly conceived set of triple counterpoints, with three fugue subjects interweaving in various permutations, no doubt a representation of the trinity in Bach's musical symbolism. And how many young female fans, literally wetting themselves in response to a performance by the Rolling Stones in 1967 would stop to think about the three-chord, 12-bar structures and pentatonic riffs which were responsible for the music's diuretic properties? It is only if we care to study music in greater formal depth, analysing its contents, that we begin to see how its structures are contained within both natural laws and culturally determined rules.

The second property of music, its *ritual function*, concerns how music works directly on the senses, not merely the sense of hearing but also on the physical body. Ritual is connected to sensate experience as distinct from emotional engagement. This is a quality which, as I hope to demonstrate, connects music with transformational experience and with the dance, articulating the intelligence of the body, locating our centre of awareness in the limbs, the limbic system, the heart and the guts, the autonomic functions. The physical immediacy which derives particularly from the temporal and rhythmic qualities of music therefore has the potential to take us into a liminal, or trance state, so it is this property of music, its pulsating force, which provides the necessary pre-conditions for ritual process.

The third property centres on its *narrative function*. Moving through time, indeed, articulating time itself, music takes us on a journey and it tells a story, not in literal terms with concrete images and characters but

---

55 In 1969, Hans Keller broadcast a composition by a ficititious young Polish composer named Pyotr Zak (a name which, in Polish, actually means 'student'). In fact, the 'music' was nothing more than random sounds created in the BBC Electronic Workshop. After some critical reviews which commented on the music's interesting structural properties, Keller published an article in *The Listener*, explaining the hoax. The critics struck back, explaining that no sounds, however they are strung together, could ever be entirely random and the power of the musical imagination ensures that structure is inevitably superimposed onto seemingly chance events.

through an unfolding and abstract series of tones, progressions, patterns and moods. When we do choose to attach music to literal narratives such as we find in song lyrics, films and operas, then these narratives instantly take on immeasurably enhanced significance, deepening our relationship to the underlying symbolic and emotional meanings of the texts, events and images and drawing out their archetypal depth. Mundane situations then become numinous and our literal stories become filled with a wider, imaginal consciousness.

The fourth, and in some ways the most deeply engaging of the four properties of music, is its *affective function*, the manner in which music works directly on the emotions, opening up channels of feeling and response. Even those with no musical training whatsoever, or who would claim to have no understanding of the mechanics of music, are nonetheless capable of being moved, sometimes to tears, by its tones and rhythms.

The balance between the four functions is of crucial importance to the way music works since over-emphasis on one at the expense of the others will inevitably distort the experience. An example of this of particular relevance to the practical aims of this book is the way in which professional musical training often places undue emphasis on technical ability to the detriment of creative understanding or spiritual qualities. In other musical cultures, notably in India, the teacher of music is also likely to be a spiritual guide, a guru. This concept feels alien to the European model, heavily influenced by a scientific, rational paradigm, which favours the graduated technical approach to learning, often ignoring the transpersonal meanings of music altogether, or at least setting them aside until a later date. The absence of improvisation in most musical training is symptomatic of strong over-identification with those archetypes which relate to tradition and theory at the expense of inspiration and spontaneity.[56] Musicology and musical analysis, relatively recent disciplines which are positively regarded within our education system, seem to distil theory to the point where the essential flavour of the musical experience becomes altogether lost, leading to sterility and dryness and often robbing the music entirely of its affective meanings.[57] Another example of the dangers of over-identification with a single musical archetype might be the way in which some rock musicians become so entangled in their own myth, fatally locked into the archetype of ritual that they burn out rapidly in a frenzy of sensory excess – of "sex

---

56 In archetypal terms this means favouring the Senex (old man, tradition, order) principle over the Puer (youth, spontaneity, inspiration.)

57 This is surely one of the main reasons for the general unpopularity of music in the school curriculum, a fact underpinned by numerous government reports.

and drugs and rock and roll" as Ian Dury encapsulated it. Syd Barrett of Pink Floyd and Janis Joplin were early casualties; Amy Winehouse and Pete Doherty more recent ones.

In Greek mythology, these four archetypal musical functions are represented by four figures whose characters and stories relate to the musical landscape in separate but complementary ways. The first of these is the god Apollo. Instructed in the arts by the muses, he is usually cited as the god of music due to his understanding of form, balance, harmony and beauty and in this sense he can be said to represent, principally, the quality of FORM.[58] He often appears with a lyre tucked under his arm, a present from his father, Zeus, (though it was the invention of Hermes). Apollo's half brother, Dionysus, also a god, represents RITUAL, encapsulating the physical and chthonic properties of music. His shape-changing abilities and his connection to transformational processes, including of course the fermentation of wine, connects him inevitably to carnival, to the dance and to the drum. Both Apollo and Dionysus, as deities, may be said to represent the autonomous natural laws which govern musical sounds. "Tis nature's voice, through all the moving world", as we hear in Purcell's *Ode on St. Cecilia's Day* (1692), reminding us once again that the art of music is based upon principles which are embedded within the laws of life itself. Both gods connect to the healing properties of music, Apollo through balance and wholeness, Dionysus through ritual transformation.

Next comes Orpheus, all too human, but with a divine gift of song, Orpheus is the prototypical musician, minstrel, troubadour, balladeer, mastersinger, rock star, whose songs possessed such beauty that they could uproot trees and cause stones to shift in their beds ('the hills are alive' etc.). The orphic myth, lyrical and tragic is, in many ways, peculiarly apposite to the European experience, though universal in its relevance. His journey to the underworld is one which we all make both imaginally and literally: it is a story of life, death and resurrection, love and loss of soul and it therefore underlines the NARRATIVE function of music. His journey, facilitated by music, leads him (and us) into the dark night of the soul[59] and back into the light of day, sadder but wiser.

Finally, the AFFECTIVE function is represented, archetypally, by Psyche who, like Orpheus, is human and, also like Orpheus, makes a descent into Hades; but where Orpheus is united, all too briefly, with his bride, Eurydice, in the underworld, Psyche is ultimately united

---

[58] The fact that Apollo is regarded as such in European culture underlines Nietzsche's argument, discussed earlier in this chapter, that the Dionysian element of music had been repressed.
[59] Some regard Orpheus as the prototype of the Christ figure, his journey and re-emergence from the underworld viewed as death and resurrection.

permanently with her lover, Cupid, in the heavenly regions: she is admitted to the pantheon, becoming herself a goddess. Her story is also about the pain of love and loss but it has, after many trials, a happy ending. Psyche both provides us with an image of the affective function in music and complements the male archetype represented by Orpheus: Psyche as Anima (soul) and Orpheus as Animus (spirit): both human, each requiring, for identical though differently articulated reasons, access to the world of the gods; each undergoing significant and painful trials in the process.

Different forms of mediation, different contexts of reception and different genres will inevitably place emphasis on different archetypes. For example, sitting down in a concert hall to listen to a symphony will inevitably foreground the formal and narrative qualities of tone, whereas dancing the night away at a rave will invariably put us in touch with our bodily senses and emphasise music's ritual functions. An orchestral concert is heavily weighted with the warm and sunny disposition of Apollo whilst a jazz club will be patronised more perhaps by his half-brother, Dionysus. Singing carols at Christmas connects people to time and memory and these personal and collective narratives expressed in song will echo with the voice of Orpheus. Solo song, and especially the female singer-songwriter will often invoke Psyche for inspiration. But we begin with Apollo.

Music and Spirit – Apollo

> *"Music exalts each joy, allays each grief,*
> *Expels diseases, softens every pain;*
> *And hence the wise of ancient days adored*
> *One power of physic, melody and song."*[60]
> (Thomas Armstrong)

> *"Thou didst the scatter'd atoms bind."*
> (Purcell/Tate, Ode on St. Cecilia's Day, 1692)

Apollo represents music as an art of grace, balance, light and form and we might add that he also represents the notion of beauty, often depicted as a blond and athletic youth. As a male sky god he represents *animus*, and, therefore, *spirit*, the questing, ascending energy which

---
60 Quoted in Bullfinch, Thomas *Myths of Greece and Rome* Ed. Bryan Holme (1981) Penguin Books.

inspires us to seek some kind of self-realisation and to improve our lot. But further than this, as Armstrong's verse reminds us, Apollo combines his musical skills with medicine and the healing arts and so music and well-being are joined at the very roots of our musical epistemology. In addition, Apollo is an all-knowing and clear-sighted god who sees everything, holding, as the founder of the oracle at Delphi, the gift of prophecy. He is also fond of sex and hunting.

The stories surrounding Apollo are numerous and point to a rich mixture of strength, athleticism, resourcefulness, courage, imagination, playfulness, arrogance and venality. Shortly after birth he becomes famous for hunting down and killing the monstrous Python, setting up the oracle at Delphi and establishing the competitive 'Pythian' games. Later on he teases Cupid and the little god takes his revenge by causing Apollo to fall in love with the nymph, Daphne, simultaneously causing *her* to reject Apollo's advances. During the chase, Daphne is turned into a laurel tree and the leaves are woven into a wreath which Apollo uses to decorate his lyre. This crown of laurels subsequently becomes a symbol of respect, awarded to athletes and warriors (and musicians no doubt) to honour their achievements.

As a musician, Apollo is often seen with a lyre tucked under his arm, a birthday present from his father, Zeus, but actually the invention of Hermes, the god associated with invention and imagination as well as with the capacity to move between the upper and lower regions, heaven and hades. Yet Apollo is instructed by the muses (his half-sisters) in the arts, sometimes appearing to be led by them and at other times seemingly taking the lead himself. This interplay between the female elements represented by the muses, and the male principle, represented by Apollo, seems to establish the prototypes of aesthetic creation and concepts of beauty, structure, craft and form as well as the contemplative arts. The nine muses between them cover all of the arts - poetry, song, dance, theatre, as well as the capacity to reflect on the world through history, memory and astronomy. So what significance does all of this have for music?

As god of the sun, Apollo sheds light on all who come into contact with him: he encourages us to rise to the zenith of possibility. We hear him perhaps at his most undiluted (and banal) forms in civic fanfares, military marches, oompah bands and even maybe, muzak; we hear him unadorned when practicing scales and arpeggios; we hear him magisterially in the music of Bach; and we hear him ubiquitously and therefore simplistically in all those pop songs which seem to be in C major, the bland anthems of Abba perhaps, or the saccharine tunefulness of Andrew Lloyd Webber. Indeed, whenever music appears in the major mode as opposed to the minor mode, Apollo is not too far distant, though maintaining the balance between major and minor modes is also his concern. The art of music as ritual is partly his domain, but rather than the deep rituals of sacrifice and transformation, which belong to his half-brother Dionysus, we hear in Apollo's music the celebrations of achievement. *The Ode to Joy* is more his domain than *The Drinking Song of Earth's Sorrow*[61] and he inevitably presides over national anthems[62], school hymns, the opening ceremony of the Olympics and competitive music festivals.

At a deeper level, the Apollonian spirit imbues us with a sense of order and of beauty. This grace and elegance is something which, particularly in a European perspective, we *require* music to provide: we popularly demand music to be pretty or beautiful although in reality, a lot of music is concerned equally with darker hues and a less ordered, more dangerous world. In undiluted form we hear Apollo in Bach's *Prelude in C*, from the first book of the *Well-tempered Keyboard*. Here, we can almost hear Bach saying, "this is what it feels like to be in C major, this is the meaning of C major, this is how it's done and it is beautiful." The opening chord could almost be a creation of Apollo's lyre itself, with its perfectly spaced arpeggio voicing and equally tempered tuning. But Apollo is also an instructor and this didactic element is something we also find frequently in the music of Bach and specifically in these Prelude and Fugues, It is as if Bach is constantly pointing out to us how it all works so that even in his most emotive music (in the Passions, for example) there is this sense of establishing a tradition, creating a canon. So the Prelude in C is also informing us that this system of composition, especially the new tuning, the equal temperament, the crowning achievement of European musical thought which makes possible key centres and modulations and all the intricate labyrinthine potential of tonality is also the future of music, representing a world of order, beauty, rationality and progress.

Bach was not actually elevated to this (Apollonian) position as the central (canonised) figure in European music until the early to mid 19th Century. The rediscovery of his music at this point in European history can be felt therefore as the expression of an archetype which was emerging collectively, politically and technologically through the

---

61 The opening song in Mahler's *Song of the Earth*.
62 Even the national hymns of non-European countries seem to have followed Apollo's example, casting their melodies into a tonal mould.

unification of the German states in particular and through economic and industrial expansion in Europe generally. Behind this cultural development and the simultaneous establishment of the musical canon, stands the archetypal figure of Apollo, providing the template, the *idea of canon* and the *notion of greatness* epitomised, even today perhaps, by the figure of Beethoven. The beauty of a tradition rests in the sense of continuity it provides, deepening our sense of ourselves through our relationship with a single thread which reaches deeply into the past. Thus Apollo connects us to time through an awareness of the significance of tradition and a history which resonates in music based on a system (tonality) which is rational, clear sighted and hierarchically ordered. This is a position of power and it appealed and still appeals strongly to the European mindset. On the other hand, the danger with any canonical tradition is that it too easily creates orthodoxy, a rule-bound ideology with a rigid, sanctified repertoire which can so easily lose touch with the immediacy of the present, with depth of soul and thus in danger of erecting barriers to cultural renewal.

For this reason, the Apollonian spirit seems to find favour within the ruling hegemonies ensuring that the major patrons of music up until the 19th Century, notably the church and the nobility were prone to use music (and musicians) as emblems of their power. This is a theme which runs through Tim Blanning's (2002) book *The Culture of Power and the Power of Culture* where he describes how musicians, singers and even highly respected composers such as Bach, Haydn and Mozart were often kept under the tightest control by their paymasters. In one passage Blanning provides evidence of how Frederick the Great of Prussia "chose not to sit in the royal box but preferred a seat immediately in front of the orchestra pit, so that he could keep a sharp eye both on the stage and the musical director's score."[63] Such control would not have been possible were not the musical system itself dominated by rule-bound processes and notated scores. So from this angle, we can begin to view the whole European musical tradition as the perpetuation of a myth which constantly replays a contest between rationality, control and order on the one hand and irrationality, depth of expression and improvisatory freedom on the other.

Apollo also provides us with the notion of music as a vessel of *celebration*. When we consider, for example, a piece such as Brahms's *Academic Festival Overture* or the pageant of music which opens the

---

63 Blanning (2002), op.cit.

Olympics or indeed a football anthem such as 'You'll Never Walk Alone', then we can be certain that the archetypal energy of Apollo fills the stadium. This civic role for music is also expressed in the tradition of music festivals as occasions where young and old compete musically in much the same fashion as they would in athletics or swimming. It is important to look at the dangers inherent in this as well as the benefits. The BBC Young Musician of the Year contest which showcases classically trained performers runs parallel to programmes such as X-factor, which seeks out talent in the popular music field. In both instances, the depth meaning of the music becomes easily swamped by the hype which attends such events and the participants submit themselves to the possibility of humiliation as they are inevitably sorted into winners and losers by judges who are considered to be experts but who are in effect merely human beings posturing as gods. What, in the end, is achieved on these occasions may be less important than what is lost. In order to cope with the humiliation which can easily attend failure, the ego builds around itself a protective wall, which renders soul invisible or invulnerable. The music then easily becomes dry and meaningless. In the reverse case, audiences become hysterical whilst performers, even those who are successful, sometimes fall apart, unable to cope, as humans, with the kind of elevation which belongs rightly to gods.

Then, when Apollo regards love as a game, he suffers the consequences. In teasing Cupid he encourages the little god to send a gold tipped arrow which inflames his desire. But Daphne's arrow is tipped with lead and she is rendered impervious to his charms leading inevitably to disappointment and loss. Apollo caught up with Daphne, only to lose her as she turned into a laurel tree. The message seems to be that if you try to hunt down soul, you surely lose her! The wreath which he then attached to his lyre and which becomes the prototype of the medals nowadays awarded to musical and Olympic athletes may be a mark of achievement but also a reminder of loss as well as a warning against hubris. Apollo idly teased Cupid and, having made light of love, paid dearly for it. The beauty of music, its aesthetic and poetic meaning, as well as its capacity to bring people together in empathic relationship, is all too easily lost when the prize being sought is a gold medallion, a framed certificate or a silver cup.

But if Apollo presides over national hymns, he might also be thought to appear in the praise songs of the griots of West African countries and in the shamanic traditions of various cultures, whether in Siberia or South America, in which traditional rhythms and sacred chants become tools for healing. The shamanic spirit in art and music has been explored elsewhere, notably by Michael Tucker in his magisterial book *Dreaming with Open Eyes*.[64] In this book and in a later discussion between Tucker, Maxwell Steer and the composer Jonathan Harvey[65] the author draws attention to the difficulties faced by anyone in the modern world who seeks to access these depth or soul properties of music, painting or sculpture. So, in some ways, the Apollonian spirit itself and the culture which arises from it views practices such as shamanism as anti-intellectual or irrational so, for example in a culture over-identified with this particular archetype, the only universally acceptable form of medicine is that which is based on scientifically proven evidence. This leaves the healing properties of music and the profession of music therapy either marginalised or in the difficult and dubious position of having to prove its effectiveness medically or in line with scientific paradigms. That music creates a sense of well-being seems central to its function but the strength of music to heal and transform goes beyond this and Apollo therefore provides a link between music and medicine, demonstrating that tone and texture in sound have the potential to heal and transform both body and mind. Music is powerful medicine and therefore its powers need to be recognised and regulated. We find this principle of order and containment in Apollo's stories as well as in his musical creations.

This brings us to what is perhaps Apollo's most important attribute, the capacity to create balance between the various archetypes and the musical qualities informed by them. Thus, in the symphonies of Beethoven, for example, we often find a perfect correlation, or rather a dramatic dialogue, between light elements and darker hues, or between the lyrical (song) and the kinaesthetic (dance). We hear Apollo's hunting horn at the opening of the third symphony (the 'Eroica') representing the command, confidence, youthfulness, simplicity and strength of the Apollonian spirit, a fanfare for the enlightenment. Yet, within a few bars, a darkening occurs, the sun goes behind a cloud and the low D flat reminds us that day is followed by night and even this god's bright sun is extinguished rhythmically by the very laws of time which he dictates. Napoleon, to whom Beethoven's third was originally dedicated, eventually suffered precisely the nemesis which comes from hubristic over-identification with the archetype. His 'Apollonian' gesture,

---

64 Tucker, Michael (1992) *Dreaming with Open Eyes, the Shamanic Spirit in Twentieth Century Art and Culture*. Harper Collins, London.
65 Published under the title Music and Inner Meaning in Vol 14 of *Contemporary Music Review* (1996) P. 9-23.

crowning himself Emperor in Vienna in 1803, so angered Beethoven that the composer destroyed the dedication page of the score. We also hear Apollo's horns in the hunting trio of the third movement of the 'Eroica' and again in the Finale, with a musical and mythical reference to Prometheus who famously challenged the gods, stole their fire and suffered a tortured fate as punishment.

In the music of The Beatles we discover an integration of the earthiness and darker colours of rock music with the humour and lightness of popular song and the sophistication and elegance of the classical tradition. There seems little doubt that much of their success was derived from this capacity to capture these balancing elements of the archetype. In *Eleanor Rigby* for example, the use of the string quartet locates an otherwise contemporary song in an older tradition, maintaining lightness despite the blues reference on the words "where do they all belong." A song such as this almost automatically becomes a classic – enters another canon. Once The Beatles gave up touring (see Dionysus below) and moved into the recording studio, their music moves away from its roots in rock and roll and becomes more measured, more balanced, more worked out and therefore less spontaneous. This feels like a distinct shift from the domain of Dionysus to the more rational world of Apollo but they managed to maintain a link with the raw energy of the touring days, achieving a remarkable blend of elements in celebrated albums such as *Revolver* and *Abbey Road*.

The Blues itself, especially in its developed classic 12-bar form, provides an elegant example of Apollonian balance, a genre which has surely been admitted to his temple. The three, four-bar phrases, the three chords, each with, typically, four notes (dominant seventh chords), the ambiguities between the light and dark through the frequent juxtaposition of major and minor modes and the combination of European harmony (the basis of blues harmony) with African scales (the basis of blues melody) are, without doubt, one of the most miraculous products of musical history. When we further consider that the blues form follows a circular trajectory, progressing through twelve bars and then restarting, the link to the sun god becomes even more apparent. Moreover, the blues is and always was, a healing form, both in an emotive, personal sense, the lyrics and melodies often charting the rough seas of sex and relationships, but also in a collective sense, drawing simultaneously on the deep, uprooted African traditions, with all of the cultural trauma and personal terror that implies (the source of blues melody), and the European experience (the source of blues harmony). These oppositions are then perfectly synthesised, creating a wholeness and a balance which works its powerful magic on the collective psyche.

If Apollo provides us with the archetypes of balance and healing he also connects us to time. As a sun god this is unsurprising but this relationship also includes the important link between time and memory. The mother of the muses is Mnemosyne – memory – and this capacity for recall, our sense of the past and how this capacity to reflect creates a sense of the self becomes a major element in the psychologising process of individual human life as well as an indispensable aspect of the collective, identity-forming process for nations and ethnic groups. It is a property which, perhaps more than any other human attribute makes possible what Hillman terms "the poetic basis of mind". Memory and time work together to create consciousness and music often takes us into our memories, of childhood experiences, of significant moments in our personal lives and of the celebrations which measure our connections to others. Like smell, sound tends to hold in its vibratory qualities instinctual memory and in the case of music, this means emotional memory as well as the ability to recall not just the events themselves but the feelings associated with them and this helps us to make sense of the past.

Music both measures and celebrates time and Apollo provides us with the tools for both. The way in which music tends towards equally spaced beats, fixed pulse rather than free rhythm is particularly Apollonian. This can be heard particularly in classical music where the melodic patterns tend to fall into fourfold patterns, squarely on the beat rather than sitting astride of the beat. Yet, in the case of bebop jazz, for example, Apollo manages to contain the syncopations within the structures, finding balance between seemingly utterly opposed elements, between the freedom and improvisational flights of melody, seeking release from the beat, and the perfectly balanced 8 bar phrases around which most be-bop tunes are constructed. In much African music, the complexity of speech rhythm finds its way into drumming patterns which overlay each other in polyrhythmic complexity, yet, beneath this fecundity of rhythm which seems to reflect the irrationality of natural processes we can still feel the underlying rationality of Apollonian pulse.

The case of jazz is particularly interesting since what existed originally as a music representing 'other', and thus standing in opposition to the norm, relatively quickly develops its own canonical status and its own theoretical 'rules'. Improvisation, especially within the bebop tradition, is precisely contained and even today, is an important focus or 'locus classicus' for many jazz musicians. Indeed, most young jazz musicians seek to "win their spurs" by learning to improvise over the "rhythm changes", a set of harmonic progressions derived from and never very far departing from the Gershwin song "I' Got Ryhthm". This 32-bar structure, a standard convention in the chorus sections of popular songs of the 30s, is a perfectly balanced AABA form within which we encounter the two basic chord progressions of western European music, the so-called II-V-I (the A section) and the cycle of fifths (the B section). On top of this, we often hear (in "Lester Leaps In" for example) a melodic line based on the pentatonic scale, which is the basic melodic building block of much African music, or even a minor blues melody over what is originally a major mode progression. Thus, within a single convention, we find a remarkable balance created out of musics from two very different traditions.

The role of the lyre in Apollo's musical landscape is of deep significance, especially when we reflect on the god responsible for its invention, Hermes. The lyre is the archetype of all musical instruments which may therefore be thought of as magical objects which transform vibrations into sound and sound into meaning (Hermes is also in effect, the god who injects meaning into things.) The instruments of contemporary music may not always seem so, especially the technologically sophisticated instruments which populate orchestras, but the electric guitar, which we may take to be descended directly from the lyre, and which has become the iconic instrument of rock, retains much of this magical and symbolic quality – intense, winged and phallic.

Yet, the instrument which surely represents more than any other the evolved Apollonian spirit in European musical culture is the piano. Laid out visibly in black and white is the map of musical history: the diatonic scale, (the white notes), the pentatonic scale (the black notes) and the chromatic scale (all the notes). Together they provide the whole cycle of possibilities contained within the tonal system and therefore the potential for grand narratives built out of different key centres which often seem to create a form of non-verbal dialectic, the sonic equivalent of Plato's dialogues or Shakespeare's plays. The keyboard itself developed into a visual symbol of the archetype of order, rationality and balance. Perhaps it is no accident that the white notes represent a dynamic European system (the diatonic scale) whilst the black notes create a static, pentatonic scale, non-European. At some stage in the evolution of the keyboard, around the end of the 18th Century, this arrangement became the norm, clearly the result of a 'decision' formed partly sub-consciously. Whether or not we subscribe to this explanation of the origins of black and white notes, Beethoven was in no doubt about the archetypal quality of the piano, writing to piano makers Broadwood and Sons in 1817 having received a gift of their famous grand, "I shall regard it as an altar upon which I will place the choicest offerings of my mind to the Divine Apollo".[66]

Richness and scope of tone make the piano the ideal solo instrument. This is also a handicap, so that whilst it represents the romantic ideal of the individual soul, which translates instantly into a social ideal, it simultaneously risks isolating the performer who may find herself locked away for hours, days or month in solo practice, (the price paid by many of the pioneers of progress and invention through the 19th Century). Conversely, the "pub pianist", master or mistress of the art of accompaniment, was, and, in some traditional hostelries, remains, the centre of attention despite the rise of the juke box. In the piano concertos of Mozart, the solo piano often appears as a playful and witty protagonist, or else as a poetic soul struggling with or supported through a drama which places the individual in a dynamic relationship to the outside world. We only have to listen to the finale of the A major concerto (K488) to hear Mozart's own irrepressible wit and diversions flirting cheekily with the woodwind of the orchestra. In the concertos of Beethoven, Liszt, Schumann, Brahms, Grieg and Tchaikovsky this role becomes heroic, the piano as a warrior or Promethian figure struggling in conflict with the gods, with destiny.

The archetype of the individual is constantly reinforced by the substantial solo piano repertoire, especially in the case of a composer like Chopin who exploited to the full its poetic and its heroic dimensions. This quality finds its way into modern forms, jazz in particular, where pianists such as Bill Evans and Thelonius Monk managed in their highly contrasted ways to capture the ambiguities of the jazz vocal style through ingenious use of chord voicings and grace notes. The keyboard today has become the basis for electronically created music where it is now the primary medium for inputting musical data into midi systems and therefore an ubiquitous cultural tool. Where the school hall once boasted

---

66 Beethoven, letter to Broadwood Feb. 3 1818. Quoted in Palmieri, R. (Ed.) (2003) *Encyclopedia of Keyboard Instruments*. Routledge, London.

a piano (many still do) the music classroom today is often populated by ranks of midi keyboards controlled by young students, each wearing headphones, each locked into their own digitally pristine, solitary, Apollonian soundworld.

As an instrument playing alongside others, the piano is indeed godlike, a controlling force which can easily swamp other instruments, not just because of its volume, but because its tonal centring and its harmonic tendencies carry powerful collective and cultural messages which become impossible to ignore. The whole concept of equal temperament which has dominated European music up to and beyond the birth of the blues, is based on a hierarchical system out of which it is possible to create tonal drama and tonal dialectic. This provides beauty, to be sure, but it also easily turns music into a branch of philosophy. Furthermore, since it is impossible for more than one person at a time to improvise tonal structures,[67] it isolates the composer and dislocates the act of creation from the participative act of music-making. Yet it also makes possible grand designs, symphonies, concertos, string quartets and tone poems.

These are the Apollonian virtues – leadership, power, strength and beauty; yet, the hubristic dangers inherent in all of this cannot be ignored. Apollo, enlightened and beautiful though he may be, is only part of the story, only one aspect of music. His sunny disposition and hunter's aim surely need to be balanced by those opposing qualities which provide darker, instinctive ambiguities and which "walk on the wild side".

Music and Intoxication – Dionysus

Essential to his worship was a spiritual release through music and dance; in the history of religion, archetypal behaviour demands music and dance as essential for the most exalted rituals.[68]

When Stravinsky's The Rite of Spring was premiered in Paris in 1913, the theatre erupted: the audience rioted and the police had to be called.[69] This kind of reaction to modernist music was not, however, at all unusual. Schoenberg's highly chromatic music, in particular, his *Pierrot Lunaire* and the *5 Orchestral Pieces*, received similar receptions in Vienna and there were often identical emotionally charged exchanges between those

---

[67] The "cleverness" of jazz depends upon the ability of musicians to improvise *around* previously existing tonal structures.
[68] Morford, Mark P. O. and Lenardon, Robert J. *Classical Mythology*, 8th Ed. OUP
[69] Stravinsky's own account of this memorable event appears in *Conversations with Robert Craft*. (1963).

audience members who supported the composer and those who were intent on ridiculing or dismissing the music as cacophony. In Budapest, Bartok's *Miraculous Mandarin* was banned on the grounds that it was obscene and Nijinsky's choreographic response to Debussy's erotic tone poem inspired by Mallarme, *Prélude a L'Après Midi d'un Faune*[70] was similarly censored for its explicit sexuality.

There is something in all of this music which offends tradition, which runs counter to prevailing orthodoxies and yet which feels deeply honest to those who can bear to hear its truth. In each example of musical modernism there is a sense that tradition is being challenged, not from outside the system but from within: the European composer, having evolved steadily from humble servant, creating music for powerful patrons, whether from church or state, had finally shaken off the last binding restrictions, allowing the music to reclaim its cthonic roots. Stravinsky was already a respected composer in the Russian nationalist tradition, producing works which were exotic and colourful though hardly revolutionary; Schoenberg was steeped in the music of German romanticism and his early *Gurrelieder*, though vast and emotionally charged, had been ecstatically received by the Viennese public; Bartok, a concert pianist who revered Bach, Beethoven and Liszt was a conservatoire musician and teacher. But very suddenly, it all changed: it was as if something which had been stirring beneath the surface, some dark energy, all of a sudden broke into consciousness and within a very short space of time this extraordinary music appeared simultaneously in more than one centre.

In *The Rite of Spring*, we are witnessing music which appears to draw its energy directly from nature, connecting with the body, with the earth, with instinctual forces and with the celebration of death and new life. Musically, this is achieved through structures based almost entirely around rhythmic development allied to a modality which is contained in small motivic cells rather than expanded into full-blown melodic lines. Gone are the grand dramas of Romanticism and the lyrical (narrative) melodies of classicism: in their place we hear the pagan drum, the shaman's rattle and bells, the static repetitions of ritual chant and folk song, the yoiking of the Sami people and the throat singing of Siberian shamans. Harmonic rhythm, the steady tread of chord progressions has all but disappeared, the composer simply building chords on top of one another to create tensile blocks which do not in themselves create any

---

70 First performed in the Théâtre du Châtelet in Paris on May 29, 1912.

sense of the kind of tonal narratives we encounter in the music of Bach, Beethoven or Brahms. The dynamic propulsion of *The Rite* is purely physical, created largely through brute repetition and an uneasy, yet somehow logically arranged, displacement of rhythmic accents. If we view this scheme archetypally, it feels as if the Apollonian spirit which, in Europe, had been represented by tonal structures embedded in the body of works which constitute the canon, has been swept away to be replaced by a barbaric energy which is chaotic, revolutionary, rebellious, iconoclastic and intuitive. The canon had exploded!

In Schoenberg's music, the tonal system is taken to the edge of the cliff and then pushed over! The increasing use of chromatic harmony which had coloured the works of the 19th Century in ever more expressive hues, is taken by Schoenberg to its logical conclusion, whereby the expressive colouration is so foregrounded that it becomes the central principle of the musical structure and the tonal logic is pushed so far into the background that it becomes virtually inaudible. Where Stravinsky's *Rite* feels brutish, barbaric and primitive, Schoenberg's *Pierrot Lunaire*, for example seems subtle, sophisticated and dreamlike. This musical language is often referred to as 'atonal' but the accurate term for it is 'pantonal' or 'pan-chromatic', both allusions to the Greek god from whose name we derive the word 'panic'.

This very different energy is presided over by Apollo's half-brother Dionysus, attended, not by muses, but by furies (Maenads), wild female followers; and where Apollo, as Phoebus, traverses the sky in neat rotations (cycles of fifths perhaps?) Dionysus wanders from island to island, changes shape, roams the forests, crosses the seas. Musically, then, we can view Dionysus more as a god of unpredictability (and therefore improvisation) but also of transformation, fundamental changes which can only come about through ritual death and rebirth, precisely the theme of Stravinsky's *Rite*. Indeed, Dionysus means literally, twice born, an allusion to the narratives of his birth (see below).

The Dionysian myths also provide a vital symbolic connection between wine and blood which become one of the primary symbols of religious symbolism and personal renewal in European culture. The mystery rites which Dionysus invented were not merely drunken orgies (bacchanals in the Roman version), but theatrical celebrations of heightened consciousness and mystic ecstasy, symbolic enactments connecting chthonic energy with human awareness. The process of fermentation itself is a symbol of the transformational qualities of decay: as the vine withers and the fruit decays so consciousness is enhanced through the intoxicating spirit released as alcohol from the dying fruit: thus, wine, and its properties, becomes a major symbol of death and rebirth. The Dionysian rites were accompanied by wild dancing and music, the equivalent of the modern day rave perhaps, bringing happiness and fulfilment for those who follow and understand the precepts and accept the rituals; madness and death for those who ignore these truths.

The Dionysian spirit permeates the first movement from Gustav Mahler's *Song of the Earth* where the sorrows of the world are condensed into a remarkable 8 minute long paean to nature and transcendence. As the wine is poured into golden goblets, the poet speaks:

> *hold back, do not drink until you have seen the world in its short-lived beauty and felt the truth, that, though spring is eternal, we have less than 100 years to enjoy the rotting fruits of this earth. Look! See the ape, howling on the gravestone, in the moonlight? Now my comrades, now is the moment, drain your glasses. Dark is life, dark is death!* [71]

The process of decay is not merely a process of transformation but it creates the intoxicating substance (alcohol) which heightens consciousness, leading to a sudden but fleeting understanding of the mysteries. As Mahler himself approached death, and as the Austrian capital in which he lived witnessed the end of an era, so life itself suddenly became that much more vivid, that much more intensely lived. As the heroic tenor sinks onto the word "Tod" (death), so the horn signal, the phallic call to life, sounds again.

The stories of Dionysus are diverse, violent, mysterious and transformational, presenting an image of a god who represents two polarised aspects of human beings: the bestial and the ecstatic. As his name tells us, he was twice born, each birth accompanied by bizarre violence, flesh eating, divine fire and magical properties. He is a shape-shifter, a wanderer, a volatile and vengeful god, who, in one story, turns a ship full of pirates, who had attempted to abduct him, into dolphins. Through his 'invention' of wine, he becomes associated with intoxication, those heightened states familiar to all but the most rigid teetotallers and represented in the ancient tales by bands of wild followers: nymphs (young beautiful and female), satyrs (male, lecherous, god-like and half

---

[71] Paraphrased from the original.

goat, half human) and Maenads, women who forsake domesticity to drink wine, have sex and eat raw meat from animals torn to pieces by their own hands. In Euripides' play The Bacchae, the young King, Pentheus, who attempts to ban the Dionysian rites, meets the same fate, as did Orpheus (see below).

The Dionysian rites were therefore sacrificial events mixing blood and wine, though little detail has come down to us since this was a mystery cult standing in many respects at a pole from the more Apollonian inclined Orphic/Pythagorean rituals which emphasised asceticism and restraint. The Dionysian spirit represents forms of truth which emerge when we strip away the masks of civilized behaviour or rather replace them with the masks of carnival, awakening the primary energy of living forms. This fundamental truth, the underlying irrationality of life, its chaotic source, resonates strongly with Schopenhauer's 'will', as it does with Henri Bergson's 'prime reality' but, as argued earlier in this chapter, it is to Nietzsche that we turn for the most eloquent understanding and expression of this spirit and for whom music was the primary medium through which this "insatiable hunger for existence" might be propelled into conscious living. Intoxication comes not necessarily from alcohol or drugs but also through those forms of music which drive to the physical heart of things – blues, jazz, rock and rap.

We can hear this quality in the music of many different genres but Rock music, in particular draws or finds its inspiration in the Dionysian archetype. Mick Jagger of The Rolling Stones, who might be said to personify the spirit of the rock idiom as well as anyone, uses music to this day as the driver for a form of theatre where the imagery and metaphors appear to strip away the veneer of civilised order revealing the authenticity of feeling and matter lying beneath. Like other white musicians before him, such as Elvis Presley and Jerry Lee Lewis, Jagger embraces the music of 'other', the blues which had its roots in the disenfranchised, nomadic African American communities, re-discovering the rawness required for an expression of the new consciousness, the transformational and often ecstatic energy of the nineteen sixties. In 'Sympathy for the Devil' for example, The Rolling Stones directly identify themselves, whether consciously or not, with Dionysian imagery, their performances becoming examples of shamanic theatre. Elvis, like the god himself, inspired thousands of young women to scream with ecstasy during his performances, inviting deep disapproval if not irrational hatred from countless white conservative Americans, baffled by how this young white boy could embrace what they regarded as the essence of bestiality in music. The Beatles, in their earlier, touring phase, inspired similar hordes of otherwise respectable young girls to leave behind their middle class homes to scream and shake in uncontrolled frenzy, often losing control of their bladders in the process. Early in their career, The Who often ended performances with a destructive orgy, smashing up their instruments and setting fire to the stage! David Bowie, another white musician/actor developed a number of alter egos, masks, (notably Ziggy Stardust) capturing the ambiguity and theatricality which is an essential element of the Dionysian rite. Once again, despite (or because of) the hermaphroditic quality of his stage persona (and his admitted bi-sexuality) it was particularly young women who were entranced by his performances. These modern day *maenads* were affected by the music, for sure, but also by the power of this particular music, rock, to open up an unconscious, symbolic need for transcendence; a ritualised drive towards renewal, fertility and ecstasy, a hunger for life.[72]

As the god of theatre we also meet Dionysus in the grand spectacles of rock, in the light shows of Deep Purple, the theatrical displays of Pink Floyd and the legendary festivals - Woodstock, Glastonbury, Isle of Wight. Some of the music which was performed at these events is etched onto the social history of the modern era, significant moments in which major transformations of consciousness took place. Somehow, we all wanted to be there; listening to recordings is insufficient. Woodstock, in particular, seemed to represent a distillation of all the unease, disillusion and trauma which surrounded the Vietnam war, the tragedy and violence of world events, mapped either subtly or consciously onto performances by The Grateful Dead, Joni Mitchell, Jimi Hendrix, The Band, Crosby Stills and Nash, Santana, Creedence Clearwater Revival, Janis Joplin, Jefferson Airplane, The Who and Ravi Shankar (to name only a selection). There is no dis-location in *this* music; no detailed attention to the refined niceties of performance; no carefully rehearsed techniques; no grace and not much balance: simply the truth.

If Apollo, despite being pictured as a handsome youth, represents the Senex or wise old man, the upholder of order and tradition, form and balance, then Dionysus is connected more with the Puer archetype or the spirit of eternal youth, disorder, rebellion, freedom and excess. The

---

72 Stravinsky's audience in 1913 may have been shocked at the imaginary narrative in which a young virgin dances herself to death yet, more recently, rave culture has produced a number of instances in which young women have collapsed and died as a result of the combined effects of a drug, appropriately named ecstasy, and excessive dancing.

emotional din and clash of his music and the unrestrained freedom and passion of his worship is often presented in direct contrast to Apollo, god of the lyre's disciplined melody, reason, and self-control. These two antithetical forces, the irrational (Dionysian) and the rational (Apollonian) are dominant archetypal motifs, inherent in human nature, which seemed to attain particular force and visibility in the second half of the 20th Century.

In the Dionysian myths we encounter this Puer energy in the Satyrs and their older brothers the Sileni, male creatures, half animal, half human, who seem to represent men who have foresworn a life of achievement and public duty in order to live libidinously and irresponsibly, drinking wine and consorting with women even at an age when most have retired on a final salary pension and devoted themselves to playing golf.[73] It is not difficult to see the figure of the satyr active in the lives of numerous rock musicians who, assuming they survive a youth of excess, refuse to grow old but continue to 'strut their stuff' well into old age. The reluctance to grow old gracefully might also be witnessed in the behaviour of their fans, some of whom are still riding motorbikes well past an age when it is neither wise nor safe to do so.[74] But Dionysus does not inspire a need for safety or security, rather, his energy, once it takes hold, whether or not as the result of intoxication, drives people to abjure the civilised, to don the masks of carnival[75] and to embrace a kind of alternative lifestyle which, whilst it may not earn medals for bravery, knighthoods for valour or a laurel wreath for achievement, imparts knowledge of those inner mysteries without which life would be dry, dutiful and meaningless.

As a god of fertility, Dionysus also inspires music which connects us to the seasons and to the cycles of growth and decay, warmth and cold, light and dark, traversing a more complex and circuitous route than Apollo's neat daily arc. In Bob Copper's book *A Song for Every Season*, he celebrates the dying tradition of folk singing which at one time allowed communities to express through song and dance significant points in the calendar as well as the rituals and festivals celebrating birth, death, weddings and funerals.[76] This tradition, as in so many European countries, has slowly disappeared, kept alive only through recordings or folk clubs

---

[73] See Philip Roth's novel *Sabbath's Theatre* for a contemporary narrative of the satyr.
[74] The so-called 'born again biker' provides an appropriate symbol for the Dionysian spirit since the god himself, as his name tells us, was twice-born.
[75] I shall be discussing music's carnival functions in greater detail in Chapter 6.
[76] Copper, Bob (1971), *A Song for Every Season: 100 years in the Life of a Sussex Farming Family*. Heinemann.

meeting in village halls and the back rooms of pubs. So we might usefully call on the spirit of Dionysus to lead us back to this primary function of music, its capacity to connect us to time, to the seasons and to the festivals which chart the annual cycle.

Yet, as folk culture decays, Dionysus re-appears through another form of music-making which emerged as an offshoot of jazz. The free improvisation which emerged in the nineteen sixties through the modal jazz of pioneers such as Miles Davis, John Coltrane, Ornette Coleman, Eric Dolphy, Pharoah Sanders, Charles Mingus and Sun Ra seems to shake off what remained of the European legacy, reaching back towards the African roots of jazz. The sixties witnessed both a broadening and a deepening of jazz both in its language and in the intentionality of its performers through a 'post-bop' style epitomised by the extended improvisatory excursions of John Coltrane and his contemporaries.

The development of Coltrane's style, painfully and painstakingly worked out through a dedicated form of practice which comes close to meditation, demonstrates how he appears to find release from the temporal expressive language of mainstream jazz, partly through a straightening out of his sound (straight tone, even quavers) and partly through a technical supremacy which enabled him to build up vast skyscrapers of tone or 'sheets of sound' as they are often called. Together with Elvin Jones he seems to find a kind of liberation from the bar-line so that within the poly-rhythmic cascades of notes a broader and much longer pulse appears. The music seems often to be both very fast and very slow, seeming to chart simultaneously the vibrations of inner life, the whirling of atoms and the long tread of the seasons or even the movement of the stars. Within this music we can hear both wildness, a release from convention, and a transcendent striving for heightened consciousness. This principle of transformation through ecstatic trance or liminal states, can be heard for example in the recorded versions of *A Love Supreme, Ascension and Mars*, modern day symbols of the Dionysian spirit.

Music and Narrative – Orpheus

According to legend, Orpheus, the prototypical musician, sang with such unsurpassed beauty that it had a magical effect not only on those humans and gods who were fortunate enough to be within range of his voice and lyre but also animals, trees, plants and even inanimate objects like rocks: all were equally moved by his music, literally or figuratively.

The story is well-known.[77] He falls deeply in love with a beautiful nymph, Eurydice, and they prepare for a midsummer marriage. But before the ceremony has even begun, Eurydice steps on a poisonous snake, collapses and dies, her soul floating downwards to the underworld. Orpheus is inconsolable and decides to make the journey to Hades himself to plead for the return of his bride. Through the subtlety and beauty of his songs he makes his journey to the depths, his singing softening the heart of the ferryman and even turning Cerberus, the fierce three-headed dog, into a yapping Dalmatian!

He finally arrives before Hades and his wife, Persephone, and sings with such passion and beauty that Hades (persuaded by his wife) agrees to release Eurydice. But of course, the stern god sets conditions: "you must walk in front of your bride, look ahead and on no account turn to see if she follows. Should you look back, even the slightest glance, then she will be lost to you for ever." (see plate section)

Orpheus agrees and sets off, his heart content but his mind unsure. Was she behind him? Could he hear her footsteps? Was that her breathing or merely the sounds of the wind? Surely one small sideways glance won't hurt? It was to be the last glimpse of her, his soul woman, her face fading into the depths of eternal night, his eyes blinded by the light of day. Fingertips reach out but do not meet. Orpheus sang, Eurydice sighed and all was lost.

Back in the upper world all has changed. Orpheus can sing only songs of grief. The furies, female followers of Dionysus taunt him and, angered by his rejection of their advances, throw their spears at him. At first, disarmed by his singing, their weapons cannot find their aim. But the women set up a wailing which drowns out the singer's lamenting with wild cacophony and they tear him limb from limb, casting his head into the river... where, still singing, it floats down to the sea.

Orpheus provides us with the prototype of the composer, singer, songwriter, musician, improviser, performer and sound healer. The entire story centres on the extraordinary musical skills gifted to him by his mother, Calliope, the foremost of the muses, though all of the muses are musically skilled. But Orpheus is a mortal and therefore the way the myth unfolds provides us (as mortals) with numerous insights into the nature of music and how this 'god-like' gift might be used. It seems particularly significant for example that his singing and playing affects not only other mortals but also the whole of the natural world, animate and inanimate,

---

77 The re-telling here is influenced by numerous and diverse sources, including the many libretti which, from the birth of opera in the early 1600s, draw upon the myth of Orpheus.

reminding us that music has a physical reality which is in some ways autonomous, linked inextricably with natural processes, with the structure of things. Beyond this he is able to charm (or enchant) the gods themselves, signifying that music connects us somehow directly to transpersonal, metaphysical reality in a way that no other art can. So whilst Orpheus' presence can be felt in a literal sense in the performances of just about anyone with a guitar strung across their body, his story reminds us constantly that when we make music we connect to *life, love, joy, tragedy, grief, descent, fear, hope, loss, death, transfiguration and transcendence* (his narrative in a nutshell). Every musical act contains the whole of life.

It is no surprise therefore that the figure of Orpheus has been a constant presence in musical development in the West and particularly in the gradual development of extended musical forms. It will be useful therefore to examine this phenomenon in a little more depth before moving on to consider the wider implications of the story. The myth of Orpheus was very important to the early Greeks in the millennium preceding the Common Era. Pythagoras of Samos, seer, shaman, mathematician and musician headed the Orphic cults which observed daily rituals and used music as a healing agent.[78] Using an instrument called the monochord, he investigated the nature of vibrating tones, discovering that each musical sound, in addition to the fundamental tone, contained a set of additional harmonic resonances arranged in arithmetic proportion. These overtones become highly significant for the development of music in the west since they underpin the way in which tonal harmony sets up tension and resolution. Thus, the way that music develops culturally seems to be dependent to some extent upon how the natural properties of sound and vibration are converted into musical form. Where the Europeans eventually devised from these harmonic properties of sound *tonality*, the hierarchical arrangement of vertically arranged chord progressions, non-European cultures, as well as the folk traditions of European countries, favoured *modal* procedures which revolve around the non-hierarchical melodic properties contained in Pythagoras' discovery.

Of course, none of this happened consciously but collectively, a gradually evolving process running parallel to social, religious and cultural patterns. In *The Republic*, Plato appears to foreshadow the development of tonality in the myth of Er in which a soldier who dies in

---

78 See Godwin, Joscelyn (1992): *Harmony of the Spheres, The Pythagorean Tradition in Music*.

battle ascends to heaven and witnesses a choir of angels singing in perfectly arranged harmonies. This belief in a heavenly harmony, a perfect arrangement of tones is carried through into medieval Europe in the concept of the Harmony of the Spheres, a powerful component of alchemical and philosophical thought.[79] It embraced a concept of music which represented certainty, belief in a divine order, a conceptualisation of the world as an elegant and wonderful machine created by a master clockmaker, a concept which of course, since Darwin, Freud, Einstein and Schoenberg, has been superseded by principles of relativity and uncertainty.

The myth of Orpheus takes the forestage again in the early 17th century where it becomes the central narrative of early opera, a conscious attempt by the Florentine Camerati to resurrect by now mythologised, traditions and principles of Greek theatre. In one way or another, many, if not most operatic themes since that time, including masterpieces such as *Marriage of Figaro*, *Carmen*, *Tosca*, *La Boheme*, *Kata Kabanova*, *Wozzeck* and *Lulu*, have been centred around the seduction, abduction or death of their heroines.[80] Moreover, the musical language which derives from these early 17th century beginnings, and which provides the basis for the western European classical tradition, also supports a narrative, albeit in abstract form, in which a hero sets out on a journey (departs from the home key), overcomes a number of obstacles (the tensions which are set up through modulation and development) and then returns triumphantly (or tragically) having defeated the forces of darkness (or not) and resolved all doubt through a return to the home key and the final cadence, which can be tragic or triumphant.

This kind of narrative or trajectory appears in virtually all of the music composed in the European art tradition from around 1600 up until 1900 (and beyond) providing a clear alpha and omega of musical form. We find it in the Preludes and Fugues of Bach, the String Quartets of Haydn and Mozart, the symphonies of Beethoven, the symphonic poems of Liszt and, magisterially, in the Symphonies of Mahler: in short, wherever serious music is being consciously created over a period of some three hundred years. It becomes the central norm of European musical form, so that any music which departs in any way from this kind of pattern or even this aesthetic is viewed as 'other'. Yet even that music which attempts to depart from the centrality of the German tradition invariably uses identical, albeit exotically coloured, tonal narratives. This would

---

79 See James, Jamie (1993) *The Music of the Spheres: music, science and the natural order of the universe*. Grove Press, New York.
80 See Clement, Catherine (1997) *Opera: the Undoing of Women*. University of Minnesota Press.

include nineteenth century nationalistic styles (Bohemian and Russian music – Smetana, Dvorak, Borodin, Mussorgsky) as well as French modernism (Debussy and Ravel), Scandinavian symphonists (Sibelius and Nielson) and English composers including Parry, Elgar, Walton and even Tippett. The narrative form even persists in the extremes of chromatic music which we witness in the late nineteenth and early twentieth century through composers like Schoenberg (his *Transfigured Night*, for example) though when his music becomes pan-tonal[81] (for example, in *Pierrot Lunaire*) the narrative enters a dream state in which tonality all but dissolves. We also find tonal narratives permeating twentieth century popular musical forms, particularly in the standard 32-bar structures (for example George Gershwin's 'I got Rhythm'), blues (especially in the 12-bar format), jazz (notably bebop) and film scores, where tonality is particularly suited to epic narratives such as John Williams's score for *Star Wars* or John Barry's music for *The Titanic* – another Orpheus tinted tale. Only in the music of the European avant-garde perhaps (Stockhausen, Kagel, Nono), in free jazz (John Coltrane, Ornette Coleman and others), rock music and, latterly styles such as hip-hop do tonal narratives finally disappear.

In all of these instances, the myth of Orpheus seems to permeate, however subtly, the functions and forms which the music takes on and the longest and most heroic narrative of all is, of course, the symphony. The 'story' of a symphony in its classic form is always ultimately the same: a heroic protagonist is introduced as a key centre linked to a musical motive; this subject is then joined by a contrasting, though complementary motive or melody, in a new but closely related key. These two themes, or subjects, are then developed through a series of transformational procedures, changing shape, encountering dramatic conflicts, moving through both quiet waters and climactic torrents but eventually arriving back at the 'home key', a moment which is always felt either as a quiet sense of relief (e.g. Brahms's second Symphony, a stern summons (e.g. Beethoven's 5th Symphony) or a triumphant homecoming (e.g. Elgar's 2nd Symphony).

It would be a mistake to oversimplify the enormous diversity and variety of symphonic thought which developed and expanded through the 19th and 20th centuries. But we can clearly detect a central principle which permeates the classical tradition and is present also in more intimate musical forms such as string quartets and solo piano works: this

---

81 The middle period music of Schoenberg and his immediate disciples such as Berg and Webern, sounds as if it is in all keys at once due to the fact that all twelve notes of the tonal system are kept constantly in play. Although key centres are hinted at, the music constantly develops and modulates leaving the listener in a state of suspension.

is the principle of dynamic development, a forward moving transformational narrative carried both through tonal procedures (chord progressions and key changes) and through the ways in which melodies and motives are metamorphosed, sometimes radically. This I suggest is the Orphic archetype at work and though we encounter it particularly strongly in the European tradition where its foregrounding represents something fundamental about the nature of the European myth, it is at work in all music, underlining the power of music not merely to accompany our life journeys but actually to change lives.

When we consider the myth of Orpheus in greater depth and with some kind of post-modern distance, a number of interesting factors emerge. Firstly, Orpheus' relationship to the women in the plot is by no means simple. To begin with, we might consider his attachment to Eurydice over-dependent or over-sentimental, a factor which is emphasised in Baz Luhrmann's retelling of the story in the film *Moulin Rouge*. Orpheus is cast in this instance, as a typical *Puer Aeternus*, a naive youth going through his rite of passage. In fact, he articulates precisely that notion of romantic love which dominates western attitudes to relationships and which therefore appears in countless popular songs, many of which are ironically recreated in Luhrmann's film. The hero feels himself to be incomplete without the object of his dreams (his 'other half'), the source of his passion (suffering). He then undertakes his heroic journey as the necessary and only means of finding the missing part of himself, something we could describe as *soul retrieval*. This journey downwards also represents a turning inwards, a journey into *anima consciousness* (represented by the image of Eurydice) without which his life is meaningless. But, lacking the necessary maturity, he mistrusts his intuitions, looks back, loses faith, pauses, misses his footing, stumbles and loses everything. This is of course, tragic – *loss of soul*.

Then, significantly, it is not Hades but his wife, Persephone, who sheds tears, whose heart is won over by Orpheus' singing and she in turn persuades Hades to relax a little and bend the rules. (Somehow it is easier for Orpheus to communicate with the wife of the boss than with the boss himself who appears totally unmusical!) But it is Hades, representing stern reality, who lays down the rule that Orpheus is not to look back. There is wisdom in this, especially for a musician whose intelligence should lie in his ears, not his eyes. Trust in intuition reaps inner rewards and when Orpheus loses this trust he consequently returns to the upper world having split off his rational consciousness (light) from his inner awareness (dark). The female element (anima) is then consigned to remain suppressed, buried in the depths, whilst the male (animus) can only sing of this tragic circumstance, replaying the journey, re-visiting the narrative, re-entering the wound. We hear this archetypal message in almost every romantic ballad of Tin Pan Alley as well as in the blues, the theatrical songs of Rodgers and Hammerstein and even, occasionally, in the faux operas of Andrew Lloyd Webber. We can think of Orpheus here as a poet in contrast to Apollo the hunter, an archetypical polarity captured in Schubert's *Die Schöne Müllerin* song-cycle, where the poet is eventually destroyed by anger and grief. Where the god chased his prey (Daphne), wanting to capture her beauty, Orpheus might even be said to have had an unconscious desire to experience this tragedy, enter this "vale of soul-making"; the deepening of consciousness which comes from such experience is after all an essential element in human development without which the poetic soul would never be accessed, the world remaining superficial and material.

Finally, Orpheus is torn apart by the Maenads, female followers of Dionysus. His rejection of the feminine (soul) and his mistrust of the dark (the unconscious) represents a double loss, the first involuntary, the second intentional. By rejecting the physical, the ecstatic, intoxication, the dance and the drum, represented by the followers of Dionysus, Orpheus, despite his capacity to make beautiful music, becomes disembodied (figuratively and literally), incapable of relationship, socially isolated, culturally dis-located. He falls apart.

Yet, most importantly perhaps, we are reminded that the Orphic myth is one of love and marriage which goes wrong – the banishing of Eurydice to the underworld is not just about loss of soul, though that is serious enough, but also about a break in the natural cycle of life and death which would have seen Eurydice and Orpheus reunited and having babies. So what we actually find is a complex set of relationships to the feminine in her various forms and, finally a loss or rejection of the feminine principle altogether, whether maternal (Persephone), romantic (Eurydice) or carnal (Maenads). Music, via Orpheus, reaches out to the eternal feminine (consider the endless list of composers' muses), but the story, like the beautiful art music of European culture, suggests an abstract, mental image rather than a bodily physical reality.

What messages does Orpheus carry into the contemporary world? In the early 17th century the attraction of the plot for early, and thence later, opera composers rests in the fact that it coincided with the emergence of rationalism and the beginning of the enlightenment. In this context we might interpret Orpheus' unwillingness to trust his ears, (his feelings, anima) and the need to see in order to believe (his rational side, animus) as a metaphor for empirical truth and the birth of science. Furthermore, the death of women, or at least the way in which the female principle was somehow culturally buried, relegated to an inferior position in culture and commerce, becomes a familiar pattern in the evolution of western thinking and habits. A cultural norm is established in which the male principle becomes dominant, underpinned by a religion based upon a male trinity expressed through music in which triads (three-note chords) arranged in strict hierarchical progressions, are the central organising principle.

The loss of soul which Orpheus suffers is often experienced in musical structure as the poignant 'otherness' of the minor mode (as opposed to the major) or the sub-dominant key (as opposed to the dominant) or the 'feminine' cadence; whilst the norm is undoubtedly represented through the march of triads which usually ends in a perfect or 'male' cadence. In order for this cadence to be achieved, in order for the music to resolve, it is necessary to *suppress* or even *repress* the natural seventh of the chord (a B flat in the key of C) by sharpening it, thus creating the so-called 'leading note'. The 'natural' seventh, which occurs in the harmonic series, or natural scale (in C), as a B flat, in modern nomenclature then becomes a B natural.[82] This seems like an enforced, even violent process, replayed countlessly at the close of both small and large scale tonal structures (e.g. the very end of Bach's Prelude Number 1 from the '48' and at the very beginning of Beethoven's first Symphony[83]). So we often refer to the 'flattened seventh' or 'modal seventh' when it appears in non-European musics, as if it was a *departure* from the norm rather than an inevitable product of the natural harmonic series.[84] But it is the Western model which departs from nature, which challenges Hades: a beautiful but, as Orpheus discovered, ultimately doom-laden project.

Central to this interpretation of the myth are the twin notions of

---

82 The use of the term 'natural' is paradoxical since we describe the alternative to the 'flat' as natural though in fact it is the so-called 'flattened' seventh which appears in nature as the sixth harmonic.
83 In this instance, Beethoven seems to present it as an "in joke", understood mainly by other musicians, a "Symphony in C" which apparently opens with a cadence in F.
84 So the very language we employ to describe music is permeated with clues as to the enculturated meanings we attach to the structure of the sounds. At the same time, it should come as no surprise that the "anima" aspects of music, which express a longing for soul, the minor key melodies of Schubert, the adagios of Beethoven, the "Liebestod" of Wagner find their way into people's hearts with heightened significance.

sacrifice and the emergence of longing: the former expressed as *loss of soul* and the latter as *feeling at a distance*. In the modern world, soul (anima) is often hidden, to the point where the very word 'soul' might be regarded as taboo, particularly in academic circles (except amongst Jungians). A good example of this is in modern medicine where the treatment of the soul is largely ignored or regarded as irrelevant or even heretical: the body is the focal point and any ghost which might be lurking in the machine is discounted. This perspective also dominates musical learning where dry theory and rigorous technical drill is emphasised at the cost of soul qualities. Like Orpheus, modern man ascends into the light to see things and reify life through vision, the certainty of all-conquering sight, not trusting merely to hear or to feel his way: we have literally lit up our world with electricity; we cannot move fast enough horizontally or vertically; we spend much time in the air (like that other famous Puer, Icarus), in the upper atmosphere, reaching ever upwards, beyond; we tend to think literally, working things out through reason, leaving the imagination in the dark; if there is such a thing as a modern myth then this is being expressed consciously through a denial of myth.

The modern world expresses itself through a desire for continual growth and a constant striving for improvement expressed through ever-increasing economic growth and consumption, a utopian dream marching from Plato to the present. Any reflective, soul-longing may be psychologised as depression and stigmatised or even medically treated. In this sense, it is an ascending curve culture with all the character of a spiritual journey, even though we mostly consider it to be godless. Youth and youthfulness is prized whilst ageing is regarded as an inconvenient though increasingly ubiquitous burden. (Ironically, it is the pursuit of youth which creates the conditions for longevity!) In a sense, we seek to become gods and, if we cannot access this enlightened, heightened state of spiritual consciousness through meditation, contemplation, discipline or prayer, we pour it, literally, down our throats, as alcohol. It might also be possible to see in this culture of excess a need to compensate for the loss or suppression of feeling. Empathy, passion and emotion have become fixed within tradition as female attributes, polarised with the male "virtues" of industry, rationality and objectivity. In science and academia, it is these latter qualities which receive positive valorisation and which are rewarded with public recognition. The softer virtues, however valuable (e.g. child-rearing) are simply not prized in the same way: they remain, like Eurydice, invisible.

So when Orpheus the musician is forced to leave Eurydice in the dark, losing (or abandoning) his very soul, he appears to represent much of what modern human beings experience. The benefits we gain in a society based upon empirical truth and the dominance of scientific method may appear all too obvious: sophisticated technology making life easier, a strong sense of control of our own destinies, the notion that science can solve everything; medicines to cure all ills, including the extension of life itself. Yet the penalty we pay for these benefits becomes all too clear when the technology breaks down and we suddenly find ourselves, literally, in the dark, helpless and vulnerable: far from being in control of our own destinies, we may feel like the alienated victims of mechanisation and globalisation; science, far from solving everything, creates ever new problems many of which defy resolution. Our mythology compels us to believe that we are the cause of global warming regardless of whether or not that may be the (rational) truth. Music itself, the archetypal voice and lyre of Orpheus, turns life into soul, animating matter, its modal qualities bringing us into harmony with ourselves and making it possible to bear misfortune and lost moments through the magic of tone. We need it therefore in vast quantities in order to compensate for what we have lost.

It is surely not insignificant either, that it is Orpheus' unwillingness to join the dance which causes his own death – though his head continues to sing, plangently, after his dismemberment by the Furies. In the eighteenth century, people began to sit still to listen to music, even when it is cast in dance forms, and the structures of classical music seem to become increasingly a disembodied discourse, locked in the head, the concept of beauty replacing the intelligence of the body. The concert hall becomes a place of contemplation rather than participation; music seems to become subject to the cultural necessities of reason and clarity, elevated above the chthonic realities of ecstasy and trance. *Orpheus ends up all head and no body*.

So where is Orpheus today and what clues can we find within this musical myth which points us in the direction of healing and regeneration? Contradictions abound. On the one hand, there is little doubt that music has become an inflated currency and, as such, its value has dropped. As previously argued, far from being viewed as vital to our well being as human beings it is relegated mainly to its function as entertainment. This applies now in some respects equally to the great 'Orphic' narratives, the symphonies, concertos and operatic masterpieces, as it does to the mass-produced popular forms which crowd out the airwaves. The marketing and mediation of both streams is becoming identical and the social meanings converge. Yet the Orphic power is still there, potential in the nature of music itself, waiting to be reclaimed and rediscovered. Perhaps the story is incomplete. Can we imagine the two elements in this myth, the lost soul and the tragic hero, coming together? Are we witnessing the re-affirmation of the feminine principle in music, a reconciliation of animus and anima, something which will surely not be possible so long as the dominant paradigm of art music holds sway and the commercial imperatives of the music industry have a stranglehold on the alternatives. Within the works of the great tradition, which represent both rationality and reason even as they reach out to soul, we encounter the dangers inherent in a cultural mode which suppresses not just the feminine principle but also those natural processes which maintain the cycles of life and nurture living process. Within the Orpheus myth we have perhaps both an explanation and a warning.

Music and Soul – Psyche

Music is the soulbird that sings in the deep heart of the listener
(Sri Chinmoy)

Psyche represents music as affect, its emotional power, and beyond this, through her unflagging and endless capacity to feel, she tells us how music connects to soul. Her story is complex, subtle and suffused with pain, vulnerability, jealousy, longing and love. Countlessly re-told, the original tale establishes a prototypical model for many of the love stories, songs, fairy-tales, poems, novels and films which have come down to us over the centuries. In her story we have references to Beauty and the Beast, Cinderella, The Sleeping Beauty, Pandora's Box. We also have one of the great archetypal expressions of the initiation mysteries through which the soul (Psyche) is bound to endure and overcome significant trials before being transformed and re-united with spirit (Eros). Here is a summary, necessarily truncated.[85]

The tale begins with beauty, the celebrated beauty of Psyche, the youngest of three daughters. Psyche's beauty comes to the attention of

---

85 The story appears first in Apuleius, *The Golden Ass*. Countlessly re-told, a fine version can be found in Bullfinch (1913/2005) and a concise version in http://en.wikipedia.org/wiki/Cupid_and_Psyche. A famous poetical version was composed by Robert Bridges in 1913.

Aphrodite, mother of Eros and goddess of love itself, incurring her jealousy. Aphrodite then instructs her son to destroy Psyche's beauty but before he can complete this task he falls in love with her himself and she with him. This presents a problem. She is in love with a god and no mortal can possibly suffice and, despite countless suitors she therefore remains single. Her parents consult the oracle as a result of which Psyche is taken to a mountain top where she is destined to marry a beast. She finds herself however, in an elegant palace where Eros, invisible in the dark, flies to her each night. Her jealous sisters taunt her and plant doubts in her mind, tricking her into believing that this invisible lover is in fact a monster. Psyche takes a lamp and a knife and prepares to cut off this monster's head but sees instead the exquisite sleeping form of Eros. He wakes and is so angry at her suspicion that he flies away and completely disappears whilst Psyche is banished, literally, to a desert of longing.

Psyche approaches Aphrodite herself for help but the jealous mother sets her a multitude of impossible tasks to fulfil as a condition for giving up her son. With the help of various insects, animals and minor gods, Psyche manages to complete these tasks but each time, Aphrodite is unmoved, setting her even more complicated and seemingly endless labours, finally instructing her to descend to Hades to bring back Persephone's casket containing the secrets of beauty. She descends, again with help from a magical source and collects the box, but, disobeying instruction from Persephone and desperate to make herself as beautiful as possible in order to win back her god, peeps inside and instantly falls into a profound sleep. Eros at last appears, flies down, pops the vanity back into the casket and Psyche awakes, at which point, Zeus himself declares enough is enough and sends Hermes to fetch Psyche. She is given wings, welcomed into the home of the gods, becomes immortal herself and is thus permitted at last to marry Eros.

When considering the variety of ways in which music affects us, most will recall at least one occasion in their lives when music has moved them to tears. When this happens, we might say, in archetypal terms, that *psyche* is present. Psyche, of course, is the Greek word for *soul* and we also encounter her in the Latin form as *anima*, the female element in Jung's theory of archetypes. Psyche is always present in music, through her capacity for emotion, through her representation of beauty and through the ways therefore that music both engages our own emotional lives and provides us with a sense of the beautiful. Psyche is also fragile, like a butterfly reminding us of the transience of beauty, the unpredictability of life and need for faith, constancy and trust if we are to achieve our heart's desire. Her tale reminds us of our own vulnerability without which we are not fully human and incapable of depth relationships. Music also has this property.

Psyche is, through much of her narrative, alone (though aided by animals, insects and gods) and the solo voice, whether in song or in the sound of an instrument such as the flute or violin, or soprano saxophone (especially when played by Jan Garbarek) often seems to encapsulate the soul quality of music. Psyche can be encountered therefore most readily across a variety of vocal genres, in German Lieder for example (where the lyric tenor is often cast as Orpheus singing to his soul image), in jazz song (where many of the most celebrated singers are female) and even in Country and Western music where very often, both male and female singers are bemoaning their fate, plaintively seeking release from some kind of torment. Indeed, whenever we open our mouths to sing, we are instantly in touch with this deeper, more vulnerable and in some ways more real part of ourselves. This is no doubt why many people find it difficult, embarrassing or even traumatic, to sing in public; it may also be the reason why some people never sing at all, even to themselves. Singing puts us in touch with our inner selves, in Psyche's case, Eros, and this, as she discovers, can be painful. Eros' arrows prick the soul.

Yet, song is essential to our well being, a fundamental musical act and everyone can sing. Those who feel they are unable to pitch a note or hold a tune may have been told as children that they are 'tone-deaf', a desperately damaging label which may well continue to blight a person well into their adult life. Or, having become comfortable with the pragmatic and material rationality of work and discourse, having received an education which largely ignored the emotive and creative life or having grown up under the spell of some fundamental religious belief which suppresses song, joy, Eros and therefore, sexual love and longing, or music altogether, many may simply feel uncomfortable with the vulnerability which singing triggers and therefore unwilling to take down the defences which keep their emotional life hidden from others or even from themselves. Nothing is more likely to cause blushing than singing, and blushing, as Jung remarked, can be viewed symbolically as the Self rising to the surface of the skin, whilst physiologically, perhaps even in evolutionary terms, it is no doubt a defence mechanism. How many people, humiliated as children, probably unintentionally, by music teachers or other adults, simply close down their singing voices for good and lose this vital source of contact with soul? The wonder of Psyche is that she continues to persevere with her quest despite repeated humiliations, setbacks and despair. She simply refuses to give up. She therefore teaches us that without this willingness to stand defenceless and open to the world we cannot achieve true relationship, which ultimately is a divine gift. At the end of her tale she becomes immortal herself and the myth therefore speaks to us of the immortality of the soul.

Hugo Wolf expresses the torment of Psyche exquisitely in his setting of a poem by the Swabian poet, Eduard Morike titled *The Jilted Servant Girl (Das Verlassene Mägdlein)*. The poem tells of a young housemaid who rises early in the morning to clean the ashes from the hearth and light the fire (a reference to Cinderella, the representation of Psyche in German folklore). As the flames begin to flicker she suddenly recalls the dream she had that night of the heartless youth who has abandoned her and, as the flames rise, her tears fall. Psyche teaches us to weep, to respond to bitter experience not with anger or violence, which hardens the ego shell and shuts down feeling, but with tears; this deepens our experience of life, puts us in touch with soul, revealing those aspects of experience which lie beneath the surface. In this respect she functions as our guiding anima and it is this capacity of music to take us into a place of emotional awareness which is surely one of its primary functions. Wolf's musical setting is full of bare thirds, stripped down, open and raw. At the mid-point of the song where Psyche feels completely lost in her sad reverie, Wolf skilfully employs the augmented triad, a device which momentarily dissolves any sense of purpose in the music, leaving us floating in a dream world where our sense of direction towards any kind of finite goal evaporates. We can sense Psyche at this moment sitting in the middle of a desert plain, or on the floor of a forest, faced with an impossible task and totally forlorn. It is as if time has been momentarily suspended leaving us in a state of pure feeling. Psyche's relationship to time is revealing in that she appears to have no regard for the finite nature of things, her sole purpose is to find Eros once more, no matter how long it takes. In the end, it is no doubt her connection to this infinity of time which becomes the prerequisite for her own immortality.

Solo song in general and the female voice in particular carries much of what Psyche represents. Male singers, especially in the rock genres often use the falsetto voice (strangely termed, since there may well be something especially *authentic* in the male voice used in this way) to project the anima state of feeling. In a celebrated track by the Canadian group The Band, titled *I Will be Released*, which expresses the longing for freedom and enlightenment which prevailed during this period, the lead singer uses the high falsetto voice throughout. The final lines of the chorus, in which he peaks on a high 'c' might be heard as an anthem to Psyche herself, begging for mercy ("any day now, any day now, I shall be released"). Other examples of female solo singers and songwriters who seem to identify closely with Psyche are almost too numerous to mention but they would certainly include Billy Holiday, Joni Mitchell, Janis Joplin, Alanis Morisette, Enya and the nymph-like Icelandic singer, Bjork. In each and every case, their songs create narratives which are personalised and internalised and there is always the inherent danger of over-identification with the archetype so that, as in the case of 'Lady Day' for example, or Janis Joplin, the singers' own lives becomes heavily and tragically involved with a re-enactment of Psyche's trials.

If I were to choose one song which seems to capture the essence of the trials which Psyche endures then it would be Bjork's "So Broken", recorded in 1998 with the flamenco guitarist Raimundo Amador who supplies an unwavering tango rhythm and fierce melodic juxtapositions to Bjork's fragile vocals. The lyrics tell of heartbreak ("In pieces, my heart is broken") of confusion ("I'm puzzling") of the impossible ("Here I go, trying to run ahead of that heartbreak train") and of hopelessness ("Thinking it will never catch up with me"). As the song begins, the small melodic cell with the falling seventh on the word "broken" might be heard as the weary sighing of Psyche as she faces yet another day of exhausting and impossible tasks, (running ahead of the train is just such a task), drained of energy and with an empty heart, just like Morike's maid. As the song progresses, Bjork's voice becomes more and more fragmented, at one point breaking into falsetto and then back into the throat as she attempts to communicate the fullness and depth of emotion. As the song ends, she wails like a nymph pinned to a wall of despair. This is Psyche as a vulnerable butterfly, struggling for survival.

Perhaps we can all feel this special relationship between Soul and time in that last, but not yet entirely lost, specialised genre, the Christmas Carol. These seasonal tunes, familiar to all regardless of their level of faith, are perhaps the only remaining example of musical taboo in our culture - it would feel totally inappropriate to play or sing them at any other time than at the winter solstice. The special quality of this moment of the year is expressed through carols in a way which internalises our relationship with ourselves and deepens our relationship with time. It is the music of Christmas which contains this special feeling more powerfully than any of the other celebratory devices we use during this time: Christmas cards, roast turkey, office parties, trees and lights, none of these would function in quite the way they do without the ubiquitous presence of those familiar tunes. The internalising function, the reflective state which is Psyche's domain, is emphasised by the 'closing in' which takes place within families at this time, a process which is often as fraught with difficulty as it is a focus for celebration. The relationship to time is quite literally at its deepest point as the winter solstice closes in, reaching a kind of zero hour as Christmas eve arrives when the acceleration of time which has characterised the previous few days suddenly finds a point of rest. It is exactly at this moment that song is at its most potent, articulating the mystery of time regardless of any specific religious narrative.

Beyond the world of song, Psyche inhabits those spaces in music where soul qualities are evident through texture and modality. The solo violin, both in classical genres and in more rooted forms, such as Roma music, carries strong emotions alongside a sense of vulnerability. The narratives in large-scale pieces such as the Sibelius, Elgar and Berg violin concertos,[86] both of which are rooted in an earlier and nowadays exceptionally popular genre of the classical tradition (Max Bruch's violin concerto is a constant winner of the Classic FM 'hall of fame' popularity poll) seem to place the solo violin, like Psyche, as the protagonist or even the victim in a tragic drama. The violin as a solo instrument has flourished in the hands of a significant number of Jewish performers as if the whole tragedy of the Jewish experience is distilled into the sound of the instrument as played by such figures as Kreisler, Perlmann, Heifetz, Menhuin and Kremer to name but a few. For the Roma people, marginalised, socially deprived and all too often despised across European cultures, banished to the margins, the violin is also of special significance, expressing a depth of soul which reminds us of Psyche, inhabiting the darker corners of life, unable to find solace and acceptance,

---

86 Both the Berg and Elgar bear dedications to anima figures in the composers' own lives. Berg's concerto bears the dedication "to the memory of an angel." The reference is to Manon Gropius who had died tragically young of polio. Elgar's, even more pointedly is inscribed "*Aqui está encerrada el alma de* ....." ("Herein is enshrined the soul of .....") the five dots referring almost certainly to one of Elgar's numerous female muses, probably, according to Dora Powell in her book *Memories of a Variation*, the American Julia Worthington.

seeking always the promised regions which remain somehow out of reach, beyond the trials of living. It is this sense of longing combined with struggle which the violin as well as the viola and the cello seem to be able to express with particular poignancy.

When we apply the anima/psyche archetype to the concept of musical renewal, we might discover that there is a real hunger in the contemporary world for the kind of experience and states of feeling which Psyche carries. The ascending curve culture and the pursuit of happiness which dominate our utopian idealism with all its emphasis on spirit, achievement, solutions and dynamism finds a necessary balance and depth in Psyche's travails. And whilst, as listeners, many people seem to be particularly drawn to, let us say, the Bruch concerto or the recorded output of female vocalists, as participants, many appear to be seeking a reclamation of song itself, as a birthright, and for participation in singing at a grass roots level. In the UK this movement towards musical self-realisation is represented in large measure by the emergence of the Natural Voice Practitioner's Network. One of the most remarkable and prominent figures in this renewal of our relationship with the natural voice is the singer, teacher and healer Frankie Armstrong whose own extraordinary journey from blindness to sight, darkness to light, might almost be viewed as a reflection of Psyche's own narrative.

The manner in which Psyche approaches her tasks offers guidance in our own music-making. Why are the tasks so complicated and so seemingly impossible that she can do little more than sit and weep at the impossibility of it all?[87] Yet, it is precisely this capacity to feel, to give up rational control, to submit herself to chance and to fate which allows the solution to present itself. When she lets go of conscious control it becomes possible for the magical animals and insects, those animal helpers impossibly sentimentalised in Disney versions of the tale, to become active and play their crucial role as intuitive guides. Making music is not about being rational and theoretical, neither is it about being heroic. A musical task, if it is to be truly creative, cannot be fulfilled without the kind of magical interventions which appear from the depths of the imagination and which figure in Psyche's tale as ants, or the river god or the voices from the tower; improvisation is always 'on-the-edge' and nothing significant can ever be achieved in the domain of Psyche without this

---

[87] In the German folk tale, *The Queen Bee*, a male figure, the youngest son, the 'simpleton', sits on the forest floor and weeps when faced with tasks his older, tougher brothers had failed to complete and who are subsequently turned to stone. This image of how concretization or objectification of a problem leads to sterility is highly instructive. The weeping youth, like Psyche, is subsequently assisted by the messengers of nature - ants, ducks and eventually the Queen Bee herself who leads him to success and to his heart's desire.

element of danger. If we try to make music safe, theorising it, notating it, controlling it, then the depth to which Psyche leads us is not going to be achieved: we remain in the shallows or else dry up altogether. Renewal is not possible without this descent and if we rely only on the regimented time of Kronos we lose the connection to *significant time* which comes from *Kairos*. In the tale of Eros and Psyche, the interventions always appear in the "nick of time" just as all seems lost.

Jung (1959) has drawn our attention to how the creative mind draws upon anima for guidance and inspiration. All art-making needs to access the unconscious area of mind which provides the artist with both the autonomous energy and the archetypal resources which make creative action possible. It also provides the sense of direction, meaning and purpose essential if heroic action is to be undertaken.

> *With the archetype of the anima, we enter the realm of the gods, or rather, the realm that metaphysics has reserved for itself. Everything anima touches becomes numinous – unconditional, dangerous, taboo, magical.*[88]

In some cases this inspirational image is actualised as a living muse.[89] Each time Psyche is confronted by a seemingly impossible task, her inner guides in the form of insects, animals or genies, like the river god, the inhabitants of the deeper recesses of the living world, come to her aid. In the ultimate task, she descends (like Orpheus) into the deepest recess of all, the dark depths of the underworld. Jung always maintained that confrontation with the shadow was the most difficult and challenging of all human tasks. For Psyche, having had the courage to make this journey she then (again like Orpheus) disobeys the instruction not to look, opens the forbidden box and is promptly 'punished' by sleep, obliged in other words, to enter her own unconscious on the way to self renewal. It is only when she has taken this plunge into the depths of her own being that Eros can again approach her, make contact and Hermes is instructed to bring her to the table of the gods. Hermes, who is, archetypally, the interpreter, who infuses music and therefore, life, with meaning, who, as *psychopomp*, accompanies us on our soul journeys and who provides us with the capacity for reflection (as in a mirror - his dual aspect) appears at the critical point in the tale: when all felt hopeless and lost, this divine intervention releases us from the torpor of unconscious living and

---

[88] Jung, C.G. (1959). *The Archetypes of the Collective Unconscious*. Translated by R. F. C. Hull. London. P. 28.
[89] Celebrated examples of this phenomenon include Berlioz' muse, Harriet Smithson who inspired the *Symphonie Fantastique* and Kamila Stosslova, who captured the soul of Leos Janacek in the last years of his life.

we also fly.

The lesson here for music makers is clear: we cannot rely on conscious and apparent rules and procedures. Music grows from these inner states of the psyche (with a small 'p' this time) and the imagination functions in those shadowy areas on the margins of the conscious life, an in-between, transitional or liminal domain. *Soul work takes place in the dark.* At every crucial point in her story, we encounter Psyche, feeling everything, often on her knees in supplication, begging the goddess for mercy, for acceptance, for delivery. When delivery eventually comes, Psyche becomes herself a goddess. Music has this capacity to transport us to a world beyond the self, to the transpersonal domain but most of all perhaps, Psyche teaches us about the constancy of relationship: her story is, ultimately, about love, the heart simultaneously broken, captivated and tormented but finally healed by the deepest and most soulful of human emotions and the one which music, according to Shakespeare, feeds.

Lifemusic and the Archetypes

I was arguing earlier in this chapter that, since music is abstract, what we are able to project onto it is the image of the dynamic of life itself. Furthermore, the forms, feelings, narratives and affects which music encompasses, the four archetypal qualities, carry a charge which connects us to time and therefore to a sense of past, present and future. The past is expressed through memory and reflection; the present through action which is driven directly by the experience of the here and now; and the future through the imagination which creates unforeseen and unpredictable landscapes. The archetypes which we have been discussing are constantly at work even though they have been described in archaic terms and, however we choose to express them, they are the connecting threads between the three phases of time as well as dictating, albeit indirectly, the musical choices we make when creating our own music. The challenge of making music may be met through reference to archetypal patterns and images: by keeping these underpinning images in focus, we arrive at generative principles which will guide and shape our music-making as surely as the muses guided Apollo and Ariadne's thread guided Theseus through the labyrinth. Ultimately, approaching music from this archetypal perspective enables us to step out of the domain of our own contemporary myths and offers the potential to create afresh a music which is not trapped within a specific set of cultural precepts. The concept of *Lifemusic* is based on the premise that this is at once desirable, achievable and inevitable.

CHAPTER 3

UNFORESEEN MAGIC

Life is flux (Heraclitus)

Improvisation is intuition in action, a way to discover the muse and learn to respond to her call.[90]

In composition, you take as much time as you like to create ten seconds of music whereas in improvisation it just takes ten seconds. (Steve Lacy)[91]

Improvisation

Improvisation is the primary act of music: it connects us to time with an immediacy and an intimacy which, whilst also present to some degree in composed or notated forms, is immeasurably stronger during improvisation. Indeed, before music can be composed it must be imagined and improvisation is pure imagination in the moment. All music is time-based, but only in improvisation is the creative process completely merged, in the 'here and now', with the sonic event, the creative product. For this reason, improvisation has also been termed 'instant composing'.[92] Creating music in the moment is exhilarating, dangerous and satisfying, a form of creative flight where the leap into the dark generates a particular and unique sense of freedom. This feeling of liberation is almost certainly linked to the way in which the improvising moment suspends the improviser in a 'liminal' space, an 'in-between-ness' which makes improvising always a threshold event. Perhaps it is only through this state of mind that the archetypes can be accessed. Hermes moves at speed and unless we join him, the imagination quickly dries up. *Improvising is making music with wings.*

In contemporary practice, improvisation generates significant debate amongst musicians, some of whom use it very rarely (e.g. orchestral musicians), some who use it within clearly defined boundaries (e.g. jazz

---

90 Nachmanovitch, Stephen. (1990) *Free Play: Improvisation in Life and Art.* Penguin USA.
91 This sentence takes exactly ten seconds to say.
92 See Evan Parker (1992) *De Motu - Man and Machine.* Printed in full on www.efi.group.shef.ac.uk/fulltext

musicians) some who use it therapeutically (e.g. music therapists) and some who employ improvisation for social purposes (e.g. community musicians). There are also musicians who, in recent decades, have developed the practice of improvisation as a specialised and unique, non-idiomatic art (free improvisation). The practice of *Lifemusic* has strong connections with all of these without restricting itself to any particular brand. Restoring soul to the practice of music is not something which is restricted to one particular kind of musical activity but it might need prevailing types of musical events to make some space for it requiring a departure from normal patterns, opening up a space in which anything can happen, seeking only to ensure as far as possible that what in fact does happen is both appropriate to the moment and collectively understood and endorsed by the participants.

In defining improvisation and in tracing its history, it will be useful to keep in focus the underlying idea that improvisation is nothing more and nothing less than an approach to music (and to life) which not merely allows for the unexpected and the unforeseen, but works *with* the absence of parameters, making unpredictability a generative force guided only by the hermeneutic capacity of the imagination.[93] Lack of planning is not synonymous with lack of structure and the unforeseen event need not be at all chaotic. Some, if not all of the finest (composed) music has this quality of being simultaneously unexpected and yet inevitable: we hear it as readily in the string quartets of Mozart as in the folk music of Tuva; in the mantric repetitions of Steve Reich as in the yoiking of the Sami people of the arctic circle; in the extraordinary circular forms of Evan Parker's freely improvised saxophones as in the symphonies of Bruckner. Perhaps it is only when we attempt to *over control* the flowing force of life (Schopenhauer's will) that chaos ensues: imposing conscious attitude onto unconscious process will inevitably create problems.[94] In attempting to control or tame elements which, by their very nature, are part of the autonomous flowing structures of life we may be courting disaster. Music, the best of it, teaches us that conscious control is far less effective than opening the heart, mind and senses to the musical quality of life itself. This is the doctrine of *Nada Brahma*, the world as a sounding force which in turn reflects and mirrors Kepler's *anima mundi*, the world soul, a universal harmony which guides and informs the human heart and the human imagination. Improvisation is therefore also an opening out, a

---

[93] Jung regarded the imagination as the primary faculty of human beings through which we make sense of the world, create the narratives of our lives and inject those lives with meaning – hence 'hermeneutic'.

[94] See von Franz, Marie-Louise (1995). *Shadow and Evil in Fairy Tales*, in particular Chapter 5. Shambhala Books, London.

temporal space left open when the hard, controlling (and protective) shell of ego has been dissolved.

Defining Improvisation

In describing improvisation as the *primary musical act*, I am defining it as not merely the first stage of the creative process but, in some senses, as the only stage, since revisiting musical material, revising it, refining it, is in effect, a process of *re-improvisation*: the truly creative musician constantly re-invents and re-visits a piece not because there is necessarily anything wrong with the original version but simply because musical forms are alive, life moves on and flux is a condition of this aliveness. Creative living is no different and to be stuck in a single paradigm, repeating the same patterns and following the same paths throughout life is not only undesirable but in reality, impossible.

> *Play, as free improvisation, sharpens our capacity to deal with a changing world. Humanity, playing through our prolific variety of cultural adaptations, has spread over the whole globe, survived several ice ages, and created stupendous artefacts.*[95]

In community music, improvisation is the essential ingredient of any workshop activity, whether this takes place in the classroom, in evening classes, in music therapy sessions, or indeed, in any context where people gather together to *musick*. The transformation of the noun *music* into the verb *musick* (see Chris Small, 2004) serves to remind us that improvisations are always musical *acts* whereas notated compositions can more often be found lying lifeless between the pages of a score, dependent upon the ministrations of a trained musician to breathe life into them or the services of a musicologist to render them totally lifeless!

Yet, despite its primary position, improvisation is curiously neglected in the training of musicians and, until relatively recently, also generally ignored in theoretical writings about music. As the late Derek Bailey (1992) remarked:

> *Improvisation enjoys the curious distinction of being both the most widely practised of all musical activities and the least acknowledged and understood. While it is today present in almost every area of music, there is an almost total absence of information about it.*[96]

---

95 Nachmanovitch. Op.cit. P. 45
96 Bailey, Derek (1992). *Improvisation: its nature and practice in music.* London.

Common definitions of improvisation tend to place a negative emphasis on it and it is not so difficult to work out why the term "composition" should have found favour in our culture whilst "improvisation" has been marginalised. As Alan Durant (1989) has pointed out:

> *the word originally meant "to act without foresight or planning" and, on entering the English language in the late eighteenth century, the term fairly rapidly acquired a "negatively valorised meaning" as in "an improvised solution".*[97]

This negative attitude speaks of a culture which tends to devalue that area of mind which is non-conceptual and intuitive. We inhabit a society where scientific method, observable phenomena and reductive thinking are dominant and in such cultural conditions, improvised forms are seen as less trustworthy, less valid than composed (i.e. notated) or recorded forms. Whereas the former are slippery, unpredictable and even perhaps, inexplicable the latter are fixed, predictable and explicable (not to mention packageable, saleable and commodifiable), all of which renders this composed music safer, more controllable and, crucially, commercially viable. When we compare this negative definition of improvisation with the vast benefits it offers to the development of the individual imagination we might also guess that some of the suspicion surrounding the practice of improvisation and the freedom and autonomy it promotes is political as well as cultural.[98] Images come to mind of practice rooms full of children dutifully practicing their scales and obediently learning and memorising the classics, the music of the European tradition. These practice rooms might as easily be found today in Japan, South Korea or The People's Republic of China as in Europe, countries where individual autonomy may be less highly prized than duty to the state. This image is only one step removed from that of the Madrassas of Pakistan, rooms full of young children rocking back and forth as they chant and memorise the Koran. This is in no way to devalue either the richness of classical music or the profundity of the messages of Islam but simply to point out how a fixed canon, social norm, orthodoxy or rigidly imposed religious creed can so easily become a tool which suppresses individual autonomy.

In less politically contentious areas the word 'improvisation' is used

---

97 Durant, Alan (1989). *Conditions of Music*. New York.
98 Jazz musicians in the former Soviet block were treated with suspicion and in some cases prosecuted for subversion. See also Josef Skvorecky's novella *The Bass Saxophone* for a description of the restrictions placed on jazz musicians by the Nazi regime. Skvorecky himself suffered from severe censorship in his Czechoslovak homeland and emigrated to Canada after the 1968 Russian occupation.

to denote situations in which 'quick-fire' solutions are required for unexpected problems. For example, "she was forced to improvise a hurried meal from the little that was available in the food cupboard", suggests something makeshift, temporary, unsatisfactory or ill-prepared (though some of the most imaginative food might result from this circumstance). This use of the word is also generally derogatory, underlined by the dictionary definition, which gives us, "to do anything without *proper* materials or preparation" running alongside a more arts-oriented definition, "to compose and recite, or perform *without preparation*". [99] As is so often the case, the dictionary definition reveals more about social attitudes, about prevailing cultural perspectives represented by common usage than about the underlying meaning, since it necessarily defines the word as closely as possible to how it is used by the population at large. The etymology, however, is far more charitable to the improviser, giving simply "unforeseen". (Hoad 1986, page 231)

It seems likely then that the negative use of 'improvisation' is somehow connected to a general mistrust of hazard, unpredictability, fear of the unknown and insecurity about the future. We tend to be particularly suspicious of any kind of activity where the patterns of cause and effect are not immediately apparent, tending to ask always, "why did that happen" in preference to, "what is going on?" Yet the question "why" ensures that we place ourselves at a distance from the experience, translating the right brain immediacy of process into the more left brain domain of explanation. "What" simply describes the experience itself and, as Hillman describes it, nudges closer to soul.

> *"What" proceeds straight into an event. The search for "whatness" or quiddity, the interior identity of an event, its essence, takes one into depth. It is a question from the soul of the questioner into the soul of the happening. "What" stays right with the matter, asking it to state itself again, to repeat itself in other terms, to re-present itself by means of other images. "What" implies that everything everywhere is matter for the psyche, matters to it – is significant, offers a spark, releases or feeds soul.* (Hillman, 1975, page 138) [100]

Neil Sorrell (1992) reminds us that 'improvisation' in common speech conveys:

---

99   The Chambers Dictionary (1993)
100 Hillman, James (1975). *Re-Visioning Psychology*. New York.

something that is insufficiently prepared and without lasting value (e.g. 'an improvised shelter'). Contrast this with another more specifically musical term which has become an irritating cliché: 'orchestrated' (as in 'an orchestrated attack') which suggests just the opposite: something calculated and contrived in detail, of which the effect is inherently predictable. The element of condescension attached to improvisation can only hinder an understanding of its nature and true value as an essential part of musical discourse. (Sorrell, 1992, page 776) [101]

So it seems then that this concern with predictability, with the planned event, is a cultural construct, a social need, collectively determined, for everything to be visible and rationally explained. In contrast to this we seem less able to appreciate patterns which have a sense of immediacy, are emergent or unconsciously determined *even though we have to deal with them constantly*. We separate out the pragmatic concerns of daily living, the "serious business" of life from what James Hillman calls "the poetic basis of mind"; and as we make this separation, we both devalue the imagination and weaken the sense of significance we derive from the business of life itself.

Thus, improvisation, the patterns of which are, by definition, unwritten, and therefore uncontained in any culturally fixed formula is regarded with a degree of suspicion, acceptable perhaps in 'lower' forms of music-making, such as rock and jazz, but surely not the stuff of serious music-making or of serious living! It is the insecurity of improvising which is perhaps the greatest barrier to its wider acceptance and which renders the classically trained musician often paralysed with fear at the prospect of playing without notation. Contemporary society is fashioned increasingly around security and safety, whether it is the material security which comes from insuring our goods against theft or our houses against fire or our lives against serious illness or early death. We often package goods so securely that it is often all but impossible to access the product itself![102] Fixations with health and safety easily rob our lives of colour and open the doors to a controlling and sometimes over-protective class of minders. Music itself, as I was arguing in Chapter 1, has become in many ways similarly packaged, fixed into notated scores, recorded forms and neatly contained, at one time in chunky gramophone records, then flimsy cassette tapes, then shiny CDs and now mapped invisibly onto

---

101 Sorrell, Neil (1992). 'Improvisation' in Paynter, J., Howell, T., Orton, R., Seymour, P. *Companion to Contemporary Musical Thought*. Routledge.
102 Significantly, perhaps, this is particularly true of CD cases.

microchips. What was originally live and substantial, people blowing tubular instruments and striking resonating surfaces was first of all reduced to scratches on vinyl, then to magnetic patterns and finally digitised, translated into electronic numbers, from physical to analogue to digital, from microgrooves to microchips, all in less than a hundred years, the content expanding as the medium shrinks.

Prepared for Everything

Yet, whilst the common definition of improvisation suggests a lack of preparation, amongst improvisers themselves, there is little doubt that 'instantaneous things can only be achieved through hard work'. As Bobby Wellins, the great tenor saxophonist has pointed out, '...whilst improvisation might be an instinctive and spontaneous activity, that does not mean that it is unprepared'.[103] In fact, the improviser has to be *exceptionally* prepared, not just for *one activity*, not just for the exam to be passed or the test to be fulfilled, but for *any eventuality*. We need to prepare, to practice, it is a condition of life. But we also need to be aware of the dangers inherent in repetition.

> *When we see technique or skill as a "something" to be attained, we again fall into the dichotomy between "practice" and "perfect", which leads into any number of vicious circles. If we improvise with an instrument, tool, or idea that we know well, we have the solid technique for expressing ourselves. But the technique can get too solid – we can become so used to knowing how it should be done that we become distanced from the freshness of today's situation. This is the danger that inheres in the very competence that we acquire in practice. Competence that loses a sense of its roots in the playful spirit becomes ensconced in rigid forms of professionalism.* [104]

Furthermore, the act of improvisation is itself a form of preparation, a process-based activity rather than a ready-made product. In music, the improviser is always prepared for the next unforeseen departure, a condition which is much more reflective of the process of life itself where unforeseen events often present the greatest challenges and almost certainly have greatest import. This places improvisation at the core of life rather than in the margins.

---

103 Bobby Wellins quoted in an interview with Nick Sorensen in Sorensen, N (1988). *Understanding Improvisation*. Unpublished MA Dissertation. University of Sussex.
104 Nachmanovitch op.cit. P. 67.

In improvised music, the unplanned might even be said to *determine* structure. A pattern of sound, a sonic event will create a musical departure which then requires a response, either repetition or else some kind of development and, eventually, a resolution: indeed, the way in which the problem is presented might well be the most significant element in the whole process. The genie which leaps, sometimes unexpectedly, from the un-stoppered bottle of the imagination becomes then the guiding spirit which leads the improviser through the maze. In classical music, for example, the famous opening of Beethoven's Eroica Symphony is characterised by the D flat which unexpectedly 'throws a shadow' across the otherwise sunny landscape in the seventh bar. This darkening element seems to contradict the prevailing key centre of E flat, threatening the survival of the tonal framework. Yet, though at first seemingly inconsequential, this single note then begins to permeate the structure and eventually becomes a determining element in the whole, complex architecture. In the field of jazz there are countless examples of notes plucked seemingly at random out of the air which then require to be somehow accommodated into the structure. Listening to Miles Davis' solo improvisation on *Freddie Freeloader* from the album *Kind of Blue*, we can hear that each musical departure, each re-entry into the 12 bar sequence, is more hazardous than the previous one. Davis begins his solo with a simple repetition of the key note but from that moment on, each new sequence starts with something increasingly daring, unexpected and unplanned, propelling the music into a deeper and more complex space. Each time this happens, Davis is compelled to follow through the consequences of his leap into the dark which is thus revealed as a leap of faith.

Inner Necessity

In such instances, the 'problem' itself, the primary event, contains the seeds of its own realisation, the clue to the structure; the event seems to be arrived at seemingly without the considered intervention of the inventor, appearing of its own accord, autonomously, by some law of nature. If we amplify this process, if one hazardous event is followed by another, we arrive at a truly improvised medium where all events are spontaneous and hazard has become the norm. The resulting form then grows and expands from a kind of *inner necessity*, a term employed by the painter Wassily Kandinsky (1910) to denote the autonomous flow of the creative process.[105] Kandinsky's friend, Arnold Schoenberg achieves precisely this kind of intuitive flow in his middle period music, (discussed in Chapter 1) resulting in a style of dissonance which many people find unsettling though others find it merely truthful. Anthony Payne (1979) described this music as a 'full-scale plunge into the sub-conscious'[106] which perhaps explains the bafflement of many listeners on first encounter. The final piece in his *5 Orchestral Pieces* of 1913 is in essence, an improvisation, where the events follow each other so smoothly, each the progenitor of the next, that the music is in a state of continuous flux, a kind of ghostly Viennese waltz spinning into a spiral of memory, regret, nostalgia, fear and longing.

Schoenberg, by his own admission, felt driven by historical necessity to compose these works, and there is little doubt that his music emerged at a pace which could only point towards it being improvised and notated almost simultaneously. The music appears to overturn the concepts underpinning European art music yet Schoenberg himself felt destined to fulfil this historical role as the upholder of the very tradition he appeared to be challenging, the torch bearer of the great tradition, as if he had no choice in the matter. This concept of *inner necessity* is locked into our definition of improvisation: we may have a wide range of choices, perhaps infinite, but we are forced to a single solution, we must go with the flow, or else the basis of the structure, its existence in time, breaks open. If we stop to think or rationalise, the brain switches into a different mode and contact with the moment is immediately lost. The archetypal depth of the music is then replaced by something constructed from the rational mind, something more theoretical and therefore removed from the essential, flowing energy of life.[107]

As a truly time-based medium, improvisation, whether of the kind that leads to composed forms, jazz, rock, or remains as free improvisation, represents this inescapable flow or force, since the speed at which the improviser responds prevents them from thinking too rationally about the event or its outcomes. Structure is felt rather than planned and form emerges directly from this feeling, dictated perhaps more by the autonomous activity of the limbic system than by the frontal lobes of the brain, and thus emerging from the deep well of the personal and collective

---

105 Kandinsky, op.cit
106 Payne, Anthony (1979), *Schoenberg*. Oxford University Press, Oxford. P. 20
107 Schoenberg relates an instance where he had to postpone working on the Orchestral Variations for some months during which time he "lost" the solution to a particular compositional problem which he had arrived at spontaneously. Coming back to the piece later, he was forced to laboriously work at the piece until the "solution" was arrived at through rational process. Whereupon, he found the mislaid scrap of paper with the original solution which was...naturally...identical!

unconscious, where the archetypes are at their most active. The act of improvisation in music, as in life, calls into play intuition ("the highest form of intelligence" according to Krishnamurti) and this provides solutions which come, as it were, in the nick of time: in improvisation every moment is the last one – and the first. This is not to say that the solutions do not themselves derive from previous preparation, training or conditioning, but the instantaneous nature of the choice ensures that the improvisatory act is never dry or lifeless, never allowed to draw merely upon available norms but always at a point where the norm is pushed into the background making way for a new foreground.[108]

Forming and Performing

Keith Swanwick (1988) defines improvisation as 'the simultaneous act of forming and performing'[109] linking music in this respect to the arts of painting or sculpture, both of which art forms would be regarded as absurd if the main activity was simply to recreate work by selected artists from a previous era. Yet this is precisely what happens in the world of classical music and Swanwick's definition therefore reminds us how improvised forms represent a divergence from the prevailing (European) model which has increasingly separated the role of composer from that of performer. This was not always the case. In his day, Bach himself was almost certainly more celebrated for his gifts as an improviser than as a composer. The division between 'former' and performer' is a relatively recent phenomenon, a cultural construct of the last 100 years or so. The image of the composer as a lonely, romantic (and probably troubled) figure labouring over his (almost always 'his') life's work, is a modern myth, more at home perhaps in Hollywood than embedded in the reality of history. Mozart was an improviser with an excellent memory and notated his music in cafes, wine bars and during rehearsals. The published versions of his music, though treated like sacred texts, are in many cases, spontaneously conceived forms which might well have been altered or played around with during performance. But how many modern pianists improvise even the cadenzas to Mozart's concertos let alone "mess around with" the published versions of his sonatas?[110]

Some commentators draw a distinction between *idiomatic* improvisation and so-called *free improvisation*. Indeed, Stephen Nachmanovitch (2007), one of the most perceptive and enthusiastic

---

108 A fuller explanation of Hans Keller's theory of foreground and background form will come in the following chapter.
109 Swanwick, Keith, (1988) *Music, Mind, Imagination*. Page 42. Oxford University Press.
110 An exception is the American pianist Robert Levin who is also an articulate advocate for a renewal of improvisational practice.

advocates of group improvising, draws a clear distinction between the two:
> *In the conservatory world, some people equate improvisation with jazz. Improvisation is not jazz. Jazz is one of the world's beautiful semi-improvised forms of music-making, structurally very similar to Indian raga-playing. In both traditions, the musician sticks to a rough template or framework derived from tradition and defined by a scale, a rhythm, a mood, and then threads a personal path within the boundaries of that framework. In free improvisation, there is no template or prior agreement. We listen to each other very intensely and support each other, and from that atmosphere of listening and support, the structure and character of each piece emerges.*[111]

Working within a recognizable idiom requires a detailed understanding of how that idiom works and thus prior learning and development of technique becomes necessary. This is particularly true of traditional and be-bop forms of jazz where an intimate knowledge of the norms needs to be built up over a relatively long period of time. Yet, even when improvising without reference to any fixed idiom, some kind of recognizable framework will inevitably develop simply from the basic human tendency to create structure and a need to be coherent and communicative. Ultimately it is virtually impossible and certainly unnecessary to avoid totally the norms which result from our musical and social conditioning.

Perhaps rather than drawing firm boundaries between *free* and *idiomatic* improvisation, it would be more useful to define the act of improvising as a spectrum of structure, some of which veers towards norms and some of which opens out into uncharted territory. In archetypal terms (see Chapter 2), at one end of this spectrum stands Apollo, representing the continuity of tradition, whilst at the other end lurks Dionysus, representing the natural flux of nature. In between the two, Orpheus constructs his narratives, drawing from each end of the spectrum, simultaneously and spontaneously. An improvising group will often begin playing within the conscious boundaries of form only to diverge from this Apollonian "holding" as the piece gathers energy, and, driven by the Dionysion necessity for release, eventually find themselves playing with total abandon. Full discussion of this phenomenon and the

---

111 Nachmanovitch, Stephen (2007). *The Discipline of Improvisation.* www.freeplay.com

theory of the Holding Form will be explored in depth in the following chapter whilst the improvisation exercises in Chapter 8 grow are all based around this principle.

A Brief History of Improvisation

Having gone some way towards defining the nature of improvisation itself, let us now look in a little more detail at how improvisational practice has been located within the European tradition and what this tells us about our own social and cultural attitudes. By examining some of the ways in which improvisation has figured (or not) historically, we might be able to get a clearer understanding of its social and cultural functions and thus clarify its value as a resource for connecting people to time.

It is difficult to be precise about the exact point in the history of European art music when improvisation ceased to be an intrinsic element of musical acts or when composers ceased to improvise in public and performance became a separate discipline. It is certainly a relatively recent phenomenon. The distinction between the two has never really been a part of the vernacular tradition of music where folk songs were always open adaptation, always given fresh life by different performers. Part of the problem in examining the history of improvisation is that we have no exact data on the nature of improvisational practice before the invention of the phonograph and therefore any examples which do exist from the past have already been notated and therefore automatically ceased to be improvisations. What seems to be clear is that notation, over the thousand years since its invention, gradually becomes more and more prescriptive so that what was originally intended as an aid to the memory, an approximation which allows for flexibility and inventive change, becomes a tool which attempts to determine totally the outcome of a musical performance. Many trained musicians are nowadays therefore entirely dependent on the notated score and have little or no idea how to go about making up their own music. Many do not even regard it as desirable and those who do often feel extremely nervous about playing music without a score as a guide. Moreover, the willingness of otherwise highly gifted individuals to submit themselves to a rigid form of training which robs them of their musical autonomy suggests that a peculiar though ubiquitous status attaches to such practice.

It is possible, indeed, likely that musicians in Europe in an earlier period improvised in a similar fashion to contemporary musicians in other parts of the world. African music leaves plenty of space for improvisation as does Indian classical music and other forms such as *qawwali*. Early writings from the Christian Fathers from the 4th and 5th centuries suggest that what *has* been notated is only an approximation, a basic form around which musicians would improvise.[112] Musicians therefore might well have improvised within the context of a certain occasion, connected to the time of year perhaps or a particular festival, articulating the uniqueness of the moment and the location through the special qualities of the musical event. Notated forms, by fixing the music in time past, inevitably depart from this sense of immediacy, losing the sense of occasion and the capacity to express the moment as it happens. The skill of an Indian sitar player, or the vocal improvisations of musicians such as Nusrat Fateh Ali Khan will be affected by the time of day, the season, the gathered company and the occasion and improvised adaptations to the raga or to the song will emerge from the sensitivity of the performer to the special conditions which surround that particular performance.

Notation begins to take hold in Europe around the turn of the first millennium through the work of theorists such as Guido d'Arezzo (995-1050) who codified contemporary practice and instituted training procedures.[113] His Micrologus (1026) sets the pattern for most later theoretical works on harmony which tend to be prescriptive, taking the common practice of the time and in effect validating it, suggesting not so much that this is what musicians happen to do as this is what the good musician *should* be doing. It is little wonder then that Guido d'Arezzo's work which facilitated the performance of Gregorian chant should have been favoured by Pope Paul XIX. Notation then, whilst of undoubted benefit to the performance of music, was from the very beginning, an instrument of cultural, religious and institutional control.

The prevailing styles in much of this early music were well suited to improvisation since they often relied on the addition of a *descant* or *altus* to a fixed melodic line, the *cantus firmus*. As counterpoints become more involved and the polyphonic styles of the Renaissance open new doors of complexity, notated works become more refined, if not more rule-bound. Improvised lines become the domain of the performers whilst the notated version, especially after the advent of printing, gains in cultural if not political strength. The ideological power of music was recognised by successive Popes to the extent that even Palestrina, deemed a musical conservative by most measures, was arraigned before the Council of

---

112 Horsley, Imogene. (2001). "Improvisation II: Western Art Music 2: History to 1600". *The New Grove Dictionary of Music and Musicians*, second edition, edited by Stanley Sadie and John Tyrell. London: Macmillan
113 See Hoppin, Richard H. (1978) *Medieval Music*. Norton, P. 194-195

Trent to explain his divergence from accepted practice.[114] Without doubt, there is a link between the development of notation and the recognition, on the part of those who were seeking to preserve their power over others, that music carries powerful meanings over which they needed to have some form of control.

In secular music before 1600, improvisation flourished amongst madrigalists, minstrels and motettists and this practice was carried over into the new music after 1600 where vocal embellishment becomes a dramatic device in the newly emerging genre of opera.[115] As the structural principles of chord progressions become more central to musical structures, as the mechanics of tonality replace the more freely flowing linearity of polyphony, lutenists and keyboard players develop improvisatory skills akin to those of modern jazz musicians, embellishing the chords and improvising over bass lines with figures added to denote which chords were to be used. In this period and for some considerable time beyond it, keyboard musicians in particular were judged on their improvisatory skill and it was only as the 18th century moves into the 19th that notation begins to be more prescriptive and the new audience for art music, the bourgeoisie, creates a market for notated music which could be performed at home by amateurs. It is possible that it was also around this time, as more and more people began to aspire to a kind of urban respectability, that notated music comes to represent the material security and fixed values which improvisatory styles, linked more perhaps in people's minds to rural folk music, could not support.

The great musical virtuosi of the 19th century such as Schumann, Liszt and Paganini were also great improvisers yet their written scores become increasingly prescriptive with liberal use of expression marks and more use of German as opposed to Italian. It was as if composers were attempting to create more precise images of their feeling states within the musical texts and were eager to ensure that others rendered performances which were as authentic to those feelings as possible. In the same period, the respect afforded to many of these composer-performers by the newly emerging public turned them into romantic heroes and the scores they created are indeed often heroic in scale. It is hard to imagine how the notation of a work such as Wagner's Ring Cycle could ever have been achieved in a single lifetime.

This lionisation of composers turns them from craftsmen into gods, a cultural phenomenon through which, in psychological terms perhaps,

---

114 Despite this, the imitation of Palestrina was and in some places, remains an integral part of the training of musicians in higher education.
115 Horsley, op.cit.

people begin to project onto composers the divine qualities hidden in their own psyches. This finds a parallel in the modern period with its cult of celebrity and the hero worship of rock artists and popular singers. Contemporary attitudes are, in this sense, somewhat stuck in the 19th century, a fact underlined by the continuing popularity of 19th century Romantic music, at least amongst the concert-going public. It may be that the notion of 'greatness' in individuals is regarded as a pre-condition for the integrity and healthy functioning of our culture and therefore it is only natural that it is precisely this aspect of music which gains greatest acceptance. Physically, this hierarchy is perfectly replicated in virtually every concert hall, where the audience sits in the auditorium, performers are elevated onto a platform, the conductor, even more elevated, onto a podium whilst the composer presumably hovers like an invisible god in the clouds, overseeing the whole ritual. The paradox is all too obvious in that the spirit of romanticism, which embodied the revolutionary ideals of equality, freedom, personal heroism and the autonomy of the individual has become the willing slave of its own idealism, falling back into a much older, culturally layered system.[116]

Little wonder then, that within this cultural layering, the skill of improvisation, which celebrates the present moment, becomes undervalued. It is entirely absent from the training of musicians in the UK's Associated Board grade system, for example. In the music academies across Europe and North America the emphasis is on interpretation rather than creative individualism and this is even more apparent in countries such as Japan, China and South Korea where the European musical tradition appears to be not merely a representation of material well-being, a reflection of the coveted values enshrined in the western economies, but also a symbol of the hegemony of the state, the preservation of the status quo in which, paradoxically, the freedoms expressed in the music are not in any way reflected in the conditions which surround its performance. The very music which was born in an age of rebellion, the romantic keyboard repertoire for example, is performed dutifully and obediently by thousands of young musicians seeking acclaim and approval, suspicious or even fearful of improvised music which is devalued if not altogether dismissed. As Chris Small has written:

It is not only that the training of musicians has almost certainly left them unequipped to engage in any kind of on-the-spot

---

[116] See Small, Chrisptopher (2004) *Musicking: The Meanings of Performing and Listening* Wesleyan University Press particularly Chapters 4 and 5 for a rich deconstruction of the concert phenomenon.

invention but it has also left them without the slightest idea that such an activity is either possible or desirable. (Small, 1987)[117]

And the creative percussionist and thinker Edwin Prevost provides even sharper imagery to express our curious fixation with the music of the past:

Classical musicians in their recreations are, at their best, celebrating and re-enacting the earlier, inner, individualistic struggle of the composer. But those ideas are now as safely contained as his body is secured by the grave. (Prevost, 1995)[118]

Yet it is entirely feasible, given the very nature of improvisation, to open it up, make it easily accessible, thereby offering the possibility of encountering life not at a safe distance (the past) but in close proximity (the present); not through the notated forms which come to us from outside of ourselves but through the motivation which rises from our own inner spaces; not via the mediation of an industry and mechanical reproduction but via our own bodies, voices and hands with no recourse to reproductive equipment; not under the direction of the 'old masters' and their contemporary advocates (conductors, teachers, concert managers, radio producers) but through each other in consort with ourselves.

Seven Steps to Heaven

Throughout most of the period we have been discussing so far, Western Europe was steadily imposing its own cultural patterns on the rest of the world, on the Americas, Asia, the Far East and Africa. The collisions of cultures and the human and cultural tragedies which emanated from them are described by Ronald Wright (1992) in his book *Stolen Continents*. He tells at one point of the way in which the sacred icons of the Incas, constructed largely of gold but of purely aesthetic and ritual significance to the Inca people themselves, were melted down into ingots by Spanish mercenaries who could not see anything in them beyond their commercial value. The precious metal came back to Europe as a commodity, stripped of its deeper significance, robbed of its spiritual depth. But music cannot be melted down in this way and the mingling and merging of European and non-European musics over the past 100

---

117 Small, Christopher. (1987). *Music of the Common Tongue*. London. P. 281
118 Prevost, Edwin (1995) *No Sound is Innocent*. Copula, Matching Tye. P. 75

years has created a potent channel of musical exchange leading to lively and revelatory hybrid forms.

Nowhere is this more evident than in the field of jazz which mixes the rhythms and pentatonic chants of West Africans, dispossessed and enslaved, with the elegantly balanced harmonic musical procedures of Europeans, dominant and colonialist. And the 'alchemical vessel' in which this mixture occurs is neither Africa nor Europe but North America where principles of individual freedom are embedded in the constitution. The resulting music, the driving force of which has always been improvisation, has surely become the most significant development in world music in the past 100 years, the generic source of the innumerable popular forms in contemporary music and thus the basis for a massive and profitable industry. Jazz is not merely a style (though some purists would have it remain so) but a way of thinking and responding musically which accommodates and adapts to whatever is happening in the moment. In jazz, in all of its forms, we feel two powerful elements at work, the spirit of freedom and the spirit of renewal.

In some ways, the history of jazz represents a continually shifting dialogue between the spiritual songs of the black population, with roots in African modality, pentatonic and rhythmically open and the chord progressions of the European tradition, rhythmically four-square but harmonically rich. Early blues is almost entirely monodic and single chord yet in the same period we find music such as ragtime which is fully notated as well as employing formal devices we would otherwise associate with Chopin or Mendelssohn. Scott Joplin himself sought approval and respectability and his syncopations may be exotic but they are essentially polite. Jelly Roll Morton, who claims to have invented jazz, also worked, as a pianist, with relatively tightly structured forms embedded in tonal procedures and W.C. Handy wrote out his 'blues' compositions almost in the manner of Schubert composing lieder.

Further into the early jazz period and into the swing era, we find a similar adherence to the tonal procedures of Europe, albeit blended in with the modal features and inflections of the blues (of which more in a moment). From Armstrong and Beiderbecke, through to Ellington, however rich, creative and inventive their music might be it is nonetheless (and understandably) tailored for an audience and paymasters who were mostly white and with whom there was no argument. Jazz was mostly, in the first half of its history, music which depended on commercial success and it grew in its fortunes and its forms, alongside the growth of the recording industry.[119] The influence of Europe is felt particularly strongly for example in the contribution Billy Strayhorn, who had studied in Europe, made to Ellington's work as well as in the self-consciously 'academic' playing of pianists such as John Lewis and Dave Brubeck.

The Ellington/Strayhorn collaborations in particular created original music out of a fine balancing act between the European manner, which notates and fixes its products and the African tradition which is aural, non-written and allows for improvisation. A masterpiece such as the suite 'Such Sweet Thunder', a celebration of Shakespeare's plays, demonstrates both a middle class education rooted in European history and a willingness or need to break free from or challenge this historical model. Despite some extraordinary improvising (for example, Cat Anderson's solo on 'Madness in Great Ones') Ellington is very much in control of the forms and the arrangements and his commercial success was based upon the repeatability of both the tunes *and* the improvised solos which are preserved in the recorded version of the work. Audiences the world over, who turned out year after year to listen to Ellington's band performing, were comforted to hear the same melodies appearing over and again. Interestingly, Ellington's 'Black, Brown and Beige', another of his numerous suites, which celebrates the history of the African American people, demonstrates a similar fine balance between European and African styles whilst the famous 'Concerto for Cootie' locates the raw and disarmingly human sounding trumpet of Cootie Williams in an elegant, 'drawing-room' tonal structure.

The bebop period, which overlaps with the swing band era, begins to accentuate the tensions between the two traditions (European tonality, African modality), extending the modal foreground so that it comes into ever greater conflict with the harmonic background. We begin to feel black consciousness asserting its rights of ownership and this has a dramatic effect on the musical forms. Charlie Parker, Dizzy Gillespie, Clifford Brown, Dexter Gordon, Sonny Rollins, Art Blakey and the other bebop pioneers took the frameworks of the thirties show tunes (minus the verses) and extended them with new melodies and ingenious use of flattened ninths, augmented elevenths and sharpened thirteenths to create a music of extraordinary vitality and tension, technically challenging, intellectually stimulating yet always, somehow, paying homage sooner or later to the 'rhythm changes'[120] – George Gershwin's 32 bar AABA

---

119 Ellington's compositions for example were often designed to fit onto one side of a gramophone record.
120 The chord progression of 'I Got Rhythm'

structure with its two purely 'European' devices, II-V-I plus circle of fifths or to the blues in its by now ubiquitous 12-bar format. Most of all, bebop established improvised solos as the core of the musical events, the 'heads' simply existing as convenient starting and finishing points.

Then, in the 1960s, a significant break occurs. The rhythmic and modal qualities of jazz which have their roots in the original African source appear to take over entirely and the contained harmonic structures of the European derived frameworks become eclipsed by pure modality, emancipated rhythm and an expressive freedom much more at home in the company of Dionysus than Apollo. In the music of John Coltrane, as with Charles Mingus, Ornette Coleman, Eric Dolphy, Pharoah Sanders, Roland Kirk, Albert Ayler, Sun Ra and the Miles Davis of 'Bitches Brew' we witness a radical departure, represented by modal freedom and polyrhythmic experiments unfettered by any tonal safety net. Coltrane's *A Love Supreme*, perhaps more than any other work, comes to represent this new-found freedom and within his music at this stage, there emerges simultaneously a neo-spirituality which stands in marked contrast to the commercial imperatives of earlier jazz output. A fuller history of the transpersonal history of jazz belongs elsewhere but it is in the "free jazz" movement of the sixties, which, unsurprisingly, but unexpectedly connects in a completely new way with European art music in its post-war developments, with the minimalism of Steve Reich, with the post-modernity of Berio and the new improvisatory freedom of Stockhausen, that the music renews contact with its deep spiritual roots.

Alongside this explosive creativity, the civil rights movement augurs a painful and violent but inexorable political, religious and cultural path towards freedom. The new found black consciousness which emerged through the sixties in all areas, though accompanied by conflict and political suppression, found expression in a new music which was neither modernist nor neo-classical but seemed to flow from a collective voice which was saying, "anyone can do this". And Coltrane is far from the only musician to embrace both freedom and spirituality in this way. Similar paths were being beaten by Miles Davis' in the recordings of *Kind of Blue* and *In a Silent Way*, in the mystical theatricality of Sun Ra, in the uncompromising power of Charles Mingus, the sacred concerts of Ellington, the primal baying of Pharoah Sanders, the searching originality of Eric Dolphy and in a re-connection with the music of Africa, India and the far east.

Throughout this whole period, the Blues colours everything. Stemming from the pentatonic chants of the early African Americans, emerging from the swamps of the Mississippi delta, its rhythms and speech melodies deeply encoded with archetypal material, with the religious and shamanic rites of distant, lost West African cultures, blending into every style along the way, into Dixieland, Creole music, boogie-woogie, swing, bebop, hard bop, cool jazz and hot jazz, jazz rock, the blues maintains a generic presence in jazz which then feeds into popular styles, through gospel, soul, country music and thence into rhythm and blues and rock and roll. The melodic basis of the blues, the pentatonic scale (major or minor) with its flattened fifths and flattened sevenths and an equivocal, ambiguous, in-between-ness of tuning, impossible to learn didactically, but which can only be felt, finds its way into virtually every style of 20th century music, even throwing its expressive cloak across composed art music (Bartok, Stravinsky, Copland, Tippett, to name but a few).

The peculiar potency of the blues stems perhaps from three main sources. First, the relocation of musical content in vocal melody rather than in instrumental harmony; second, the tensions created when this modality is combined with the basic chord sequences of tonal music. Once this principle had become framed in the, by now ubiquitous, 12-bar blues sequence we hear the dynamic resonance which gives blues harmony its particular frisson. It is in its melodic inflexions and ambiguous modalities that blues carries its deepest human messages, perhaps, in what Mike Zwerin calls 'The Cry', an authentic, passionate, rooted, pagan, angry, sad, but above all emotionally honest call from the collective heart: an expression of simultaneous grief and joy which defies any theorising. This brings us to the third and most potent aspect of the blues, its transpersonal power: its capacity to hold within its unique yet comparatively simple framework the expressive energy required to fly beyond the ego self into the domain of the gods. Blues carries us beyond grief, beyond longing, beyond despair and beyond even the tragic, into the divine. The Blues, more than any other 20th Century musical innovation, is infused by the spirit of Psyche herself, who, all alone, took those seven, painful steps to heaven.

Whilst the inflections of the blues permeate numerous other genres, the blues form itself has an extraordinarily broad range of expression. Compare, for example, Howlin' Wolf singing "Back Door Man" in which he presents himself as an anti-hero, a creature of the night, a shadowy, snakelike antidote to the white urban dream, with Ellington's miniature masterpiece "Transblucency" where the mellifluous charm of the trombone is blended with a clarinet and high soprano voice to create an image of the very urbane values which Howlin' Wolf rejects. The gravel voice of Howlin' Wolf could not be more different than the smooth tones of trombonist Lawrence Brown yet, in each case, the blues framework provides a musical canvas which blends the bitter with the sweet. It prevents the dark from descending into despair and protects the light from becoming too innocent. Or compare the punchy and primitive blues harp of Brownie Mghee in tandem with Sonny Terry with the complex cycles of fifths and extended chord voicings of Charlie Parker on his 'Blues for Alice'. Or place side by side the great British bluesman John Mayall, blending the textures of Hammond organ with blues harp, guitar, saxophones and his urgent vocalese with one of the great early blues singers like Bessie Smith to hear how, over a half century and across continents, the blues maintains its integrity of expression and form. Such immediacy and such adaptability could only be achieved through improvisational practice, through trying things out and "messin' around 'til it comes right". Given the primary importance of the blues in 20th Century music it seems lamentable that it is not present in every music syllabus, not as something to be learned *about* or taught in the schooled way that is the norm in so many classrooms, through analysis, notation, theory and practice, but within a totally fresh paradigm of experiential learning, an approach which is itself improvisatory, spontaneous, flowing and, above all, rooted in the moment, in direct contact with life.

The forms of jazz and blues which emerged in the 1950s become the primary influence on the development of rock music and other popular forms in the following decade. But, as Evan Eisenberg (1987) describes it, "the heady new wine of sixties music needed bottles – records – to contain its bouquet."[121] So the music industry inevitably homed in on the popularity of the new music and the "recording angel" descends, guiding, facilitating and, above all, commercially controlling and dominating the air waves with what only too easily becomes noise. (Attali, op.cit.)

Yet the free jazz of the sixties gave rise to an alternative totally *non-commercial* kind of music which attempted to transcend barriers of style or genre and which, in some of its forms, attempted to subvert the capitalist system itself. So called *free improvisation* begins to emerge. In

---

121 Evan Eisenberg (1987), *The Recording Angel*. Picador.

Europe this was represented by the work of groups such as AMM, the Spontaneous Music Ensemble, the Instant Composers' Pool and the Willem Breuker Kollektiv (to name but a few) whilst in the US pioneers such as Pauline Oliveros,[122] Stephen Nachmanovitch, David Darling and Butch Morris begin to work with a free approach to sound, creativity and improvisation, linking their musical experiments directly to people, places, communities and self-realisation. We can make strong links and similarities of approach with the avant-garde emerging from the art music at the same time – with John Cage, Morton Feldman, Christian Wolff in the US, Cornelius Cardew in the UK and Karlheinz Stockhausen in Germany – all of which points the way towards a form of music-making which develop its own rules, its own language, as it proceeds.

AMM for example, committed themselves never to rehearse, making every musical event a fresh departure. Keith Rowe, the guitarist with AMM, developed an aversion to what he termed 'fingerprinting' – falling back onto previously learned habits or patterns, the fingers automatically seeking out previously learned chord shapes for example (something which guitarists are particularly prone to do). To avoid this, he developed the habit of laying the guitar on the table and using a variety of implements with which to excite (or torture?) the strings - various plectrums, brushes and even a personal battery operated fan! Stockhausen moves (surprisingly perhaps) from closely notated total serialism to electronic experimentation and then to pieces like *Ylem* which are little more than sets of instructions to his players. *Stimmung* (1968) is a tone essay for six singers, worked out in substantial detail, which draws on the archetypal qualities of overtone chanting mixed with quasi-mystical magic words and improvisatory interactions. It employs a single chord (B flat 7/9) for the entire length of performance, which may be as much as 2 hours. In place of a conventional score, notated onto staves, he published a set of loose pages some of which can be cut into sections and laid out for the performers to choose at will.

These developments in free improvisation, though invisible to many at the time, have slowly filtered through into the lives of more people through the pioneering work of people such as the late John Stevens. The practice of community music developed within this frame of musical reference and it is no accident that the modern practice and profession of music therapy, which is also based around spontaneous improvisation, begins to take shape at the same time, thanks to the guiding lights of

---

122 Together with Stuart Dempster and David Gamper, Oliveros went on to form the legendary Deep Listening Band in 1988.

experimental practitioners such as Carl Nordoff, Clive Robbins, Juliet Alvin and Mary Priestley. Thus improvisation finds, in some ways, its most potent applications in areas of community building, self-realisation, psychotherapy, complementary medicine, healing and neo-spirituality.

The idea that people, whether trained musicians or not, can make music together without recourse to notation, with no direct reference to any pre-existing, imposed structure, with nothing to guide them except for the natural properties of sound and the feel of the moment, the space, the gathered company, sits uneasily, even today, with prevailing notions of music and its mediation. Yet, as AMM and many others have shown, the structures of music are etched into the fabric of human consciousness: they exist in the forms and shapes of speech melody; they vibrate in every corner of the natural world; they sway with the rhythms of our bodies and the beating of our hearts; we only need to listen. This atomistic approach to music-making, though virtually ignored in the commercial and classical arenas, has a steadily gathering profile as people become more aware of its values and its functions.

This then leads us back to the phenomenon of improvisation itself. How does it function as a therapeutic or healing medium? What actually takes place in an improvised musical event? How does the structure of the musical event relate to the emotions, relationships, inner lives and outer connections of those participating in or creating such an event? In the search for a guiding theory which informs and underpins improvisation, the notion of the *Holding Form* emerges. So in the next chapter, I want to dive directly into the improvisation pool, trying to work out what happens, how it happens and, equally importantly, in what contexts? What is the nature and direction of the musical pathways along which people travel when they are improvising?

CHAPTER 4

PATHWAYS TO HEALING

The dance between the conscious and unconscious is choreographed in the transitional space of the imaginal realm. Creative arts therapists have long known that transformation towards wholeness can only happen through experience within this symbolic realm.[123]

Thus, without our imposing a preconditioned intention on it, a musical improvisation can dynamically structure itself.[124]

[The group began playing with very little energy: one participant almost imperceptibly scratching the surface of a hand drum, another making soft shushing noises, whilst a third played the odd, random sound on her violin. This continued for some moments before, perhaps more by accident than design, a longer note on the violin was followed by two drum strokes. This sounded like a point of contact and the players looked up at each other, smiled and repeated the same pattern. Another player, who had been silent until that point, joined in with a two-note chord on the keyboard which just happened to harmonise with the violin note. The improvisation then picked up and developed around this three-way pattern with little development at first but gradually venturing further and further outwards. At the climax of the piece, a new energy emerged and the participants (6 in all) converged onto the exactly the same rhythm for about 10 seconds before fragmenting and going in different directions. As this moment passed, the woman who had been shushing began to sing a wordless phrase and gradually everyone joined in, singing softly, the different voices blending and harmonising in spontaneous and surprising ways before coming to rest on an extraordinarily beautiful chord.]

Group improvisation creates tone-based narratives which both move us, emotionally and move with us, temporally. The emotional content connects with the Self whilst the temporal patterns appear to be universal,

---
[123] Lewis, Penny (1993). *Creative Transformation*. Wilmette, Illinois.
[124] Nachmanovitch, op.cit P. 103

collectively imagined and thus connected with the archetypes. As we improvise, we seem to be creating a connecting pathway, or rather, a series of connecting pathways between the deep self and the outer 'world soul' or, putting this in reverse, between outer ego consciousness and the inner core self. Each musical narrative is potentially fresh and original, uniquely located in its own time and space: this is in the nature of improvised structures. Performing or listening to previously composed music may put us in touch with the grand narratives of our past, but when we improvise, we open up a more immediate and intimate space in which our personal narratives can emerge. We each have a story to tell and whilst words can describe events or paint images, it is to music that we turn for the expression of imaginal events, moving closer, as I suggested in a previous chapter, to the unconscious, archetypal source of the Self.

Improvised music has this *integrating function*: it takes the raw material of sound as it emerges from people's bodies and voices, and from the magical objects we call musical instruments, and fashions it, quite spontaneously and often with surprising ease, into structured forms. The forms articulate narratives which unfold within specific time-frames, the moment by moment shaping of temporality which is music. At every level, however seemingly banal or complex the music might be, this process of integration, articulated through time (the musical event), connects the personal to the universal and the dual elements of the psyche, inner and outer, are thus brought together, opposites are reconciled and complex, dualistic tensions resolved. The connection to time is therefore in essence, a pathway to healing.

So what actually takes place during improvisation? What kind of 'event' is it and what are the available tools which can both assist us in making an improvisation happen and help us to make some kind of sense of what is happening? How can improvisational structures be explained or understood and how might we reflect on the process? Furthermore, within cultural activities such as music therapy and community music as well as during the primary, creative stages of composition, where improvisation is central to what is taking place, what kind of links develop between musical structures and personal or psychological transformations? Can this be *measured* in any meaningful sense of that term? Although it is not difficult to list responses and reflective comments, there are so many variables, innumerable other factors in the lives and experiences of participants (which may be quite unrelated to the time spent making music) that it is virtually impossible to tell exactly how the music-making itself might be responsible for behavioural or affective changes. Yet it is obvious that making music with others creates instant changes in mood and almost invariably a sense of well-being. So by analysing the nature of (improvised) music itself, it may be possible to discover links between, on the one hand, musical structures – the dynamics of the music – and on the other, affective, transformational and relational structures – the dynamics of the relationships within the improvising group. It might then be possible to draw significant parallels between musical transformations, the changing patterns of musical form and transformative processes within individuals.

This chapter also introduces a theory of improvisation which underpins the *Lifemusic* method, the theory of the *Holding Form*. Theories of improvisation have been various though not numerous. Improvisation, by its very nature, is a slippery phenomenon and it does not submit as readily to analysis as composed, printed texts. Much theoretical work has centred on its use in educational and community music contexts (e.g. Paynter and Aston 1968, Regelski 1986, Stevens 1988, McNicol 1990, Dean 1992, Paton 2000, Vella 2000, Agrell 2008). There are also numerous instructional texts connected with jazz, (notably by American educators such as Jamey Aebersold[125] and Jerry Coker). Some writers have concentrated on the social and ideological aspects of improvisation (e.g. Blacking 1976 & 1987, Small 1977 & 1987, Durant 1984, Orton 1992, Bailey 1992, Prevost 1995) others on the nature of improvisation from the perspective of cognitive psychology (e.g. Sloboda 1986, Pressing 1986). Stephen Nachmanovitch (1990), in his unique and exuberant book *Free Play*, actually places improvisation at the heart of life and love, not so much a theory as a song of praise!

Improvisation finds a natural home in the practice of music therapy and it is in the realm of "clinical" improvisation that theories of improvisation proliferate. Wigram (2004) provides a comprehensive guide to the improvisational resources and techniques required of a music therapist whilst an earlier book by Kenneth Bruscia (1987) provides a useful basis for understanding how improvisation can be therapeutically effective. Yet, as Pavlicevic (1995) has pointed out, measurement of the effectiveness of improvisation in therapeutic contexts has tended to ignore musical process in favour of changes in non-musical behaviour in therapy clients. Given that such change is a major aim of music therapy

---

[125] Jamey Aebersold has a global reputation for his extensive series of playalong jazz albums and instructional books and workshops.
[126] Nachmanovitch, op.cit P. 103

as a complementary discipline to medicine, this is unsurprising and therefore, where musical structures are examined this tends to be anecdotally, within the context of case studies. Typical of this approach would be the brief chapter on musical structure in Priestley (1975) where descriptions of musical characteristics are linked to a variety of behaviours within a psychoanalytical framework. Pavlicevic (op. Cit. and 1997), in common with many others) draws upon research by child psychologists, particularly Trevarthen and Stern, into infant/mother interactions "in order to comprehend more fully the complex musical processes that generate and enrich the therapeutic setting" or in an attempt to devise a useful schema within which the link between musical process and affective or physical transformation can be understood, something which Ansdell (1995) and Ruud (1995) have also attempted.

By its very nature, each improvisation provides unique conditions, creating musical and affective narratives which have relevance in a whole range of contexts - therapeutic, healing, relationship enriching, team building and community cohesion, to name but a few. The narratives which emerge through improvisation are quite distinct from the kind of musical narratives which are contained, typically, in composed, fixed, notated or recorded forms. The difference lies not merely in the shift of consciousness which takes place when we are exposed to music (which all music prompts) but perhaps more in the *direction* in which this shift occurs and the manner in which we then negotiate and traverse the pathways which lead in a variety of directions through the maze of the psyche. We might argue that when *listening* to music we may be led *towards* archetypal feelings: the music transports us from the external, everyday world towards a more internalised world of reflection, dreams and memories. We can say then that music is designed to *entertain*, maintaining us in a particular affective state. But when we actually *participate* in the creation of music, improvised music, something much more complex is taking place: we move perhaps in the opposite direction or in a number of different directions as the music is brought into consciousness, emerging from an unconscious (archetypal) source. In this sense it travels both outwards from the centre and back towards the source, simultaneously creating and following a diverse route and choosing the pathways in accord with, *attuned* to, our immediate, affective state. This seems to represent something much more akin to the actual process of life itself with all its diversity, surprises, unpredictability and hazards.

So I am suggesting in this chapter that, through creative improvisation, the imagination creates a number of pathways which connect the conscious with the unconscious, integrating the literal and the imaginal realms, (the dance which Penny Lewis is referring to above). Music seems to possess the phenomenological capacity to bring together the cognitive and affective domains, to integrate subject and object, potentially breaking down the dualisms which inevitably create tensions and disharmony in the soul. It therefore leads us in the direction of wholeness and makes possible a unique, personalised framework in which pathways of healing can be created spontaneously and experienced in the moment.

The Dynamics of Improvisation

Composed music says 'I', improvised music says 'we'.
(Joachim Berendt)

Group improvisation is rather like having an abstract conversation in which everyone is permitted to speak at the same time: the patterns of sound we are receiving from others mingle with the sounds we are making ourselves to provide a resonating field which lies between listening and creating, other and self, outer and inner. The sense of 'other' is engaged with the sense of 'self': at some moments we may be more aware of leading, at other moments of following but we are constantly, in a very real sense, "feeling our way." This experience is rather like being in a maze or labyrinth – a common enough symbol in literature, myth and dreams for the unconscious. Although these interpersonal dynamics are created from abstract patterns of pitch and pulse, texture and dynamics, the *feelings* are very tangible and the co-creation of the music develops affective relationships which are unique. These musical/imaginal relationships inhabit a very different space from the verbal/literal relationships which we experience at other moments. Too much talking at the beginning of an improvisation session will make it increasingly difficult to make the leap from the literal into the imaginal, from logical dialogue into musical dialogue: words, initially, feel somehow safer than sounds, we can control them with the weight of logic, so we tend to cling to them for security. But improvised music is seemingly illogically, irrationally structured, growing out of a randomness which may feel confusing or even frightening. Yet it is this very quality which creates magic and which ultimately allows us to 'solve' the riddle, emerge from the maze.

Many improvisation sessions (like the one described at the head of this chapter) begin with idling or 'noodling', chatting, messing around with instruments, curiously, casually tapping or humming. These opening moments, far from being inconsequential, are nonetheless significant, precisely because they are often performed, to a large degree, unconsciously. 'Playing around', 'messing about' or 'scribbling'[126] is a childlike activity, linked perhaps even to the repressed aspects of the mind, so it can be fruitful for the facilitator (or therapist) to take note, be aware and to respond appropriately, albeit unobtrusively to these dynamic cues, reflecting and supporting them musically. Such beginnings may feel chaotic but the idle, the unintentional, the accidental and the unconscious are so closely linked that it seems especially important at this point in an improvising session to be fully alert, listening out for the unintended motifs or patterns which, springing spontaneously from the imagination may provide a generative shape, a clue to the *holding form*, for the improvisation which follows.

Whether it is during the idling period or at a later point, something will always emerge which provides a basis for musical coherence. Very often, participants will, at a certain point make a collective unspoken decision to stop 'fiddling around' and silently wait for the session to 'begin' (whereas in fact, the process is already under way). The players might then fix upon something or the facilitator might introduce an idea – perhaps a game, a fixed pulse, a rhythmic motif or a pitch shape – which then becomes the new point of departure. 'Motif' in a purely musical sense runs parallel to 'motive' in a psychological sense: so there is an *intentionality* or *motive-ation* present in the group, often latent and thus unconscious, which will inevitably influence the unfolding form. Music therapist Gary Ansdell (1995)[127] describes a number of such beginnings in music therapy sessions, each of them different, some of them moving, some hilarious, but all sharing the same feeling of *breakthrough* – the moment when the group realises that they are empowered to shape the music, or where the sense of the music suddenly becomes *autonomously* apparent.

This point of departure may be largely random, or it may be provided by the facilitator or, as in the case of much jazz, by a pre-existing melody and harmony, but however it begins, the dynamics of the improvisation

---

126 "Scribbling" is the title of one of the workshop exercises in John Stevens' legendary workshop handbook 'Search and Reflect'.
127 Ansdell, Gary. *Music for Life*. 1995. Jessica Kingsley.

will then develop accordingly, revealing something about the nature of musical process as well as the relationships between the players, a psycho-musical dynamic which is always present and active. All performance is process. Simon Proctor[128] has written of this dynamic in music therapy as a "two-sided affair" drawing particular attention to the ways in which music therapists respond to their clients in co-improvisation and explaining how this generates simultaneously *musical form* and a sense of *connectedness*. In Proctor's music therapy world this may be related to the 'predictability' of a therapist's playing in comparison to the often chaotic playing of a client yet this relationship between chaos and structure, between hazard and predictability is a common feature of all improvisations. It is in the interplay between these two poles that we experience the *dance of transformation* where each gesture seeks to develop further the relationship between unpredictability ("I have no idea where this is leading") and musical coherence ("but it makes sense"), an idea which is absolutely central to any understanding of creative process and which I shall be dealing with in greater detail further on in this chapter.

[The session began with a lot of chatting and "scribbling" which felt chaotic and rather frustrating. But very soon a definite pulse emerged though it was unclear who started this going. As the pulse became stronger and clearer someone started humming and this developed into a kind of jazzy scat singing with a clearly defined modality. The improvisation built up more energy and volume, the group responding readily to the musical patterns, echoing some motifs, challenging others and developing spontaneous harmonies. The fixed pulse was maintained throughout, it felt like a securing anchor whilst the textures, (tuned percussion, xylophone, glockenspiel, plus drums and keyboard), together with the humming and singing, created a rich mixture of sustained, human sounds (voices) mingling with elemental sounds (wood and metal). The overall mood of the piece was playful and mercurial, unpredictable yet somehow entirely coherent. Everyone seemed to know when to end and this was very satisfying. The group sat silently for a minute and then everyone laughed!]

Individualising and Generalising

Robert Witkin (1974), in his ground breaking book *The Intelligence of Feeling*[129] suggests two aspects of the creative mind which appear to feed

---

128 Proctor, S. The Therapeutic Musical Relationship: A Two-sided Affair? *British Journal of Music Therapy* 13:1 1999
129 Witkin, Robert (1974). *The Intelligence of Feeling*. London

the dynamic of the imagination. The first of these he labels the *generalising abstraction*, a function which leads to rational understanding, in which experience can be externalised, categorised or systematised as theory. The second aspect he describes as the *individualising abstraction*, a function which internalises experience, crystallising it as part of the inner world of image forming and fantasy. This internalising process leads to what he calls a "quality of absorption" placing the *individualising abstraction* at the centre of a person's sense of Self, infusing external experience with a sense of meaning and significance - it makes things "numinous". The *generalising abstraction* can be seen therefore to have a taxonomic function – helping us to make rational sense of the world; in contrast, the *individualising abstraction* has an ontological (self-realising) function – it helps us to make sense of the Self.

We can see that these two aspects of mind also represent two poles of the *musical* imagination between which there is constant flow – a sonic field connecting the outer (generalised, theoretical, socialised, public domain) with the inner (individualised, active, personal, private domain). Music grows out of the dynamic between these two poles, creating pathways which can never be directly or consciously mapped: not only do they form a maze (see above), but they are not particularly well-lit, so it is necessary to *feel* one's way. The emphasis on feeling[130] is significant since music is primarily a *language of feeling*. Witkin's perspective is undoubtedly informed by the "human potential movement", a number of related humanistic approaches to psychotherapy which emerged in the 1960s and which are aimed at *self-actualisation*. The underlying principle here is that within each and every one of us there lurks not a beast but a genius.[131] This emphasis reflects Jung's concept of individuation, not merely as a goal of therapy but as an inescapable and inevitable aspect of the inner journey each of us makes in the course of our lives. *Lifemusic*, both as a concept and in practice is not framed as therapy but it does embrace the notion that music provides a means through which people can come together to chart this personal and collective journey. Through a deeper understanding of the musical interactions and personal transformations which take place through improvisation we may be more readily equipped to enter this transformational space.

[A 14-year old boy being held in a secure unit for young offenders showed particular enthusiasm for Beatles' songs many of which he knew

---

130 In the introduction to his book Witkin pays tribute to one of his own teachers who pointed out that the Descartes' "cogito" could more usefully be expressed as "I feel, therefore I am."

131 See, for example, Rowan, John (2001). *Ordinary Ecstasy*. Routledge, London.

'by heart' from his father's record collection. He initially displayed little interest in improvisation but he was very eager from the very first session to record his singing. He decided on "Come Together" and I switched on the recording machine, sat down at the piano and asked him to "count us in".

He sang with confidence and with unique tone and texture to his voice, which felt like a musical imprint of his inner qualities, vulnerability mixed with defiance – "this is me, listen!" Then, between each verse, spontaneously and surprisingly, he vocally improvised drum-kit accompaniment to the piano riffs. Though the form of the song belonged to the outer world, representing an attachment to external culture, world of father, fixed form and so on, the actual performance was entirely individual, both in its vocal textures and in its divergences from the original: the familiar 'out there' working simultaneously with the previously dormant 'in here'. The choice of song ('Come Together') seemed particularly appropriate for a young man whose life had seemingly fallen apart.]

Foreground and Background Form in Music

Art arises where the arbitrary and the predictable are superseded by unpredictable inevitability. (Hans Keller 1994) [132]

Before moving on to his notion of the holding form, it will be useful to place Witkin's ideas alongside Hans Keller's theory of foreground and background form. For Witkin, generalising leads towards theory, *explaining* what happens, whilst individualising leads to action, *realising* the musical event. Or, as I expressed it earlier, a taxonomic function (generalising) moving via an unpredictable series of transitions towards an ontological function (individualising). For Keller, the former (generalising) is expressed as *background form*, the hidden or even repressed underlying principles, whilst the latter (individualising) is audible in the work itself and expressed as *foreground* or what actually emerges as the piece created by the individual or group. Keller argues that it is the dynamic tension between these two poles which provides the transitional space of creativity:

I have pinched two terms from Heinrich Schenker, at the same time lavishly changing their connotations, in order to describe

---

[132] Keller, Hans (2005). *Essays on Music*. Edited by C. Wintle and B. Northcott. Cambridge University Press.

the two dimensions or levels along which musical meaning develops: background and foreground. [133]

I am now, in turn, "pinching" these terms from Keller, burdening them with the responsibility for uncovering some of the musical (and psychological) meanings carried by improvisation. So in the following quotation, take the liberty of adding bracketed references to improvisation:

> *The background of a composition (improvisation) is both the sum of the total expectations a composer (improviser) raises in the course of a piece without fulfilling them, and the sum total of those unborn fulfilments. The foreground is simply what he does instead – what is actually the score (the improvisation)...the foreground is that which suppresses the background – often even represses it in the dynamic, psychoanalytic sense, so that the composer (improviser) is unaware of what has happened.*[134]

In other words, when improvising, it is necessary to abandon any *conscious* attachment to given norms or theoretical constructs and spontaneously allow the music to flow. The norms have to be buried so that the unconscious can emerge. It is as if theory and adherence to conventions create a kind of lid which sits heavily on the container which is the soul. Only by removing this lid, or upending the container, can the soul content be poured out.

Keller had devised a method (which he called Functional Analysis) stemming in part from his psychoanalytic roots, which revealed, through live performance, the underlying, hidden unity of a musical work (the stuff that has been buried). For trained musicians especially, but also for anyone enculturated with prevailing social, musical and cultural norms, the *background form*, that is, the expectations of musical logic (or musical norms), is well-defined and will have been consciously or unconsciously absorbed. The fixed nature of these musical and cultural norms ensure not only familiarity with procedures but almost certainly deep conditioning which only too easily rules the musical mind and over-rules the imagination. A simple example of this conditioning process would be the endless diatonic scales which classically trained musicians are compelled to practice assiduously in the course of their studies, often with no reference at all to their expressive potential. Of course, it would be absurd to play only scales and then claim that this is music, so what

---
133 Keller, Hans (2005).Ibid.
134 Ibid.

actually happens during the creative process is that the scales themselves, though present, have to be forgotten, relegated to the *background*, so that the music itself can emerge, inventively and spontaneously, as *foreground*. In an important sense, this fore-grounded material also represents a challenge to the norms (the buried material, the "old school"), opening the way for creative renewal and personal growth. In therapy, it may well be traumatic associations with this "old stuff" which causes clients to seek therapeutic support so it is then through creative improvisation that transformation and healing become possible.

If the background is buried particularly deeply (as, for example with Schoenberg's previously discussed atonal music), or with players who improvise with little or no strong conditioning, an improvisation may initially feel like a 'massa confusa' a sea of chaos. This can feel decidedly uncomfortable because, even with no specialised training, people inevitably come to music-making with an embedded sense of "background form", an accumulation of musical expectations, (previously absorbed material which has become internalised in the same way that the rules of speech are carried in deep, largely unconscious structures) and it is only natural therefore to want to play within the parameters of this conditioned musical understanding. So it may be necessary to provide a space in which both attachment to musical norms and uneasiness with musical chaos are suspended. For trained musicians this can be more challenging than with untrained musicians: the training itself makes it more difficult to suspend belief in musical norms which have not merely become deeply embedded through practice but which form a powerful component of the person's identity, the ego self. In such cases, the tension between background and foreground will be more strongly defined which goes some way towards explaining why many classical musicians, who never improvise and whose attachment to the norms, particularly when contained in notated scores, are obviously very strong, are particularly inhibited around improvisation, their professional and social identities indelibly mapped onto the given norms of musical history. The untrained musician does not have anything like this personal investment in the established norms of musical structure and may consequently find improvising less daunting.

Sometimes, as described above, an improvisation will grow out of randomness, idling or uncontrolled playing. The unpredictability and whimsy of such an improvisation, where conscious control is at a minimum, may also be a reflection of inner chaos and the improvisation will often develop its own foreground in ways which can feel difficult and would probably be inappropriate as public performance for example.[135] Yet there is always a latent musical/emotional logic which an improvising group can work with and develop through the course of a piece. The structure of the imagination is such that it provides a pathway between foreground and background, between conscious and unconscious process and this pathway is both "holding" and "wriggly" in its direction. *Before finding the structure in the chaos it may first be necessary to enter the chaos.* As Keller paradoxically puts it "musical logic depends upon unpredictability". Improvisation is inherently unpredictable.

Jeff Pressing (1988), expressing the same point writes:

It is precisely the indeterminate prospects involved in music's play that are its attraction. And if certain comfortable familiarity concerning the 'fixed rules' or structure of the play-form is ever to 'come into play', it will be effective only to the degree that it is psychologised in personal (unique) ways and only to the degree that it facilitates the indeterminacy of the outcomes. This is why children engaging in free play find it necessary to invent the imaginative parameters that guide their play for the occasion.[136]

So children, Pressing reminds us, especially before they go to school, "grow up" and become imprinted with norms, have to invent this background form for themselves. This is exactly what takes place in improvisation: the "rule-book" is only there to remind us to break the rules and invent new ones.[137]

Since Keller's reference point seems largely informed by Freud, his emphasis on the composer as a singular musical mind refers more or less directly to the concept of a personal unconscious. Yet it seems equally appropriate to talk of background form in terms of the Archetypes which, according to Jung, inhabit the *collective* unconscious and thus belong to the underlying patterns of life itself. Indeterminacy, unpredictability and chaos are all symptomatic of this underlying irrationality (Schopenhauer again), the sea of chaos in which the archetypes swim, yet, within this

---

135 There is virtually no audience for purely improvised music and since, for most people, public performance or the commercial availability of recordings is the most familiar form of mediation, it might be difficult for many to see what role improvisation can possibly play in social discourse beyond the therapy room. Yet, as I argue in Part 2 of this book, new paradigms rapidly appear as soon as we begin to think outside of the box and remove musicking from its consumerist fixations.

136 Pressing, Jeff (1988). Improvisation: Methods and Models in Sloboda, J. (Ed.) *Generative Processes in Music.* Page 194. Oxford University Press.

137 Participants may be encouraged to break the rules yet, when a rule is "broken" it is always in actuality simply a new rule replacing the old one.

theatre of unreason, the narratives we create are both structured and significant. The fundamental elements of musical structure are shared by all: the music therapist is on equal terms with the client and the musician/facilitator is present only to open up a space and maybe provide some generative springboards. The motifs and musical patterns which emerge spontaneously from improvising are no less logical for being intuitively or unconsciously produced: sometimes the logic may be difficult to detect but it will be there, embedded in the psyche, hidden perhaps in the chaos itself.

The *foreground* of improvised music is the unpredictable (unforeseen) and indeterminate element whilst the *background* form (in Keller's terms) is predictable (foreseeable), determinate and theoretical. How we choose to inhabit this space between these poles, between predictability and unpredictability, provides us with many clues about ourselves and our relationships: it is a map of the individual and collective imagination and a resonating board for the dynamic structure of the psyche. In an improvising group, this space can reveal much about the dynamics of the group itself, something which makes it an ideal tool for team building and group development. Analysing or reflecting on the musical transformations which occur during an improvisation using this kind of model may reveal something about the interpersonal and emotional transformations which run parallel to the music. It may also lead us to a deeper understanding of the transpersonal nature of music, its (and our) soul qualities.

There is nothing fixed or rigid in this process. Sometimes the piece will be predictable and safe, at others chaotic and messy. Moving through its own time frame, an improvisation may well start with a consciously conceived idea which, through the course of the improvisation, gradually or suddenly disappears into the background to be replaced by freshly conceived, unpredictable and surprising foreground. *This is always a moment of extraordinary interest and importance.*

> *Nor are backgrounds and foregrounds static entities: in the course of development of the composition (improvisation), individual structures are formalised, de-individualised, turning foregrounds into backgrounds.*[138]

In other words, once the initially conceived motive or rhythm loses its ontological function, it *has* to be repressed! Children at play do this

---
138 Keller, Hans (2005).Ibid.
139 Ibid.

automatically: they simply lose interest and switch off once the game loses its mystery. This capacity to constantly re-invent and refresh, to work with the unforeseen with the *as-yet-to-be-discovered* is a primary function of the imagination pointing us in the direction of forms which are in constant flux, where new pathways are constantly opening up between background (repressed/unconscious) and foreground (revealed/conscious). Improvisation, by its very nature, provides a framework within which these two areas of mind may be integrated through a constantly flowing musical structure – connecting to time. Often, participants will consciously avoid the "obvious" which has emerged, perhaps through repetition, as a momentary "norm" (background) and move off in another direction; significantly, they may also resist following someone else's "norm", seeking instead tension, conflict and separate identity and this can also lead to music which sounds chaotic to an outside ear.

[The group begins by improvising around two opposing principles - one half of the group playing constantly moving tones, the other half playing longer sustained tones. Gradually the two principles are to be allowed to merge. The piano begins by simply repeating a low C in a steady pulse. One or two players begin to play sustained sounds but the original principle is almost immediately abandoned. It is as if the anchor of the piano allows all the other players (about 8 in all) to invent with maximum freedom and the piece suddenly sounds like an eastern marketplace, full of calling, whooping, bantering and bartering. A trumpet and cello begin to exchange swooping glissandi whilst a horn and clarinet seem to engage in serious discussion. Gradually, all the players converge onto the regular pulse of the piano, yet, no sooner than this happens, everyone sets off again in their own directions until even the piano abandons the anchor of the pulsating C to fill out the texture with strident atonal chords. The other instruments scurry and flurry in all directions. When all seems about to dissolve into chaos, the cello plucks out a pulse and the others, suddenly remembering the original "background" idea converge onto sustained and rather beautiful chords. The piano then remembers the opening and returns to the low C (this about two thirds of the way through the piece) and the other players also seem to then recapitulate material which they played earlier. The piece winds down and finally fragments into a coda which, though opening up lots of space, never loses that opening sense of pulse.]

Killing the King

The principle of musical renewal depends upon the capacity to create new patterns out of old. In fairy tales this would be symbolised perhaps by the killing of an old king who had become too rigid and tradition-bound. In a Jungian sense, over-identification with the Senex archetype (the old patterns) leads to rigidity and one-dimensionality and in music this creates academically rule-bound forms and rigid, uninspiring teaching models. Conversely, over-identification with the *Puer* (new ideas, freshness, inspiration) can easily lead to a melting pot of sound and a sea of chaos, reminding us inevitably of the story of Icarus whose youthful enthusiasm turned to arrogance, landing him in the soup! In freely improvised music, however, background is being freshly created from moment to moment and foreground both *emerges from and merges with* this background material. As the old patterns become fixed, so new ideas are invented to counter this, sometimes gradually emerging, sometimes appearing instantaneously and surprisingly. As an improvising group becomes more used to playing together (and this can happen within a very short space of time) they will discover a balance, a way of playing in which the invention of fresh foreground and the repression of background becomes autonomous – at this point, the music itself might be said to be leading the group.

If background is defined as a musical 'norm' then any divergence from this norm can be regarded as foreground. This is where the art of the improviser/composer, according to Keller, resides. During improvisations with non-schooled musicians, the sense of chaos that often arises is only felt as such because of the existence of this (background) norm. But whose norm is it? As a trained musician, I might be tempted to respond to chaos by 'tidying it up'. My own schooled approach is then in danger of over-riding my own imagination or even worse, of creating a sense of superiority over less schooled participants so that I impose my own view of how it should go on others, the manner of the dictator and something which is commonly experienced amongst those music teachers only too eager to ensure that their students do things properly. So my instinct is to stay with the chaos, allowing it to persist until the group *itself* collectively seeks to 'tidy it up', or not.

In practice, it is never quite this simple. The so-called chaos always contains structures, even perhaps, archetypal shapes which are not immediately apparent; or, the group might simply be more interested in the taste of chaos, identifying with the Dionysian energy which can be both transformative and exhilarating; or, conversely, the group, frustrated with their inability to produce something which corresponds to a norm might move towards something recognizably idiomatic. In fact, is non-idiomatic improvisation ever fully possible (logically) except for the very first time someone plays? Once a musical idea or principle repeats itself it is already on the way to becoming a norm. Furthermore, musical experience is so ubiquitous and enculturation so profound that cultural norms are deeply embedded in most people's musical minds. Even the freest of free improvisers often seem to be creating an idiom out of precisely the techniques designed to avoid idioms altogether!

[It is the week before Christmas and the group (9 academy music students) decides to improvise a ten minute version of Bach's Christmas Oratorio! With no decisions about key, chords, text, language or instrumentation, one member of the group starts vocally improvising a bass line. The others join in one at a time, creating a rough counterpoint which, though in no particular key, has all the characteristics associated with Bach's music – dynamic, forward moving rhythms, sequential repetition, distribution between high, middle and low voices and so on. Then, all of a sudden, a key centre spontaneously appears and everyone seems to be singing in perfect harmony. There is even a hint of a circle of fifths. This continues for a full five minutes until the 'oratorio' finds its way to a long held triad. The piece ends and everyone roars with laughter!]

[A (learning-impaired) teenager aged 14 improvised with chaotic abandon, exclaiming: "this is better than Baa-baa black sheep", grateful, no doubt, to be rid of a 'norm' which had been thrust upon him all too often by well-meaning but unimaginative carers. Another teenager returned often to the songs of Freddie Mercury and George Michael, moving between these and his own extraordinary and totally original improvised monodrama. A third teenage boy was obsessed with the 'Dallas' theme and spent much of the session banging out the rhythm of this bland tune on a bass drum. Yet, at one point, he began to play quietly and the drum sounded like a heartbeat. I followed this idea, moving away from Dallas towards more ritualised unchanging chords and a simple pentatonic tune. The transformation lasted only a short time but the emotional effect was profound.]

Coherent Unpredictability

I have spent some time discussing Keller's theories of background and foreground processes in music since I believe them not only to reveal fundamentally important qualities of the musical imagination but also to relate directly to the way we live, our personal and social relationships, our game playing, our politicking as well as our musicking. Here is a summary, in tabular form, the first two columns representing positions which present barriers to creativity whilst the third column is intended to reveal the kind of balance and dynamic flow which provides the potential for creative improvisation:

1) If music is entirely predictable and coherent, as described in column 1, it is all background and therefore stuck rigidly in norms. There may be some comfort in this kind of over-theoretical security but the potential for change is absent and, ultimately, the lightness of the event will be unsatisfying. The constant emphasis on convention will prevent new material emerging and the imagination will atrophy. Meaning, which depends on some kind of conflict, will be overstated, obvious. It may even be, in an autistic sense, fixated on a single principle, resulting in social isolation and relational atrophy.

2) If the music is totally unpredictable but also incoherent it is all foreground, chaotic, with no anchors in either cultural referencing or even perhaps in archetypal structure. The event will be uncomfortable and the absence of any reference to conventions or norms will ensure that the experience is unlikely to create a sense of identity. Moreover, the constant change will be unlikely to create the conditions in which identity, musical or otherwise, can be formed. For the same reasons, meaning, which also depends upon repetitions, will be absent. It may even be, in an autistic sense, out of control.

3) If the music is unpredictable yet coherent then the logic of unpredictability emerges from the fine balance between foreground and background, a balance which can only be achieved by intuition and flux: just like riding a bicycle! The flow between identifiable conventions and the surprising challenges to these conventions creates meaning. The combination of openness, flux and adaptability opens the potential for relationships and creates a transformational canvas.

None of this is prescriptive: the table merely summarises the discussion. The purpose of this chapter is to shed some light on the creative process and on the structure of the imagination, moving towards a theory of improvisation which hopefully sheds some light on its potential for healing. It may well be the case that healing, in the sense of 'making whole' depends upon precisely such a balance of qualities within the imagination as described here but most importantly, these ideas provide a basis for the practical suggestions which appear in Part 2 of this book.

PREDICTABLE/ COHERENT	UNPREDICTABLE/ INCOHERENT	UNPREDICTABLE/ COHERENT
All Fixed	All flux	Flowing
Theoretical	Chaotic	Imaginative
Standardised	Formless	Inventive
Comfortable	Uncomfortable	Surprising
Over-controlled	Out of control	Spontaneous
Light	Dark	Multi-coloured
All Unity	All Diversity	Diversified Unity
All consonance	All dissonance	Attuned
Regimented	Fragmented	Rhythmic
Fully Notated	Non-notated	Improvised
Unimaginative	Unimaginable	Imaginative
Obvious	Meaningless	Meaningful
Conventional (i.e. strict adherence to conventions)	Non-conventional (i.e. lack of awareness of conventions)	Unconventional (i.e. conventions are challenged)
Artificial	Absence of artifice	Artful
Dictatorship	Anarchy	Democracy
Stuck	Loose	Transformational
All background (repressed)	All foreground (chaos)	Moving between background and foreground (balance)

The Notion of the Holding Form

The holding form is merely the seed of which the realised form is the flower. [140]

---

140 Witkin. Op.Cit.

Holding Form (HF) theory informs both the practice of *Lifemusic* and the reflective analysis which flows from and into practice. Thus, the HF provides the *Lifemusician* with both a modus operandi, a way of working and simultaneously, a template for understanding or rationalising what is happening. Witkin begins with what he terms the "sensate problem" which grows from the need to transform *a feeling impulse* into *significant form*. This is what we do – it is what makes us human. If music is understood as the direct representation of the forms in which feelings are cast (Langer, 1947) then achieving this musical goal depends upon the capacity to create structures whilst maintaining contact with the feeling impulse during the process. In some way, inner process (feeling) and outer product (form) need to be brought into close proximity, something which improvisation automatically achieves. As Keller argues and as the above table demonstrates, if the balance between elements is not maintained, the feeling impulse is swamped, either with theory, rendering the piece dull and lifeless or with chaos which can lead to frustration. This is where the HF becomes an essential tool, maintaining balance between the two poles, or rather, creating a dynamic field which integrates these two aspects of the creative mind and it is through this integrating process, perhaps, that healing may occur.

To summarise Witkin's argument in musical terms, all musical acts take place in time, connecting the creative participant to time, where "sensate experience" does not stand still and wait for something to happen: it all happens at once.

> *If the sensate impulse is not contained then it will quickly dissolve into other sensate experiences. For a problem to be resolved it needs to be held for the duration of the process of resolving it. As soon as the sensate problem is encountered it becomes necessary to establish a Holding Form for it. This is a vital part of the creative process and without it the sensate problem itself would change out of all recognition and defy resolution. One cannot resolve so volatile and protean an event as a sensate disturbance unless one encapsulates it in a holding form.*[141]

But, moving beyond Witkin, let us consider the HF not as a static principle, but as a dynamic, shifting process which changes its shape and direction during the process, which renders the outcome unpredictable

---

141 Witkin, op.cit. P. 180-1

and unforeseen, pointing quite literally to improvisation. The "holding" is present from one moment to the next yet, because it is happening within a "time hole", it is constantly shifting, making the outcomes unpredictable. In the language of Keller, any process governed by an HF is both unpredictable and coherent. The HF may provide an access point, boundaries, even limits of style and scope but this is only a part of the story. Because it is not yet realised, without losing in any way its integrity, this initial shape can constantly change, one rule replaced by another in succession, a process governed entirely by feeling in time: the form of this feeling *preceding* as well as *accompanying* the realisation, the fluctuating, affective context out of which the music emerges. The secret of creativity is not to cling for comfort to any particular rule so during an improvisation the HF is functioning not merely as a generative, conscious motive or idea which sets the piece going (though this will be part of it, an "access point") but also something partly hidden, barely conscious, even *magical*, which autonomously kicks in as the improvisation gets under way, guiding the music away from any fixed or rigid framework, carried forwards in time by a sensate or emotional or inter-relational imperative, by an archetypal force.

The HF is not to be confused therefore with the kind of chordal frameworks used by jazz musicians such as the 12-bar blues progression. These are precise and predictable frameworks which then become *background form* as soon as the musician begins to improvise. In this instance the HF is not the chord structure but something more subtle, a hidden structure of soul which conditions the finite choices made by the musician out of the infinite choices available[142]. These choices are finite only so long as boundaries of style and genre are preserved. If a musician chooses to push these boundaries to breaking point then the HF leads towards freedom and perhaps a kind of musical truth.[143]

The HF is then the *flexible* tool through which transformations occur. In improvisation, the HF is encountered as a moving, changing, guiding, underpinning, unpredictable but inevitable force which allows the music to journey through time in spontaneously realised forms sometimes lasting well over an hour. There is always a collective sense of when the piece must end; a point is reached where the HF is spent and this is always

---

142 This inner device, the precise mechanism through which musical choices are made from one moment to the next is impossible to fix or describe precisely but, archetypally, it conjures up the image of Hermes as a guiding figure: playful and quixotic, mercurial and whimsical but able to negotiate the pathways which criss-cross the transitional space between conscious and unconscious. Hermes might also appear in his role as a reflective presence, a deep silvery pool in which we can see the reflections of our own inner light.

143 In the case of the blues, this seems to be what happened in the later music of John Coltrane which appears to abandon the conventions of blues in order to embrace a kind of metaphysical reality.

felt by everyone (though not always acted upon). But very often, when the piece comes to its natural end, there will be a significant silence, a reflective pause, during which one can almost sense Hermes, as an invisible shaman, taking his/her leave.

[A group of six musicians are improvising in an octagonal room which has floor to ceiling windows. The improvisation is based upon the idea of flight and birdsong. It begins with some steady drumming interspersed with staccato chords on the piano. As the intensity of the drumming increases, the piano begins to play faster, broken chords and a flute and oboe join in with birdsong type motifs. The music picks up in intensity and volume and as it does so the players notice that a large flock of seagulls has appeared, wheeling around outside the building and making a considerable din. As the music dies down they fly off. And then I notice a lone crow taking off from the branch of a tree just outside the window.]

Prime Reality and Intuition

Where does the HF come from and in which area of mind can it be located? Many visionary thinkers as well as more pragmatic philosophers refer to the essentialist notion of an underlying unity which dissolves the duality of reasoning which determines more conscious patterns of thought. Henri Bergson (1859-1941) describes this as "prime reality". Pirsig (1976) calls it "quality". Jung (1916) refers to it as "pleroma".

> *In his visionary* Septem Sermones ad Mortuos, *written in 1916, when he was going through a period of personal turmoil, Jung refers to the underlying reality as the pleroma, a term which he borrowed from the Gnostics. The pleroma cannot be described, because it has no qualities. In the pleroma, there are no opposites like good and evil, time and space, or force and matter, since all these opposites are created by human thought.*
>
> *Anthony Storr (1992).*

Intuition is perhaps the surest means of accessing this undifferentiated space since intellectual reasoning is bound by the dualistic nature of thought. Improvisation, which is a largely intuitive act, provides a potential field therefore in which participants can feel their way towards this primary form, giving voice to, or sounding out its patterns without the intervention of the intellect. Intuition enables us to bypass the intellect in order to open a pathway between our conscious lives and the internalised narratives which build up through our personal histories – memories, dreams, fantasies. Perhaps then, the function of the HF is inextricably linked to these intuitive patterns of feeling stored in the unconscious. They may be identical both to the internalised fantasies of ourselves and the world (in a Freudian sense) which have formed as the result of introjections and also to the forms of feeling which Langer (op.cit.) suggests exist in music - those deep structures in which feelings are felt and cast. They may even be linked to 'neuronal assemblies' as suggested by music therapist Julia Usher (1998) who provides an equation between musical 'gestalts' and improvisation. We certainly *perceive* music as a 'gestalt' (a unified experience, the whole form) so maybe we can argue equally that music can also be *conceived* as a gestalt, reflecting Witkin's description of the HF as a seed which contains the image of the flower yet to blossom. The act of improvisation places trust in this process, yielding up intellectual thinking in favour of intuitive perception in order to access the HF and thus steer a course towards this prime reality as it finds expression in the elaboration of tone, rhythm and timbre. And since time itself is a vital component, perhaps the most determining component of Bergson's prime reality as well as Jung's pleroma, improvisation, by connecting us directly to time, creates an instantaneous link with this underlying, unifying aspect of mind.

Letting go of the intellect or yielding to intuition means abandoning, as far as possible, the conscious ego self. Unless this happens it is not possible to access the other layers of the psyche let alone the archetypal domain with its potential for releasing alternative selves. Roger Dean (1989) describes improvising 'schemes' as 'Gathas', a Buddhist term which places emphasis on chance procedures and thus egoless-ness since, when we allow chance to take over the game, the controlling function of the ego dissolves. This principle of indeterminacy might also be at work through the numerous 'accidents' which inevitably arise in improvisation:

> *Accidents, which from a restricted viewpoint represent momentary failures, can be turned into success by their incorporation into the musical performance, through acceptance, integration or even emphasis.* (Orton, 1992, page 766)[144]

We might even regard accidents as the musical equivalent of Freudian slips which provide instant clues to unconscious processes which, far from being accidental may be the vital clue to the next step in solving

---

[144] Orton, Richard (1992) 'From Improvisation to Composition'. In Paynter et al. *Companion to Contemporary Musical Thought*. Routledge, London.

the riddle. Brian Eno and Peter Schmidt in 1975, devised a whole set of schemes for creative problem solving which they called 'oblique strategies', brief instructions, many of which appear like koans, designed to catch the ego off-guard. One of my favourites, which reflects this Freudian slippage is "honour thy error as a hidden intention" There is no reason to reject any musical ideas which appear during improvising, even focussing perhaps on those sounds generated during 'idling', allowing them to become integrated into the holding form.

[A middle aged woman joined the group for a day of improvising. As a child, she had had the unhappy experience (not uncommon) of being forced to practice the piano under parental pressure and had even achieved Grade VIII. She had not touched the piano since that time. During the session, she sat (sideways) at the piano, idling, fiddling, casually fingering the keys. By chance she came up with a tiny riff which very gradually flowed into and increasingly permeated the playing of the whole group becoming finally the guiding theme of the whole improvisation. She was moved to tears by this experience yet, on reflection, it was apparent that she had been totally unaware of her crucial role in creating the magical outcome of the piece.

On another occasion, a member of the group, playing the xylophone, can be heard attempting to replicate the well-known pentatonic motif from the film 'Close Encounters of a Third Kind.' She makes a tiny 'mistake' (saying "oops" as she does so). She then becomes disheartened and falls silent. Yet, as the other players in the group begin to establish the improvisation through a gathering series of musical dialogues, she returns with greater confidence playing entirely her own music and, at the vocal climax of the improvisation, her voice can be heard sailing through the texture with total abandon.]

These examples demonstrate transformations where an 'accident' has led to creativity. It is only the ego part of the self which, seeking control, says "oops" when it goes wrong. In Chapter 1, I was suggesting how the musical act, so often culturally encountered as an externalised, ready-made object, might be re-construed as an internalised yet-to-be-made experience. This would require the HF to be located in empathic, trusting relationships which are not bound by ego. Only then perhaps can the 'metaphoric' qualities of the imagination be liberated and allowed to emerge collectively and creatively. Cox and Theilgaard (1987) in *The Aeolian Mode*, constantly emphasise the importance of this aspect of trust in creative arts psychotherapy through which the therapist maintains the capacity to engage in dynamic play with the client or group. *The Aeolian Mode* describes a means by which metaphors and poetic playfulness emerge in support of people's inner narratives.

> *The calling into existence always implies the crossing of a threshold, and the threshold to be crossed may initially be that of the patient's capacity to trust the therapist and, subsequently, the patient's capacity to trust himself. From another perspective, it declares itself as the movement towards insight gathers momentum. Poesies may thus be the process whereby inner emptiness, initially experienced as insecurity, fragility, and hollowness, is gradually transmuted into affirmative depth.*
> *(Cox, Marray and Theilgaard, 1987 pg. 24)*[145]

What this passage seems to be saying is that the self can only begin to be fully encountered once the defensive mantle of the ego is replaced by the poetic basis of mind. This requires trust and empathy but once this threshold has been crossed, once the need to control has been relinquished, intuition takes over and we are provided with a "glimpse of glory".[146]

Integrity, Soul and Spirit

In a previous section I was arguing that the HF acts as a mediating factor between foreground and background. If we examine this idea more closely, we can see that these two poles are arrived at through the application of dualistic thinking to music. This creates difficulties, since musical process resists the dualist frame. So it might be more useful to regard dualism, not in a classical sense, as an image of opposites which are somehow irreconcilable, but as a dynamic field which provides the kind of flow essential for the functioning of the imagination as well as the potential for healing, a unifying of conflicting poles.[147] In archetypal terms, referring back to Chapter 2, this would mean simultaneously honouring the two related gods, Apollo and Dionysus. If we lean too far towards the procedural, Apollonian mindset, then music easily becomes dry and locked into conventions. The condition of spirit is dryness, its medium is air. If Dionysus is allowed to take over completely, then the music easily drowns in chaos. The condition of soul is wetness, its

---

145 Cox, Murray and Theilgaard, Alice (1987). *Mutative Metaphors in Psychotherapy.* London.
146 This expression belongs to T. S. Eliot discussing the function of poetry in his essay on Matthew Arnold.
147 An idea offered to me by Michael Tucker, professor of poetics at the University of Brighton, during one of our numerous enriching discussions.

medium is water. The HF therefore can be seen to have a potentially integrative function, allowing for creative freedom yet maintaining the integrity of the structure at a deep level: light and dark, wet and dry, soul and spirit.

'Integrity' is the keyword so it might be useful to look more closely at its meaning. In fact, integrity has two meanings, one structural, the other ethical. In the first sense, it is applied to objects and ideas which hold together or which demonstrate the clarity of logic. "The machine had an integrity of design which ensured its efficient functioning". Or, "his arguments, lacking in integrity, were unconvincing." In music, integrity of structure is expressed in phrases such as, "Mozart's String Quintets demonstrate an integrity of form in which diverse melodic ideas are unified with surprising ease." Or, "Miles Davis' *Bitches Brew* demonstrates how musicians from widely differing backgrounds can be integrated into a single and original creative force".

The second meaning of 'integrity' centres on personal attributes of reliability, consistency, honesty and truthfulness, suggesting that we place high value in people whose behaviour demonstrates the same kind of qualities which the structural meaning carries. These should not be confused however with *predictability* (see Keller, above) since there may be hidden factors, as is often the case with complex or unfamiliar music (and people), of which we are initially unaware whilst the apparent integrity which shelters behind predictability, conscious academicism, imposed structure or a rigid rulebook, is not integrity at all, merely *encasement*.

The integration of the personality (or the process of individuation, in Jungian terms), is a process through which conflicting elements (or unresolved complexes) are reconciled and music provides abundant, living metaphors for this process. For example, throughout the tonal period, integrity of key is of primary importance and all music composed roughly between 1600 and 1900 establishes challenges and finally restores the triad which belongs to the home key. Beethoven's Symphonies represent these narratives on a universal scale. Dane Rudhyar may well have had Beethoven in mind when he wrote the following passage:

The musical solar hero passes from one sphere to another. As he reaches the end of the transformation – the seventh step, the "leading tone", the Initiation – he is able to hear the "music of the spheres", to re-experience the succession of challenging tests that nearly destroyed his being as what the Greek culture called a "harmony", but which in terms of the European culture should be called a "soul-melody."   *(Rudhyar, 1982)*[148]

The most influential musical innovation of the twentieth century, the blues, demonstrates perfectly how fruitful, how powerful, and how liberating it can be when two radically opposed traditions are integrated. The pentatonic melodies of African music combine with the basic tonal procedures of European classicism, the "three-chord trick" to create a form of music which has healing properties etched into its entire fabric. The blues idiom is soul-full (see previous chapter), informing much of what we hear today in popular music. Academic language, conscious of the metaphysical problems with the term "soul" is more resistant to its use but, as so often, the common use of the word, as in the musical idiom described as "soul" belies a collective understanding of the way in which the integrative structures present in blues and its offshoots provides the necessary conditions for "soul-making". Music then, with its unique and archetypal qualities, is capable of integrating these poles of rational and irrational, dark and light, chaos and structure: a form of sonic alchemy.[149] In music, we discover that the dualisms which pervade so much of the business of contemporary life and thought are not merely resolved but synthesised: it is through music that the two meanings of integrity become one.

This special quality of music has already been discussed in relation to Schopenhauer and Nietzsche (in Chapter 2) but here is Rudolf Steiner driving the point home:

The other arts must pass through the mental image and they therefore render up pictures of the will. Tone, however, is a direct expression of the will itself, without interpolation of mental image. When man (sic) is artistically engaged with tone, he puts his ear to the very heart of nature itself, he perceives the will of nature and reproduces it with a series of tones. In this way, man stands in an intimate relationship to the Thing-in-Itself and penetrates to the innermost essence of things.   *(Steiner, 1983, pages 2-3)*[150]

---

148 Rudhyar, Dane (1982). *The Magic of Tone and the Art of Music*. Shambhala, Boulder.
149 Fascinatingly, in alchemy the transformational shift between the albedo and the nigredo is referred to as the "blue transit" (see below).
150 Steiner, Rudolf (1983) *The Inner Nature of Music and the Experience of Tone*. Anthroposophic Press, New York.

And, from the same essay:

When the musician improvises, he cannot imitate anything. He must draw the motifs out of the musical creation of his soul.[151]

This soul quality is surely at its most potent at the precise moment when the music is being created. However beautiful and uplifting recordings might be, however praiseworthy the interpretations of classical scores, there is no comparison to the live event. One can only imagine how exciting it must have been to hear the B minor Mass or Mozart's Prague Symphony or Beethoven's Fifth for the very first time. The freshness of the blues as an idiom is maintained through its capacity to carry the feeling of the moment through improvisations which are woven around the basic, archetypal structure. Yet, as I have been arguing, this kind of spontaneous musical act is not in any way confined to any precise idiom or style, it is merely a matter of will and intention. Where the basic structure is wedded to an archetype, the more likely it is that the resulting music will be soul-full, or numinous.

The Transitional Space

Once we cross the threshold of conscious intention and move towards the sea of unconscious imperative we enter a different kind of space altogether, a space in which change becomes not merely possible but inevitable. It is as though we are swept into a flowing current which carries us towards deeper waters. The quotation heading this chapter comes from Penny Lewis but it was the post-Freudian psychologist Donald Winnicott (1971) who linked the notion of the transitional space with play and art making. His detailed study of the relationships between mothers and infants provided many clues about the structure of the imagination. He describes the link between the newborn child and the mother as an 'illusion of oneness' which, as the infant grows and separates from mother, is necessarily dissolved, though not without trauma. He goes on to suggest (in the wake of Freud's own observations) how it becomes necessary for the child to compensate for this ensuing dis-illusion by creating a 'transitional space', an internal realm of fantasy, assisted by 'transitional objects' – comforters, toys, musical instruments, objects whose function, whilst purely symbolic, leads to the potential for healing and psychological balance.

---

[151] Ibid. P. 3.

> *Transitional objects and transitional phenomena belong to the realm of illusion which is at the basis of initiation of experience.... This intermediate area...constitutes the greater part of the infant's experience and throughout life is retained in the intense experiencing that belongs to the arts. (Winnicott, 1971, page 14)*[152]

Abstract and intuitively perceived, music is the primary medium perhaps through which we can encounter and map this rich and vital domain of mind. In this maze of pathways between the conscious world of reason and rationality and the unconscious world of irrational impulse and archetypal drama we encounter the "daimons" who lead us, playfully or otherwise, into the realm of infinite possibility. Improvisation, imagined forms, the tones and modalities which carry our memories and dreams through structures of feeling are the healing agents which Winnicott describes:

> *The searching can come only from desultory formless functioning, or perhaps from rudimentary playing, as if in a neutral zone. It is only here, in this unintegrated state of the personality, that which we describe as creative can appear. This, if reflected back, but only if reflected back, becomes part of the organised individual personality and eventually this in summation makes the individual to be, to be found, and eventually enables himself or herself to postulate the existence of self.*
>
> *This gives us our indication for...creative impulses...which are the stuff of playing. And on the basis of playing is built the whole man's (sic) experiential existence. We experience life in the exciting interweave of subjectivity and objective observation, and in an area that is intermediate between the inner reality of the individual and the shared reality of the world that is external to individuals.*[153]

The Blue Transit

How does Winnicott's transitional space, an aspect of the individual's ability not simply to cope with personal experience but to turn this coping mechanism into an act of self-realisation, equate with the collective and archetypal patterns out of which music emerges? In his essay *Alchemical Blue and the Unio Mentalis*, James Hillman provides perhaps an even

---
152 Winnicott, D.W. (1971) *Playing and Reality*. London.
153 Ibid. P. 64

Wassily Kandinsky, Improvisation 28

reproduced by kind permission of the Solomon R. Guggenheim Museum

Kratzenstein-Stub, Orpheus and Eurydice

Antonio Canova, Cupid and Psyche

The Piraeus Apollo, 6th Century Bronze

broader perspective on the nature of the transformational process:

Transitions from black to white sometime go through a series of other colours, notably darker blues, the blues of bruise, sobriety, puritan self-examination; the blues of slow jazz.
(Hillman, 1980/1981 pg. 132)[154]

In this rich and extraordinary essay Hillman places emphasis on how feeling finds expression through metaphor and how these metaphors of feeling then lead to a deepening of the understanding of self (the trials of Psyche as viewed through the alchemist's mirror perhaps). As Hillman puts it, "sadness is not the whole of it...there are patterns of self-recognition forming by means of horror and violence. The soul's *putrefactio* is generating a new anima consciousness, a new psychic grounding that must include underworld experiences of the anima itself: her death and perverse affinities."[155] For Hillman, alchemical blue is associated with bruising, trauma, woundings, decay, descent, with "falling apart" and this, in turn, leads to an opening up, a deepening of the capacity to experience things, a journey therefore into the *source* of feelings in *anima consciousness*. This is not an easy journey. Encounter with anima is always associated with psychic trials, the pain of not *being in control*. In archetypal psychology, anima, as an image of the deep feminine is equated with the capacity to feel and this inevitably means descent, just as it did at the crucial point in the tale of Psyche when she has to go down to the lower regions to bring back the box containing the secrets of beauty. This is white (innocence, rationality) moving into the dark (experience, intuition). Eurydice, Orpheus' bride also makes this descent, condemned (or choosing?) to remain in this dark, erotic space, a confinement which may be seen as inevitable and therefore tragic. Orpheus could only sing his grief.

We might consider music itself as a kind of acoustic alchemy, a series of experiments which, whilst ostensibly attempting to form gold from base matter, or simply entertaining us, is in fact forming powerful and abstract symbols representing both the soul-making function of the human mind (descent) and the transcendent qualities of the human spirit (ascent). Perhaps we can now re-imagine the Holding Form as an alchemical vessel, hermetically sealed and containing not merely the base emotions (the feeling impulses) but, when heated to the correct

---
154 Hillman, James (1980/1981) Alchemical Blue and the Unio Mentalis. From *Spring: An Annual of Archetypal Psychology and Jungian Thought.* Spring Publications.
155 Ibid. P. 133

temperature, catalysing into a transformational process which leads eventually towards an epiphany. The alchemy of improvisation mixes and balances tensions between different sonic elements: in rhythm, between the fixed pulse of the march and the random rhythms of speech; in texture, between the ritual violence of the drum and the plangent echoes of the flute; in pitch, between white notes, representing the diatonic scale with its hierarchies and black notes which form the primal equilibrium of the pentatonic scale. Intriguingly, should we care to superimpose the pentatonic scale directly onto diatonic harmony or simultaneously mix major harmony with the minor mode, in both cases mixing black with white, we suddenly, automatically even, find ourselves playing the blues. And, as Hillman reminds us, the blues is not only about sadness but about the capacity to deepen our relationship to life, to experience the tensions between sadness and joy, to journey to either end of the spectrum, finding balance between extremes of experience and innocence and to be healed in the process. In Hillman's aphorism: "blue protects white from innocence".[156]

Summary of Holding Form

The HF is a device for *containment*. In the words of Malcolm Ross (1978) it "holds the expressive impulse both in the sense of containing it so that it is not lost sight of, and in the sense of capturing its essential structural character".[157]

The HF delineates the space between conscious and unconscious and holds the journey through its entire length. Kandinsky suggests three stages in this process linking outer states with inner understanding:

1) A direct impression of outward nature expressed in artistic form. This is called 'Impression'.
2) A largely unconscious, spontaneous expression of inner character, the non-material nature. This I call 'Improvisation'.
3) An expression of a slowly formed inner feeling which comes to utterance only after long maturing. This I call 'Composition'. In this, reason, consciousness, purpose, play an overwhelming part, but of the calculation, nothing appears, only the feeling.[158]

The HF is primarily a function of intuition which is capable of sensing the deep structures which attach to the feeling impulses lying beneath the surface of rationality.

---

156 Ibid. P. 133
157 Ross, Malcolm (1978) *The Creative Arts*. Heinemann Educational, London.
158 Quoted in Ross, Malcolm (1984) *The Aesthetic Impulse*. Pergamon Press. P. 110

Not that unreasoning instinct rebels of itself against firmly established order. By the strict logic of its own inner laws it is itself of the firmest structure imaginable and the creative foundation of all binding order. (Jung, 1944/53).[159]

The HF provides a 'gestalt', a complete, sensate image which then seeks realisation, not through intellectual effort but through the spontaneity of improvisation.

One lays foundations, prunes, constructs, organises; but one does not arrive at the whole. The complete work is not the rule – it is above the rule. Art exists in the place where secrets begin and the intellect is (tragically) extinguished.
(Paul Klee, quoted in Geelhaar, 1974.)[160]

The HF functions within the spirit and patterns of play. The play is the important thing, its autonomous, self-justifying, self-contained quality. Considerations of form, structure, technique, expression, performance, audience are irrelevant. It is the quality of absorption which is central.

To get to the idea of playing it is helpful to think of the preoccupation that characterises the playing of the young child. The content does not matter. What matters is the near withdrawal state. The playing child inhabits an area that cannot easily be left, nor can it easily admit intrusions.[161]

Transformational Process

...liminality is frequently likened to death, to being in the womb, to invisibility, to darkness, to bisexuality, to the wilderness, and to an eclipse of the sun or moon.[162]

If *Lifemusic* is to have any effect beyond the sheer energy and enjoyment of music-making, then we might expect it to be transformational, to broaden our perspective on life, on relationships and on our own actions. In the following chapter I will be suggesting contexts in which this might be useful, some fairly obvious, some less so. But for the moment, I am focussing on the link between transformational processes in improvised music and affective or psychic transformation

---
159 Jung, C.G. *Psychology and Alchemy*. CW Vol 12. Routledge.
160 Klee, Paul (1915) quoted in Geelhaar, Christian (1974) *Paul Klee, Leben und Werk*. Koln.
161 Winnicott, D. W. op.cit.
162 Turner, Victor (1977). *The Ritual Process*. London. P. 95

in the people who are making the music. Music therapy, both in its modern professional forms and in its more ancient guise as a healing ritual, grows out of an empirical base which takes it for granted that this happens, that there are in fact direct links to be observed between the music people make (in the therapeutic space) and the affective, psychological or physiological changes which inevitably result. Some schools of thought lean more strongly towards the importance of the *therapeutic relationship* which develops through the music-making whilst others place emphasis on the *power of sound* itself to initiate change. But whatever the variations in approach, people are drawn to therapy and to music most often because they desire change; because the old ways of adaptation no longer suffice; because projections which, in an earlier age, functioned adequately to shield us from psychological reality, are being re-integrated. And this hurts.[163]

Lifemusic as concept and as practice, is based on the inescapable fact that change is the primary component of life: connecting to time means connecting to the flowing pulse of living process and it is only when we lose touch with this natural flux, when we attempt to resist the changes which are inevitable or when we fail to understand the symbolic quality of life that we become stuck. The modern world too often pours concrete over areas which would be better left as green fields both literally and figuratively. To observe an eclipse and measure the resulting refractions of light is useful and no doubt fascinating but to celebrate an eclipse as a life changing opportunity is something which we probably believe belongs to antiquity or to a more primitive form of culture. We believe that access to seasonal foodstuffs all year round is a good thing and fail to notice that we also lose some fundamental contact with the nature of time when we eat strawberries out of season. In Disneyland, every day ends with fireworks, is constructed to feel special, like Christmas, with the result that every day *ceases* to be special and the inhabitants end up, like Goofy the Dog, with rictus smiles on their faces. To be in harmony with the moving pulse of life is to also to be equipped with the capacity to transform ourselves and our cultural habits in balance with the flowing changes and fluctuating qualities of time which are a constant in our worlds.

In his descriptions of liminality and the ritual processes through which initiates are taken in the development of social bonding (communitas) Victor Turner (op.cit.) lists a large number of binary oppositions which

---

[163] See von Franz, Marie-Louise (1978). *Projection and Re-collection in Jungian Psychology, Reflections of the Soul*. Stuttgart.

create a dynamic between liminality (the limbo of not knowing) and the status system (the fixed reality and laws of the tribe). Although many of these dualisms are symbolised by social rank and position (e.g. absence of status/status) there are strong resonances with the kind of dualisms I was describing earlier in musical terms. The status system, for example, equates with the musical canon and with the background form from which develop the fixed laws of musical theory. Absence of status equates with the limbo of not knowing, the innocence as well as the wisdom of the "fool". When Turner cites "communitas/structure" as a dualism, we might translate this, musically speaking, as "improvisation/composition" or as "foreground/background" in Keller's terms, since the foreground represents the fluctuations of the imagination with its potential for renewal whilst the background represents the fixed conditions of musical and thus social tradition: the former is a state of unknowing (the unforeseen), the latter a state of knowing (the familiar). This is a theme which has been developed by Norwegian music therapist Even Ruud (1995) who suggests that during an improvisation participants enter a liminal state where prescribed forms (tradition) are abandoned in favour of transitional or even chaotic states (transitional space) and then replaced with "new meanings".[164] According to this argument, improvisation creates the precise conditions necessary to move the traditional forms, structures, procedures into the background, clearing the way for renewal or freshly imagined foreground.

This liminal state bears a strong resemblance to what Achterberg (1987), Harner (1980) and other researchers into shamanism would call the *shamanic state of consciousness* (SSC). In describing auditory aids to altered states, Achterberg cites the use of "bells, rattles, sticks or other percussion instruments"; chants and songs, where the former are often "phonemes strung together" (developed by jazz singers into "scat"); but most importantly "the shaman's drum reigns as the most important means to enter other realities, and as one of the most universal characteristics of shamanism". She then goes into some detail, citing medical research and evidential support to demonstrate how rhythm and tone create altered states of consciousness.[165]

There seems little doubt that, as an improvisation develops, the feedback created by constantly repeating and evolving sounds have a significant effect on the consciousness of the participants. This feedback is all-embracing since it is in the nature of sound to completely envelop

---

164 Ruud, Even (1995). Improvisation as a Liminal Experience. Chapter 12 in Bereznak-Kenny C. (ed.) *Listening, Playing, Creating - Essays on the Power of Sound*. SUNY Press.
165 Achterberg, Jean (1987). The Shaman: Master Healer in the Imaginary Realm. In *Shamanism* (ed. Nicholson). Wheaton. P. 118

the listener. It seems to be this quality, this shift away from the everyday conscious state towards the liminal area which provides a clue as to why the *Holding Form* appears to shift and change its generative function. It is entirely possible that, as the rhythms and tones of an improvisation develop, the autonomic system of the improviser becomes more engaged and consciousness deepens to a point where the players seem to be functioning with virtually no direct conscious control.

Sometimes, this can affect players to the point where they almost fall asleep. In one session a teenage girl flopped with apparent fatigue but continued to play the xylophone whilst lying on the floor. After about 15 minutes of improvising, with one of the other participants playing quite loudly on a drum, she closed her eyes and appeared to be asleep although she was still playing. In another instance, working with a group of mothers and infants, a three-year old placed his ear right against the skin of a frame drum which was on the floor, having discovered that it resonated with all the other sounds and chants that were taking place around him. He promptly fell into a deep sleep.

Liminality appears to provide a potential for transformative process which speech cannot provide, though rhetoric can. Rational language is always dualistic since it is bound to subject/object distinctions presented in linear, logical and literal forms, nouns, bound grammatically and given energy by verbs. But improvised music is *all verb* – all doing and the subject/object dichotomy dissolves in the dynamic flow of energy without need for explanation. The question "why" is replaced by a deeper sensation of "what". Ultimately liminality is about being able to let go of understanding altogether and to open up that space in which anything is possible, trusting that this will not result in meaninglessness. As Jonathan Kay, actor and mime artist once put it, "if you cannot understand it, stand under it".

Summary - Pathways and Narratives

Behind all of this discussion is the idea that the structures of music reflect and represent the structure of the imagination. The image-forming capacity may be uniquely human, but the forms in which music is cast grow out of the natural properties of sound which began to be charted as long ago as Pythagoras. This direct link between music as a language of feeling and music as an autonomous language of the universe is an ancient theme which has been explored more recently by Joachim

Berendt (op.cit.), Dane Rudhyar (op.cit.), Peter Michael Hamel (op.cit.), Hazrat Inayat Khan (1921/1996) and many others. Music is created spontaneously through improvisation and the dynamic energy of music charts both the dynamic of the psyche and simultaneously equates with the dynamics of natural processes, mapping the complex space, those pathways which are constructed like a maze between conscious and unconscious, a non-verbal yet comprehensible medium for the actualisation of the Self. This is the *imaginal realm* and the structure of the imagination is precisely charted by the structure of music. It is like a labyrinth and the closer we approach the centre, the unconscious core, the more differentiated, unfamiliar and labyrinthine it becomes: improvising music therefore inevitably means dissolving our attachment to the familiar and diverging from accepted norms making possible fresh narratives of the Self.

The imaginal realm is also a *transitional space* (Lewis, Winnicott) and this can be equated with *liminality* (Turner, Ruud). Archetypally, this is a function of Hermes and therefore a domain of playing and playfulness. The liminal state of "not-knowing" provides the conditions for musical and psychic transformation, and thus for healing since it renews our contact with creative life. All that is necessary is for the *feeling impulse* to be maintained (Witkin, Langer). This process can also be expressed alchemically as the "blue transit" (Hillman) and thus as *anima* which, expressed musically, has an Orphic (hence, lyrical) quality. The imaginal and creative tool necessary for negotiating the rhythmic and tonal pathways which criss-cross this maze and which lead us safely through is the *holding form* felt as a flexible, slender thread, though very strong and expressed archetypally perhaps as Ariadne's silk, spun out through love and devotion.

[At the beginning of the improvisation, H. is playing a strong, rhythmic motive on the bass xylophone. She seems oblivious to what is going on around her, with the others talking and settling down and generally "idling". I accompany her playing with some simple piano chords and gradually the rest of the group joins in. The improvisation moves through a series of changing "grooves" but this opening xylophone motive keeps returning in a variety of transformative "disguises". Sometimes, other players seem to be (unconsciously) challenging with hard drumming rhythms, cymbal crashes or even at one point, someone scraping the radiator with wooden drum sticks. At other

moments, an ocean drum is played in a way which feels by turns swamping and soothing. The group has worked together for 10 weeks already and the playing feels confident and purposive.

About 20 minutes into the improvising I suddenly feel an intense fatigue coming over me and find myself, literally "flopping" over the keyboard playing whatever comes out. The result is a series of quite dark chords. Eventually, H. settles onto a single note, an 'A' obsessively repeating it. I find myself playing a series of changing chords whilst the ocean drum washes over and under the sound. It feels like a drawn out valediction, a deep reluctance to let go, accompanied by a sense of sadness. As the music ends the group sits in complete silence for about ten minutes and the young woman is in tears. Later on, she reflected that she had both wanted it to end but had not been able to let go; it was as if she was being held by the music, led into a space where she would be able to release some wordless feeling. It was as if the music had invited the whole group into a closed arena of pure feeling where it could encounter some rarely visited sensation of what it was to be held, to be safe or simply to be.]

The journeys of Orpheus and Psyche may provide symbolic clues to the archetypal source of musical healing but ultimately it is in our own music-making that the conditions for renewal and personal transformation can be created, leading us individually and collectively to the soul of things. The young woman who had been so moved by the experience of this improvisation later wrote a poem about her feelings ending with the words...

Understanding without meaning
Meaning without understanding.

This hermeneutic pathway, this form of understanding which words are inadequate to express, but which is carried by music, this connection to time and to others within the musical space is the central theme of this book. The second half is therefore devoted to a form of music-making which is participatory, inclusive and creative, a means through which people can experience for themselves and with surprising ease, the archetypal qualities of music, sharing the soul quest with each other and thus restoring to music its primary function as a pathway of healing and renewal.

PART TWO

The Practice of *Lifemusic*

CHAPTER 5

DEFINING LIFEMUSIC

Lifemusic in practice employs participatory music to promote well-being, deepen awareness, enhance relationships and enrich the sense of our connection to life and to time. It is about people coming together, in a wide variety of contexts, to make entirely fresh and original music. It is not about learning an instrument (though it may include this) or singing in a choir (though any choral director could usefully employ the method) or playing in an orchestra (though an imaginative conductor might usefully introduce creative improvisation into a rehearsal). This suggests not merely a contained method but a broad philosophy which can permeate any form of music-making. Yet, the music-making itself is only a part of the concept since the philosophy advocates extending the use of live music-making into many activities where participatory music may not traditionally have any presence at all, such as in the workplace, the hospital ward, the boardroom, or even the cabinet office. In other words, it suggests ways in which we might invite Psyche into social arenas where she is perhaps most absent and most needed. This range of applications for the method will be explored in more detail in the next chapter. For the moment I shall concentrate on defining and describing the method itself.

The Four Precepts

The four precepts of *Lifemusic* describe a form of music-making which is natural (everyone can do it) non-judgmental (there are no wrong notes), revelatory (every sound has meaning) and therapeutic (serves individual well-being and promotes healthy relationships). At the core of the method is the notion that the primary function of music is to turn life into soul.

Everybody is musical.

During the 1960s a distinguished and highly regarded music educator called Arnold Bentley devised a series of tests intended to provide an indication of musicality in children.[166] The "Bentley tests", as they inevitably came to be known, were based on the assumption that some children were more musically talented than others and that therefore these talents could be identified in a quasi-scientific way fairly early on in their schooling so that appropriate resources could be channelled in their direction. On the face of it, and at the time, this seemed laudable. Most would probably agree that some people are indeed more musically talented than others and that, since resources are finite, the most able should be offered the best support.

There seems to me to be two major flaws in this approach, the first cultural and the second musical. In cultural terms, by assuming that some children are more musical than others the Bentley tests were automatically divisive, providing academic support for situations in which many young children would be labelled as *unmusical* or musically weak and would therefore be discouraged from participating in musical activities. This is to say nothing of the emotional damage inflicted on a young soul when told that they cannot hold a tune, sing sweetly or play rhythmically. Furthermore, the privileging of the musically gifted was also a way of enhancing the status and exclusivity of one kind of music since lessons were mostly about learning orchestral instruments and feeding the school and youth orchestras (always a useful showcase for education authorities) with bright young musicians. For the exceptional few it meant training for the music profession. The second flaw, linked to the first, is that the Bentley tests were designed around precisely the kind of musical models and content, styles and genres, represented by the choice of rhythms, melodies and harmonies in which the tests were cast, which belong to the European classical tradition. In effect, this meant that children were being selected or de-selected on the basis of tests which were by their very nature culturally specific. White middle class children please apply![167]

---

166 Bentley, Arnold (1966). *Musical Ability in Children and its Testing*. Novello.
167 Most formal music education in the nineteen fifties and sixties completely ignored the revolution that was taking place in the rest of the musical world with blues, jazz, rock and roll and popular idioms relatively if not entirely absent from the school curriculum. As a result, music became generally unpopular as a school subject.

In contrast to Bentley, it can be argued that music is a birthright and that the specialist musician is in fact a purely cultural product within a society which itself encourages specialisation. Many people leave music-making to "musicians" largely because they were brought up to believe that participation in the creation and performance of music is for the gifted few and thus they deny themselves the significant joy and satisfaction which would otherwise come from making music themselves. (Even highly trained professional musicians often ignore their own creative selves, only ever performing music composed by others.) However, in order to develop an inclusive approach, to broaden participation in music so that it encompasses all members of society it may be equally necessary to broaden the definition of music itself. This may mean steering away from some deeply embedded ideas about what constitutes musicality. For example we may need to abandon the notion that musicality is solely about the ability to handle a complex musical instrument, or to sing perfectly in tune (in tune with what?) or keep strictly in time (in time with whom?) or understand the complex narratives of tonal structures. It may mean embracing the notion of music as an activity which is very simple technically though highly significant emotionally; it may mean loosening our ties with the complex instruments of orchestral music, such as the violin or clarinet, and giving equal status to "instant access" instruments such as drums, shakers, xylophones, rattles, lyres, penny whistles, ukeleles and harmonicas. Most of all, perhaps, it means deconstructing the notion of the composer as a god and realising that, given the right conditions, we can all be composers.

This is a historical problem which I already touched upon in Part 1 of this book. As the nineteenth century got under way, composers became less reliant on patronage and more reliant on public concerts and the publication of their manuscripts in order to make a living. The concert-going public (principally the emerging middle classes and the intelligentsia) identified increasingly with the individualism of the composer: after all, it carried the zeitgeist, the spirit of Romanticism. With simultaneous advances in science and technology, music became at once both aesthetically beautiful and technically complex. In the same way that, for example, engineers were elevated as pioneers of industrial design, explorers were admired for charting unknown regions of the planet and poets were worshipped as revolutionaries of the soul, the composer became a lionised figure and Beethoven in particular emerges as a "great composer" just as the notion of greatness itself was being born. He came to epitomise the *composer-as-hero*, a concept which dominated the 19th century and persisted well into the 20th. Even today, this notion is far from dead with ample public money available for performances and commissions as well as for training and development. We are reluctant to let go of this particular condition of music.

Ruth Finnegan (1989), in her study of music–making in an English town, discovered an extraordinary wealth of composing amongst the population of Milton Keynes. But this composing-in-performance, as she terms it, most of it in rock, jazz and related forms, was largely underrated or ignored since it did not belong to the accepted canon which, in most people's minds is associated with the term 'composition'.

> *When only one mode of composition is held in mind – often the widely revered classical model – it is tempting to speak of the 'passivity' of the population or the lack of originality of the youth. But once one understands the validity of these differing systems for creating original music, each autonomous in its own terms, it becomes clear that there is indeed a remarkable amount of musical creativity at the grass roots.*[168]

A further problem with the elevation and lionisation of the composer in the European tradition concerns technique. The European canon itself, had developed a set of highly specialised technical procedures which remain a mystery to most of the listening public even though the emotional power of the music is audible and accessible. This is rather like being able to appreciate the joy of riding a motorcycle whilst not having the least idea of how to maintain it.[169] The greatest of them all, and the figurehead of the canonic vessel was of course, J. S. Bach, virtually forgotten until he was rediscovered or rather re-invented by Mendelssohn and others in the 1830s. Bach's music has the peculiar distinction of being at one and the same time highly complex and very beautiful. In Bach's own time and in the 19th century when interest in his music was revived, his work represented familiar religious imagery and spiritual narratives. In the 20th century the tradition which he comes to represent begins to separate the music from its original social functions. Not only is the music of this "synthetic-analytic" tradition ideal material for intellectual analysis and the relatively new discipline of musicology

---

168 Finnegan, Ruth (1989). *The Hidden Musicians. Music-making in an English town*. Cambridge University Press. P. 179
169 A metaphor for dualism developed by Robert Pirsig in his 1976 book *Zen and the Art of Motorcycle Maintenance*.

but it also begins increasingly to appear out of context, played on the airwaves, or in in-car stereo systems with little regard for its deeper contextual significance.[170] European classical music becomes beautiful in a platonic sense, abstract and ideal, elevated in status and imbued with absolute values: pure, abstract and somehow beyond social meaning. At the same time, the concept of "beauty" (which lies at the heart of the European aesthetic) assigns to music a significant value for the listener, who then becomes the passive partner in a transaction within a larger political economy. The end result of this historical accident is that the majority of people came to believe that the creation of music was best left to specialists who would provide for them, at a price, a beautiful experience. In such a system, people, by and large, became consumers rather than creators. The development of the recording industry feeds on and is fed by this aesthetic.

It is little wonder, then, that people have come to invest heavily in the cultural belief that music is a commodity which is provided for them by others. After all, this corresponds fairly precisely with the innumerable other commodities which form the basis of a market economy: cars, cosmetics, clothing, furniture as well as vital utilities such as water, gas and electricity and life-sustaining services such as health care. The mindset surrounding this consumerist philosophy combines with the canonical tradition of music, discussed above, to create a situation in which people in general simply do not themselves make or create music or even believe that it is desirable to do so. Furthermore, there are few readily available contexts which enable them to do this. Despite developments in music education which promote and support the notion of composing, whatever creativity might exist in the classroom tends to be fragmentary and unsure of its own direction; and for most people, this involvement, in any case, disappears once they leave school.

In the UK of the 1970s, the traditional 'Bentleyite' approach to music education was challenged by a whole new set of concepts. It is extraordinary to note that only 5 years separate the publication of Bentley's work with that of John Paynter and Peter Aston's *Sound and Silence*[171] yet they are worlds apart. *Sound and Silence* was a seminal text which set out to demonstrate that children are intrinsically creative and, given the right kind of stimulus, can make original music themselves. In the world of *Sound and Silence*, everyone is a composer. Paynter's ideas fed into a major Schools Council project which he

---

170 Some years ago, I heard, by chance, a startling example of this dislocation of context and meaning on Sunday morning radio, Classic FM's "Classic Romance" series where the music chosen to accompany a real life story of a young couple falling in love turned out to be the Mozart Requiem!
171 Paynter, John and Aston, Peter (1970). *Sound and Silence*. Cambridge

directed from York University between 1973 and 1978 and which strongly influenced the development of the national curriculum in the following decade. Yet, whilst *Sound and Silence* represented a significant breakthrough in attitudes and perceptions about music with young children and about nurturing the imagination, many, if not most, teachers, have failed to take up the challenge it offered and when eventually the national curriculum did emerge, creative freedom tended to be swamped, partly by the defenders of tradition (including, of course, politicians) and partly by bureaucracy. The riches of creative improvisation and imaginative composition are still very dependent on the skills and enthusiasms of individual teachers rather than something which has permeated schools in the general way which was intended by these pioneers. In addition to this, the technological revolution has filled schools with keyboards and midi equipment, further complicating the picture. It is not at all unusual today to encounter music departments populated by young people engaged in a curiously isolated relationship between themselves and the keyboard to which they are connected by a pair of headphones.

The ideas represented in *Sound and Silence* are rooted both in progressive attitudes to arts education and also to some degree in the music of the European avant-garde, a world away from your average classroom. The riches of rock music, popular forms and jazz are less evident though never excluded. But the other wave which built up in the sixties and which then trickled into wider cultural practice in the seventies came from the world of free jazz and the kind of experiments in improvisation which emerged through the work of musicians such as Derek Bailey, Evan Parker, Phil Wachsmann, Tony Oxley, John Stevens and groups such as AMM (Eddie Prevost, Keith Rowe, Lou Gare, Cornelius Cardew, John Tilbury and others) as well as the Spontaneous Improvising Ensemble which led to the formation, in 1975, of the London Musicians' Collective. One of the leading thinkers behind this progressive educational and social movement was the writer and educator Christopher Small whose book *Music, Society, Education*[172] stands alongside *Sound and Silence* as a major exposition of the new thinking which was taking place around the social uses and cultural meanings of music. Small employed improviser and drummer John Stevens to run workshops at Ealing College of Education where he pioneered a fresh and entirely person-centred approach to improvisation based upon free expression,

---

172 Small, Christopher (1977/1996). *Music, Society, Education*. Wesleyan University Press.

autonomy and group energy. This in turn led to the formation of Community Music, London and Stevens' concept of "Search and Reflect" a philosophy enshrined in his otherwise purely practical book of the same title. Chris Small's foreword to this now legendary book speaks of "giving back to people the music that belongs to them" ten words which express a major potential turnaround in cultural attitudes and in the political economy of music.[173]

Restoring to people the belief that they can make music themselves, that everyone is musical, is no simple task. It requires not merely support for the innate musical skills which each and every one of us possesses, the kind of techniques and approaches pioneered by people such as Paynter and Stevens, but in addition, some kind of tectonic shift in cultural perceptions as suggested by Chris Small. It might also require a minor battle with those who have a vested interest in the status quo, namely music professionals. After all, if everyone is empowered to create music themselves, where does that leave composers? And if whole populations suddenly begin to realise the incomparable joys of self-made music and improvisation, where does that leave the recording and publishing industry, not to mention the manufacturers of hi-fi and other playback equipment? Once we accept that everybody is musical, we return to the primary definition of music itself as *intentional time* reminding ourselves that it is not necessary for music to be technically complex, perfectly recorded and reproduced or even beautiful in order for it to be socially useful. We are all musical because we are all connected to time, simply by being alive, being aware and being human.

There are no wrong notes in music.

The celebrated jazz improvisation teacher, Jamey Aebersold begins his highly successful series of books and play-along recordings with the statement "there are no wrong notes in music – only inappropriate choices". Thus, in one sentence, he simultaneously opens and closes the door to true improvisation. An "inappropriate choice" is actually the same thing as a "wrong note" and therefore, what this statement in effect means is that the sounds a musician plays, his or her choice of notes, must conform to a previously established norm in order to be heard as "appropriate" or "correct". In this case, the norm we are speaking of is jazz. The learning method which follows then takes the norms of jazz one by one – blues, modes, standard jazz tunes with their often complex

---

173 Stevens, John (1987) *Search and Reflect*. London.

but systematised harmonic circuitry, rhythmic phrasing and expressive inflections and primes the eager learner with the toolkit needed to imitate the great figures of jazz history. And there is, of course, enormous satisfaction to be had from this process and correspondingly a large market for these learning materials. Aebersold's approach is successful because he is able to unlock the potential of motivated young musicians who wish to improvise within a chosen set of musical norms.

Aebersold enjoys the same kind of success as that other stronghold of musical training in the UK, the Associated Board of the Royal Schools of Music. Once again, we find a set of familiar musical texts, the European tradition of melody, harmony, tonality and rhythm, fixed within fully notated forms, contained within a precisely defined set of technical hoops and hurdles (the grades) and disseminated through a large-scale, international network of centres, teachers and hopeful, if not proud parents. Equally, there is enormous satisfaction to be gained from taking up and meeting this kind of challenge. No-one would deny that the achievement of a Grade VIII on any of the designated instruments within the AB domain requires considerable skill, application, determination, musicality and nerve whilst learning to improvise jazz with some degree of fluency is surely the musical equivalent of climbing Mount Everest. But what do these norms represent? Why preserve them in this way? Why are some people excluded from these achievements or why do others simply find them irrelevant?[174] And what happens if and when they are discarded?

The first result of letting go of norms might well be chaos, or seeming chaos. John Stevens's already cited book *Search and Reflect* (which in some ways stands at an ideological extreme from Aebersold's "new" approach), includes an exercise called "Scribbling" in which small groups (3 or 4 at a time) are encouraged to play randomly as fast as possible on any instruments until one of them stops, whereupon all stop. Then when someone starts playing again, they all join in, scribbling merrily, until someone stops playing...and so on. Initially, this appears to create a form of chaos. Yet, within a very short space of time, structures begin to emerge quite spontaneously. The group quickly discovers that more is to be gained from listening and responding coherently to each other than simply adopting an "anything goes" approach. If the process is allowed to continue long enough, given space and freedom to expand and provided there is sufficient trust to do this, the scribbling rapidly transforms into coherent, consistent, expressive, integrated, structured

---

174 Many young people begin learning instruments via the grade system when children only to abandon the process, dropping out of music lessons as teenagers.

and even moving musical pieces. The act of "scribbling" is eventually replaced by the innate musical integrity of the trio or group and the ensuing improvisation can become as contained and disciplined as anything within the pages of an Associated Board examination list or Aebersold instructional disc. The difference however is fundamental in that the structure is now defined by a set of spontaneously conceived rules which have emerged during the playing, from the inner motivations of the players themselves: the participants have connected to time and therefore to the archetypal patterns of sound which have been created within this precise "time-hole". At such moments, there ARE no wrong notes and every sound has a meaning within a set of freshly conceived norms. This suggests a holistic definition of music as simply a series of norms and divergences from the norm, free of any specific historical style or genre (though reference to these may still exist). Within such a definition, any sound can be validated since it can define its own terms, create its own norms, within the moment of conception - a newly arrived-at set of principles; or it can abandon them and create afresh. Music does not have to adhere to a *particular* norm to work as music and imposing such strictures on somebody else from an external source might be viewed as a political rather than musical act.[175]

None of this is intended to deny or devalue any of the remarkable and original music which works within recognizable cultural frameworks. The norms of music grow out of historical imperatives and it is inevitable, therefore, that musical idioms which carry the myths of specific cultural areas are preserved and repeatable. It is then only natural for people themselves (especially children perhaps) to strive for some kind of identifiable form of musical expression for which they will receive acceptance into the community and praise for their efforts. At a simple level this might be represented by being able to play "chopsticks" or "Für Elise" on the piano or by demonstrating the ability to sit at a drum kit and hammer out the ubiquitous "backbeat" of rock. It is always intrinsically satisfying to master a skill and the display of such expertise may result in an equally satisfying though probably short-lived form of social acceptance. At another level, the capacity to play a successful jazz gig or to sit in an orchestra and play one's part in a performance of a symphonic masterpiece can provide a significant pay-off, emotionally and socially. Identifying with and successfully working within such cultural norms provides a sense of security as well as a form of social

---

175 The fate of numerous composers and musicians unfortunate enough to find themselves living and creating in totalitarian conditions (e.g. Shostakovich and others in Soviet Russia, jazz musicians in the former Eastern bloc, serial composers in Nazi Germany or just about any musician under the Taliban in Afghanistan).

recognition, conferring status and identity and great music is always enriching for the soul.

Yet there is always a danger, as I was arguing in the first chapter, in clinging to norms to such a degree that they become first fetishised and then fossilised! So what happens if we choose to discard these identifiable norms? What kind of *alternative* 'pay-off' can be derived from playing 'wrong-note' music? What kind of music results from such an activity? Who does it belong to and where is it located, culturally? And is musical progress possible without a return to this ground zero of music-making? Consider the character of Caliban from Shakespeare's *The Tempest*. Caliban is an ambiguous and melancholic figure, very much, though not entirely, under the control of Prospero (who had liberated him from a curse). Yet, at the same time, he is resentful, restless, rebellious. Caliban's gripe with his master is that he was in so many ways better off without the learning, without the speech, without the precepts and controls of civilized behaviour which Prospero had gifted him. Caliban longs for the innocence which gave him direct access to, and understanding of, the sounds and shadows of the island. His longing to return to his former state, to feel, to experience and to live in a more primal condition is, in a very real sense, pre-socratic or non-dualistic; it belongs to the *undifferentiated Self* of Jungian psychology where subject and object, ego and projection are fully integrated, what Robert Pirsig labels as "quality".[176] In such a world there is no conflict between reason and emotion or between life as it is and life as it is imagined. Wilfred Mellers (1968) writes perceptively of this in his book about musical renewal *Caliban Reborn*:

> *To be conscious is to be aware of difference – between self and not-self, life and death, love and hate, flesh and spirit. ...In so far as the new primitivism, whether as manifested in the work of Boulez, Cage and Stockhausen, of Britten and Stravinsky, of Ornette Coleman, or of the Beatles and Bob Dylan, may evade the strife inherent in consciousness, it may evade too our human responsibilities. But this does not alter the fact that some healing of division within the psyche has been necessary before new life can be born.*[177]

Caliban then, reminds us of the price that is to be paid when we are forced to conform to a social or cultural norm, placing us in danger of

---
176 Pirsig op.cit.
177 Mellers, Wilfred (1968). *Caliban Reborn. Renewal in Twentieth-Century Music*. London. P. 181

losing touch with our true nature. In this passage, Mellers is suggesting that whilst we have some kind of human responsibility towards conformity it is equally vital to be able to shed this skin of normalcy when necessary. In fact, when creating from this deep self, playing "wrong" notes actually becomes impossible: the sounds may not conform to the prevailing culture, but they are, in a deeper sense, profoundly "right" since human instinct is itself a part of the dance of nature and the humanising spirit leads naturally towards contact, community and identity. The artist Alan Davie (who is also an improvising musician) writes of his experience as a teacher of fine art in Glasgow in the sixties, trying to persuade his students to paint "badly" in order to free them of the conformity which stands in the way of originality. They produced some of their best work when trying to "get it wrong".[178]

In maintaining that wrong notes simply do not exist we arrive at a point where every sound carries meaning: they are either heard as part of a developing or existing identity, corresponding with a recognisable norm or they resonate in contrast to this identity, diverging from the norm. Either way, every sound has a meaning. The sounds of nature, of birdsong, of waterfalls, of the wind in the trees and the rain on the stones all carry meaning even though they are beyond our control. Some traditions of music (Tuvan singing for example) draw directly upon the natural soundworld for inspiration and *Lifemusic* is so-named partly because, as a method, it attempts to draw upon direct contact with the forms inherent in nature. Caliban's companions,[179] who were intent on murder and mischief in Prospero's garden, were frightened by the primordial sounds (created by Ariel) which were yet music to Caliban's ears.

Be not afeard, the Isle is full of noises,
Sounds, and sweet airs, that give delight and hurt not:
Sometimes a thousand twangling instruments
Will hum about mine ears; and sometimes voices,
That if I then had wak'd after long sleep,
Will make me sleep again, and then in dreaming,
The clouds methought would open, and show riches
Ready to drop upon me, that when I wak'd
I cried to dream again. [180]

Caliban appears here to refer to the music of the spheres, that heavenly music which enters the heart which is open to the sky and resonates in

---
178 Davie, Alan (1997) *Towards a Philosophy of Creativity*. University of Brighton.
179 Trinculo and Stephano.
180 Shakespeare, *The Tempest*. III.2

our dreams, in our ego-less, fearless, vulnerable, sleeping state. Perhaps it is only when we are able to let go of our fear of the 'wrong' notes that it becomes possible to re-connect with this undivided song of the healed psyche, with Ariel's archetypal 'tabor and pipe.' The resulting music may then resonate with even greater and more revelatory meaning than the loftiest symphony.

Ultimately perhaps, it is a matter of ego. Identity and civilized conduct are ego bound. Caliban's 'liberation' from his primal state provides him with an ego as he sees himself in the mirror and a superego in the form of Prospero's autocratic rule but in the process he loses touch with fantasy; and he reminds us that only when we let go of this controlling element are we able to access the archetypal gold waiting to be released from the ore. As James Hillman (1975) writes,

> *The imaginal realm has its own paths of exploration which start with whatever comes to mind – any fantasy or image – much like alchemy, which begins with a primary material called by at least sixty different names. Since it starts anywhere, it can break off anywhere. Fantasy does not need to achieve a goal. Fantasy work is closer to the arts, to writing and painting and making music, than it is to contemplation and yoga. Imaginative activity is both play and work, entering and being entered and as the images gain in substance and independence, the ego's strength and autocracy tends to dissolve. But ego dissolution does not mean disorder, since all fantasy is carried by a deeper, archetypal order.* [181]

Making music is an act of trust.

Music, like life, is about relationships: between sounds, between sounds and people and between people and people. Trust is the essential ingredient in any healthy relationship, between individuals, within groups of people and also therefore in the musical space which develops out of these relationships. Trust relies upon integrity and in the previous chapter I was discussing how the twin meanings of this word are revealing: on the one hand 'integrity' has a purely structural meaning as applied to things that hold together; but on the other hand 'integrity' has a moral meaning which we assign to those whose behaviour is consistent and reliable. The link between these two meanings demonstrates how much we value consistency of structure both in things and in each other. When we release music-making from external controls, for example from

---

[181] Hillman (op.cit.) P. 178.

previously notated scores, or from the direction of a conductor or even from the fixed principles which define genres, responsibility for this consistency then depends entirely upon the integrity of the participants. The improvising group then becomes like a prototypical tribe in which the rules of engagement develop within and alongside the music-making. At such a moment, the structure of the resulting music rapidly becomes a representation of the integrity of this tribe (the way it holds together, the way it bonds) and in turn the developing mythos (the internal or psychic narrative) of the tribal group becomes embedded in or expressed through, the vibrating, resonating structures of the music.

But what kind of musical structures are we referring to? In earlier chapters I cited Stravinsky's *The Rite of Spring* as an example of music which provides us with a highly sophisticated yet strangely primitive example of how music which belongs to 'the tribe' might sound. Whereas the structures of tonal music reflect the hierarchical relationships and mindsets of the post-Enlightenment period through a form of tonal dialectic which carries the heroic narratives of the European canon (Shepherd, 1990)[182] the musical language of *The Rite* represents a radical departure from this, replacing, at a stroke, the concept of the individual as hero with the collective energy of the tribe. This holds true to some extent for any music which is non-tonal or modal. Modality is often described as a divergence from tonality whereas in fact, ALL music is modal and tonality itself is a unique and highly specialised use of one particular mode (the 'Ionian' mode or diatonic scale). Modality, unlike tonality, can be employed spontaneously with much greater freedom, both rhythmically and harmonically than the strictures of tonal procedures allow[183]. It is possible to improvise more readily within modal systems since the rules of engagement are much less dependent on a fixed and complex system, the hierarchical series of chord sequences and cadences which have to be tightly controlled in order to function. In fact, the term 'functional harmony' is commonly used to describe the tonal norm, as if all other uses of harmony were somehow 'dys-functional'. This only serves to further underline the superiority complex which inhabits European musical thought: *Tonality is autocratic, modality is democratic.*

Furthermore, modal melody emerges largely from the cadences and

---

182 Shepherd, John (1990) Music as Cultural Text, P. 135. In *Companion to Contemporary Musical Thought*. Ed. Paynter, Mellers and Swanwick. London

183 The discussion here is necessarily simplified. The language of tonal music is itself a form of modality and tonal narratives develop around the conflicts between modal expression (melody) and tonal necessity (chords), chromatic ambiguity and cadential resolutions. But the rules of harmony always prevail and these rules are by their nature hierarchical. Tonal music only works when these rules are fully understood and agreed. However inventively and skilfully creative musicians employ the techniques of tonal expression, the tread of chords is always, of necessity, unwavering.

intonation of speech, a characteristic which finds its apotheosis in folksong, whilst release from the four-square harmonic progressions of the tonal system emancipates rhythm, resulting in music which is more somatic or body-centred, capable of expressing the intelligence of the limbs, the spine and the limbic system. In larger-scale modal forms such as *The Rite of Spring*, Miles Davis's *Kind of Blue*, the later music of John Coltrane or the spun out improvisations of *The Grateful Dead*, the long *march* of European music (that least subtle of dance forms) is replaced by a Dionysian freedom which invites us to participate, to move, to leap or to whirl. The tradition of audiences sitting quietly and politely to listen to beautiful music is replaced by a new (and much older) aesthetic in which people dance, clap, chant and stamp. The Apollonian spirit of the classical ideal, ruled from the head, and lit by the sun of the enlightenment, has been replaced by the chthonic energy of Dionysus (a polarised 'endarkenment' perhaps?) Caliban is reborn. Trust then necessarily emerges from an inner space, a heart space, as opposed to something that is imposed from on high, from the head, from composers, from a male God or, heaven forbid, from some transient Pope. *Tonality represents male hegemony. Modality engenders equality.*

Discussion of modality need not be confined to the relationships between pitches: it is also about feelings, responses and attunement. Child development guru Daniel Stern (1985) has written of 'affect attunement' between infants and adults in terms of 'modalities' describing how a bond of trust may be established through a variety of non-verbal signals, gestures, responses and interactions, including the modulations of the voice, as well as the modalities of movement and facial expressions.[184] *Lifemusic* draws upon this natural capacity, present from birth, to communicate non-verbally, to reach out to others and call for a response. During group improvisation, musical structures emerge within a similar variety of modal interactions, gestural, expressive, vocal and visual, cementing relationships and suggesting the existence of an *improvisational state* - a continuum of not knowing, of unforeseen events and thus a suspension of ordinary, everyday identities. This, as I was arguing in Chapter 4, entails the abandonment of the absolute (which attaches to prescribed form) and the embrace of uncertainty (which flows from transitional form). Participants, in such moments, may be only partly conscious of what is happening though they experience a deep connection to the here and now, to time. Whilst in this state, they are also likely to

---

[184] Stern, Daniel (1985). *The Interpersonal World of the Infant*. New York

develop a strong sense of shared purpose, or *communitas*, a term originally used by Victor Turner (1977) and subsequently applied to the process of group improvisation by Even Ruud.[185] Ruud describes how improvisation can be employed to facilitate rites of passage, transformational events which operate as social and communal levelling agents through which people can confront each other in honesty and truth, freed from the kind of game-playing which often arises when people are merely talking to each other. Turner's concept of *communitas* provides us therefore with a revelatory way of viewing this function of music. It underlines the primary role of the imagination both in forming relationships and in creating communal identities; once we begin to explore such links between the structure of the imagination, liminality and improvised music, we can perhaps begin to understand more fully the potential role of music in promoting and developing bonds of trust.

Music turns life into soul

In discussing soul we return to the central idea that music connects people to time. 'Soul' is neither a fashionable nor an easy concept to work with in a literal-minded, scientifically-oriented culture such as ours, but in the context of this discussion, it can be regarded as perhaps the most important function of music – literally, its *psychic* function. There is an equation, both complex and readily experienced, between time, memory, imagination, the Self and music. Time past is experienced through memory and memory hovers in the imaginal domain, that aspect of mind which carries images, in this case, of the past. The contents of the imagination, filtered through time, thus become fantasy, meaning all those perceptions, events and experiences which we have internalised, processed and held onto since birth. This fantasy of who we are, this personalised narrative, this *mythologising* of our own experience is what defines the Self. Music draws us towards this memory-laden inner world, deepening our consciousness and shifting our awareness away from Kronos, the literal world of clock time and into the domain of Kairos – imaginal time. This is a soul-making process since it leads us towards wholeness, towards an image of the Self which is complete and which connects with the *anima mundi*, or world soul. I believe that this happens every time we come into contact with music. So I am defining Soul, not as a fixed entity, not as an object, not as a neural assembly or a vaporous substance but as an aspect of time, a constantly developing awareness of

---

185 Kenny, Caroline. (1995) *Listening, Playing, Creating. Essays on the Power of Sound.* New York. P. 105

Self, what Jungians call *individuation*. As time passes, as we internalise and react to an increasing number of experiences, we create an ever expanding internalised picture, develop an ever-greater understanding of who we are and how we relate to the world in all its mystery. Finally we begin to sense how we are integrated into that world. Music facilitates this soul-making process.

How does it do this? We can classify the act of making music, archetypally, as an "Orphic" event and thus, by definition, an expression of what James Hillman (1977) quoting Keats, calls "soul-making". The tale of Orpheus was more fully explored in Chapter 2, so it suffices here to remind ourselves that Orpheus descended into the realm of Hades, into the shadows, to retrieve his lost soul in the form of his bride, Eurydice. The narrative therefore reminds us that soul work involves a journey downwards and inwards, a deepening of our senses accompanied by a connection with the female aspect, or *anima* (this applies equally to women) and a renewal therefore of our capacity for feeling. We can say that music, in this context, has a hermetic[186] function, transporting us to this inner space: when we make music, like Orpheus, we travel downwards. Psychologically this means an encounter with the unconscious without which soul-making would be impossible. It also means an encounter with feeling, with vulnerability, with compassion and also, ultimately, with delight – the tale of Psyche (soul) herself!

I have often begun an improvisation session with the question "what is your earliest musical memory?" The question is usually allowed to hang in space, providing time for reflection. Some will answer immediately, others will wait until well into the session or into the next day and sometimes, memories are retained as closely guarded secrets. This variety of response is itself an indication of the soul-intimacy which surrounds music and the protective veil that some will automatically use to shade the inner world from too much light. Soul work takes place in the dark. The question prompts people to travel backwards in time but also downwards into their feelings and into the fantasies which linger and gestate, often exposing the vulnerability of childhood. Some will be unable to recall initially anything further back than the early years at school; some will choose something insubstantial or insignificant, the veil of memory, or in this case, forgetfulness, protecting the inner child. Others will find it possible to be more open, more exposed and may even become tearful. The memories themselves are coloured with different aspects of the

---

186 Hermes is credited with inventing the lyre but also accompanies souls to Hades. His function as a god was to connect different realms together, to reconcile opposites and through this process of connectivity we derive a heightened sense of the meaning of things, a deepened sense of significance.

developing Self and the degree to which this is allowed to be brought into the light varies. We hear of parents, grandparents, siblings, nursery schools, religious worship, the radio, the ice-cream van, gramophones, pianos, music boxes, musical clocks – and of course, song.

For N. it was hearing, with mounting excitement, the ice-cream van approaching from a distance on a Sunday. For M. it was a music-box, a present from an aunt who looked after her after the death of her mother; for C. the sung devotions at Catholic nursery school and the pressure to "get it right"; for S. a memory of how her father became a completely transformed person when he picked up his violin; for L. a memory of childhood illness accompanied by the all-too-jolly theme tune of the Archers; for L. it was the unbidden and unwelcome sounds of Edmundo Ross on the radio; for R. his grandmother singing "Bessie the Blacksmith"; for I. who was from a family of musicians, the feelings of inadequacy and fear at not being able to come up to the level of his siblings; for W. the voice of her mother singing whilst accompanying herself on the zither; for L. her Finnish grandmother singing a lullaby in Swedish – a distant memory of a forgotten tongue; for A. it was bedtime and Beethoven on the gramophone or else samba "always in the air"; and for E. it was her sister playing Chopin on the piano which "made me feel everything!"

To "feel everything" is then to be in touch with soul, making this fourth precept the most significant of them all since it drives to the centre of what music is for, why it exists and why it remains such a valuable resource for human life. Each and every one of us is capable of creating this unique blend of sound and vibration, making the connection to time audible and coherent. When this happens, when we make it happen, even what may seem like the least significant events in our lives become enhanced, numinous, charged with meaning and we suddenly become more complete, more human and more god-like. As Rilke expressed it:

Take your practiced powers and stretch them out
Until they span the chasm between two
Contradictions. . . For the god
Wants to know himself in you.[187]

These four precepts represent the philosophical and aesthetic pillars upon which *Lifemusic* rests. The following ingredients attempt to realise these ideas in practice.

---

187 From 'As once the winged energy of delight'. *The Selected Poetry of Rainer Maria von Rilke*. Translated by Stephen Mitchell (1999). P. 261. Picador.

The Four Ingredients of Lifemusic

Improvisation

Improvisation is an instantly accessible musical tool which brings people into the moment, into the 'here and now'. As defined earlier, (see Chapter 3) it means literally "unforeseen" yet whilst it might be regarded as unplanned it is never unstructured. The structure may not be immediately discernible but it is always present and is likely to be both surprising and revealing. The whole question of improvisation, how it works as music and how ubiquitously yet uneasily it sits in a culture obsessed with planning and appraising, was dealt with in a previous chapter. So how does improvisation work in the practice of *Lifemusic* and what kind of improvisation does the method employ?

Primarily, *Lifemusic* seeks to empower the improvising group to find its own route into creative musicking and thus its precepts are embedded in principles of autonomy and self-realisation. Improvisation is perhaps the only musical practice which truly allows for this, opening up the potential of the individual to choose from whatever spontaneously presents itself in the moment of creation. This means that sometimes, even within a single improvised piece, a number of different styles of music might be referred to without in any way destroying the overall integrity of the structure. What is more important perhaps is the integrity of the group, the sensitivity and empathy which ensures that at some point in the piece, whether this is near the beginning or near the end, there is a sense of cohesion – the musical form reflecting the nature of the group experience precisely within the moment that the piece emerges.

So the method does not define improvisation in any stylistic sense, (there is no orthodoxy involved) but rather seeks to uncover principles which contribute to the unity of the improvising group. This makes every session unique and every improvisation a fresh opportunity for the group to establish its identity and make its own connection to time audible. By avoiding pre-determined stylistic frameworks and allowing for pluralism, the archetypes which underpin and inform musical forms are more easily accessed. This suggests a kind of musical 'Gnosticism' where orthodoxies and doctrines are not allowed to interfere with the direct path towards (musical) understanding. Improvisation is embraced therefore as a practice which is free of doctrine even where particular idioms or styles might be chosen as a guide: the point is not to consciously avoid idiomatic play altogether (which would be both unrealistic and over prescriptive) but neither to fetishize, privilege or make sacrosanct (canonise), any particular musical style or genre.

Improvisation is the primary musical act, instant composition: no music comes into being without first being improvised. In addition, improvisation is located in the "here and now", providing a sense of immediacy, belonging to the moment. Thirdly, improvisation both gives people autonomy and is, of itself, an autonomous music. In other words, whilst the improvisers are responsible for bringing the music into being, an improvisation often takes on a life of its own, the participants following the genie into the maze.

Improvising music in groups is something which people, in general, rarely do. This is in some ways surprising since not only is it a peculiarly enriching and satisfying activity but since people spend much of their lives improvising in non-musical ways (when conversing for example) why not do it in music? Untold benefits might arise once we restore to improvisation its true value, understanding it as central to musical activity rather than peripheral. Furthermore, improvised music might be seen to have a valuable function in other areas of life, acting as a conduit between the world of the musical imagination and social contexts where music-making is currently absent. As Stephen Nachmanovitch (1990) has pointed out, what begins as music rapidly takes on significance for the rest of life.

> *When we think of improvisation, we tend to think first of improvised music or theatre or dance; but beyond their own delights, such art forms are doors into an experience that constitutes the whole of everyday life.* [188]

Participation

Lifemusic is entirely about music-making – actively creating as opposed to passively *consuming*. Anyone, regardless of background, belief, or ability is able participate instantly and equitably. There is no audience, or rather, the participants themselves become the audience, creating, listening and communicating collectively. People who have learned to play musical instruments with some degree of skill can improvise alongside those who have only their intuitions to guide them. The use of "instant access" instruments, (tuned and untuned percussion

---

188 Nachmanovitch, op.cit. P. 17

plus voices) and access points based around the concept of the Holding Form[189] provide frameworks for improvisation which makes full participation possible. In addition to the social and psychological bonding which such musicking promotes we find ourselves also in the realm of "Carnival" perhaps, where music provides for a celebration of community in relation to those events, festivals and points of the calendar which mark the significance of the passage of time.

The concept of Carnival will be dealt with in more detail in the next chapter but it is worth noting that the celebratory function of music-making has become largely dislocated from life in the modern age. Seasonal celebrations in particular have been replaced by all-year-round music, in exactly the same way that we are able to eat all-year-round bananas! Fruits and vegetables appear out of their natural season, either forced into growth through agricultural technology or flown in from parts of the world where the desired product happens to be *in* season. Such dislocations (literally so in the case of bananas) may well be convenient and consumer-friendly but it is also worth considering what is lost in the process. It is not only the carbon footprint which increases when we eat food which comes to us from such distant communities: there is also a significant distortion of our relationship to the cycle of growth and decay, disrupting the link between time and taste buds!

Our ears are perhaps even more sensitive to such dislocations (can we term this 'dis-temporality'?) than our sense of taste. Very few taboos remain in the global music industry: perhaps only the Christmas Carol is still weighted sufficiently with its collectively understood meanings to render it inappropriate to be heard at the wrong time of the year. Significantly, the Carol is also one of the few remaining instances where people are still motivated to participate in music-making, even where their lives are otherwise entirely secular. We can listen to a Bach Mass in the concert hall, love songs in the kitchen and Mozart in the shower, but people still turn out onto the streets or into candlelit churches at Christmas to sing carols. The midwinter taboo is extremely resilient, surviving (just) even where it has been weakened by endless repetition, across the airwaves, through crackling loudspeakers in every department store and at every town cross. Sadly, this inflationary process seems to start earlier each year, with carols audible as early as the end of November. Yet, the potency of the carol at the solstice itself remains somehow intact. Perhaps this has something to do with the special relationship to time which exists

---
189 See Chapter 4.

at the winter solstice, the peculiar mystery of the zero hour when the world seems to shift on its axis. It is then that the carol reminds us of the deep value of participation, not merely in the joy that it brings, or the good company it fosters but ultimately in defining our connection to time.

Communication

Participating in group improvisation develops a special kind of listening but what exactly are people listening to? Initially, the sounds they are making themselves; then the sounds made by others; and finally the sounds made collectively by the group. As these connected layers of listening expand and deepen, the structure of the music also grows. This creates a web of communication which is non-verbal and through which each literally attunes to the other. The structure of the resulting music then becomes a reflection or an analogy of the structure of the relationships forming and developing within the group.

In discussing the third precept (trust) in the previous section, I was suggesting that communication in improvised music takes place at a liminal level of consciousness where the musical dialogues are neither consciously controlled nor entirely haphazard. Rather there is a spectrum of communication between participants which, at one end of the scale may be self-absorbed and disengaged from the group, whilst at the other end is blended into the collective voice and fully engaged in group process. What is particularly interesting is how the sound of the music itself invariably reflects this spectrum of communication. When each participant is absorbed in their own playing, the resulting sound is so diverse that to anyone listening from outside it may sound like pure chaos. Yet it is essential not to devalue the importance of this element in group improvising since the music may need to pass through the gate of individual ownership before it reaches the garden of shared expression. At each point of the journey, the form the music takes will reflect the quality of communication at that moment. *In order to find the structure in the chaos it may first be necessary to enter the chaos itself.*

This whole communicative spectrum was perfectly demonstrated during the very first improvisation session with a group of around 15 adult participants on a professional development programme mainly intended for counsellors and therapists. They had been invited to play together whatever instruments were available in whatever manner they chose for about ten minutes. It became rapidly evident that each player, for whatever reason, had decided to stick to whatever they were doing individually with no wish to blend or communicate with the others. Furthermore, no one seemed to want to stop playing and the piece continued in this manner for about 30 minutes with no collectively agreed rhythms, modes or textures emerging at any time. Afterwards, when the group was reflecting on what had happened, someone happened to drop the remark that to her, the music had seemed to give off a bad smell! Thus was born the concept of *poo-music* in which the group members remain, like very young babies, absorbed in their own functions, unable or unwilling to find a collective voice. Indeed, some reflected that they had been aware of the general lack of attunement but had been reluctant to lose themselves in an attempt to follow or become blended into a separate (musical) identity. The session revealed, perhaps, that communication is not simply about listening politely and responding appropriately but first about identifying or getting in touch with the autonomous self and then, at a later stage, discovering how that identity might blend, spontaneously and naturally, with others. Had an externally-imposed, unifying principle been introduced early on this would never have happened and the process would have been artificially truncated. Later in the day, the group improvised together again, purely vocally, achieving an extraordinary and totally spontaneous sense of attunement, singing like an angelic horde!

Well-being

The intended outcomes of *Lifemusic* are therapeutic but this is not, in any strict sense, music therapy since the focus is on participation rather than pathology and on creativity rather than trauma. Where music therapists may want to support their clients in working with difficult or painful experiences, *Lifemusic* seeks to generate well-being through celebration and, ultimately a sense of delight. Even so, sessions inevitably expose people's vulnerability and painful or sensitive memories and reflections are in no way avoided. It is in the nature of music to express the truth of the soul and this means the vales as well as the peaks.

Improvisation can be transformational in a number of ways, personal and collective. Individuals may feel an enhanced sense of well-being whilst groups may experience an increased awareness of togetherness and shared purpose. Sessions may be at one and the same time stimulating and relaxing. The imagination is regarded as a primary human resource and the creative energy from musical participation may stimulate creativity in other areas of work and relationships. The interactive and reflective nature of the activity means that participants may learn about each other experientially – a musical, non-verbal and affective means of creating harmony, self-realisation and collective identity.

The Four Levels of Musical Perception

In summary I want to draw together some of the ideas contained in the precepts and ingredients and propose a four-fold framework linking the structures of improvised music with perception and trust. Four levels of musical perception seem to emerge which I intend to label as *hearing, listening, sensing, feeling*. These are not intended in any way as definitive but are offered rather as a potential guide to the links which exist between trust and musical communication. The definitions apply particularly, though certainly not exclusively, to group improvisation.

LEVEL 1 - HEARING

At the external level, people perceive sound with their ears and whilst responses may be variable in relation to what is heard, there is no obvious structural connection being made at an internal level. Much, if not most music is currently consumed at this level, very often when we are doing something else such as driving, washing the dishes, eating or cleaning our teeth. We hear music in this way mainly through recorded media, the radio, hi-fi equipment, MP3 headsets and so on. For trained musicians, an externally-imposed structure (e.g. a notated score) might ensure coherence but, robbed of the score and unless expertly memorised, the music may well fall apart, demonstrating that the relationship to the music is largely superficial. With no internal guide, responsibility for musical structure has to remain either with a composer (external to the context) or with strong leadership from a musical director. Thus the element of trust is invested almost entirely in an external figure.

Virtually all of the music which stems from the European classical tradition is based upon this kind of external source, the notated score having been created by someone who may no longer be alive or who belongs to a different sub-culture or nationality from the performers. This is not to disparage the often profound aesthetic results, the 'great' music which may result from performance of music by what are still, in some circles referred to as 'the old masters'. Yet, it is all too easy for the musical consumer to be sufficiently disengaged from the process that at a key moment (literally perhaps in the case of tonal music) in what might be a significant musical argument, in the middle of a symphony or a string quartet for example, it is all too easy to interrupt the piece at the flick of a switch or by turning down the volume. That key moment might have come inconveniently just as the listener reached the end of a car journey or finished a meal or wanted to remind their partner to take out the rubbish! Even in the concert hall, it becomes all too easy to drift off into another space altogether, momentarily losing track of the musical argument. In defining 'hearing', I am tempted to quote Sir Thomas Beecham when he remarked, "the English do not really like music, they just like the sound that it makes!" But of course, this capacity to hear without depth of understanding or participation is not just confined to the English. The sheer volume and range of currently available music and the ease with which it is mediated, encourages people to hear at this relatively shallow level of perception. It is unsurprising therefore, that ears and minds conditioned in this way will also function at this level within a participatory group. There is no judgment intended here, merely a reflection upon the way we live and the way we have chosen to mediate sound.

'Hearing' then, is defined as an external aural response: *listening with the ears.*

LEVEL 2 - LISTENING

At this second level, the ears are still the principal organs of perception. However, the inner ear is now engaged in response to what is being heard and the performer/improviser can respond coherently. Where hearing was passive, listening is active: there is both intention and attention in the act of listening, the musical mind is engaging with the sounds and welcoming them into an inner space. To listen in this way is to engage the composer's ear. providing the groundwork for creating musical structures which are entirely original. Improvisations may be short and possibly formulaic, but the imagination is kindled. The element of trust may well be contained in a previously agreed structural boundary, ensuring that the music makes sense though this does not necessarily unite the players at a deeper level. Much modern jazz is performed in this way - with chordal frameworks ('the changes') providing a previously agreed structure within which invention can take place.

I define 'listening' as the internal aural response: *listening with the mind.*

LEVEL 3 – SENSING

Listening with the ears, whether the outer ear or the inner ear, suggests an emphasis on the cognitive and specialised functions of the brain. But our potential to perceive sound exists within a more holistic framework. People who are profoundly deaf can still sense the structures of music in remarkable detail whilst the quality of an improvisation is always enhanced when the participants are able to respond to others' movements and gestures. Sensing is about being aware of total bodily action and interaction. The non-verbal language of others provides not merely clues to what is about to happen - the next moment of improvisation - but 'invitations' to respond in various appropriate ways. But more than this, sensing is also about *intuiting* what others are likely to play in the moment that is just beyond the threshold of the present. This kind of sensing derives from the capacity we all have for synchronicity of action, something which only appears perhaps when working at the somatic or autonomic level. Sensing therefore creates a language of trust from the body and mind working in unison.

Sensing will inevitably enhance the quality of the musical act in whatever form it takes. In the performance of classical music, great soloists, some string quartets and other chamber ensembles strive to achieve this 'magical' rapport whilst certain legendary jazz performances no doubt grew out of similar levels of trust. In participatory group improvisation the resulting music can often be breathtakingly surprising in its synchronicities.

I define 'sensing' as the external holistic response: *listening with the body*.

LEVEL 4 - FEELING.

The deepest bonds between people are often described as *empathic*. Truly to be able to feel what another feels is in fact a supreme feat of the human imagination and when trust breaks down, whether between individuals or between nations, it may well be because the imagination has dried up, rendering any kind of communication impossible. The challenge of relationship is therefore primarily a challenge to the creative imagination. *Feeling* goes beyond sensing in that it involves knowing and trusting to a degree which makes structure not merely coherent and synchronous but truly significant. As defined earlier, improvising is like being in a maze as well as in the dark and it becomes necessary therefore to 'feel one's way'. If we imagine the maze as a metaphor for the unconscious we might then argue that improvisation which revolves around *empathy* is likely to reflect the deepest levels at which human beings are able to connect: the resulting musical patterns will be archetypal structures of trust.

I want to define 'feeling' as the internal holistic response: *listening with the heart*.

Having defined *Lifemusic* and suggested some of the ways in which improvisation functions, I now want to turn to some of the ways in which this form of musicking might be applied. Throughout the book, I have been drawing attention to how we use music or maybe, how we abuse music in the contemporary world. Yet, as I was arguing in Part 1, this is not necessarily to prescribe how music should be used and certainly never to proscibe the way it is mediated. Rather it is a plea to become more aware of exactly what is happening when we place music within particular frameworks, teach it in certain ways and mediate it without sufficient regard for its inner value. The chapters that follow are therefore intended to suggest new paradigms, some of which are already evident in social practice and some which may be yet on the horizons of cultural development.

CHAPTER 6

THE USES OF LIFEMUSIC

Music and Communities

This chapter explores how music might bring people together. In doing so, it explores the role participatory music might play in the process of renewal at a number of levels, personal, social and cultural. If music is to be socially useful as well as enjoyable, then this almost certainly involves breaking down some of the barriers and distinctions which have developed between 'musicians' and 'non-musicians' and dissolving, or at least questioning and modifying, social practices which perpetuate and sustain these divisions. A community of music might emerge when people from diverse backgrounds and training are provided with the means and the conditions in which to make music together or when groups who are actively dedicated to music-making join up with groups for whom creative music-making is not on the agenda. Currently, such opportunities are relatively rare since cultural development has resulted in relatively rigid and divisive customs. However, the forms of creative participation advocated in these pages are intended to be of benefit to all kinds of groups, both those whose existence is dedicated to creating music, either themselves or with their clients; or groups who would probably rarely if ever consider that part of their time together might be spent making music. For convenience, I label these as "active" and "inactive".[190]

Musically Active groups would include:
- professional musicians (both classical and other styles)
- music teachers
- community musicians
- music therapists
- choirs (both traditional style choral unions and the newly emerging community choirs)
- school pupils and students

---

[190] The terms "active" and "inactive" are used here for convenience to describe social categories within which music does or does not have an automatic role to play. It does not mean that individuals within any particular group are necessarily musically deprived. We are all, potentially or in fact, musically active.

> o amateur music makers (countless blues, rock and jazz musicians as well as amateur orchestras and chamber groups)

Musically Inactive groups might include:
> o Social workers
> o Care workers
> o Health professionals
> o Office workers
> o Managerial staff
> o Call centre staff
> o Public service professionals (e.g. police, firemen, soldiers)
> o Civil servants
> o Politicians

It is likely that many of these groups (both categories) do not instantly perceive the need for or understand the benefits which might come from participating in improvised music. So many musically active groups, such as choral societies or amateur orchestras will be entirely dedicated to the performance of pre-composed, notated music whilst professional musicians, in order to survive, need to devote their energies to the performance of music which will attract as large a public as possible. In the first list, it is probably only music therapists for whom freely improvised music constitutes a core discipline. In the case of other professionals (inactive), the time and energy involved in the average working day makes it all but impossible to imagine how, why or indeed where, improvised music-making could happen. Some active musicians, school and college students for example, or jazz and rock musicians, will use creative improvisation as part of the process of putting together musical ideas, often in preparation for performance, whether in pub, village hall, school assembly or busking on the street. This is all part of the kind of diverse and vibrant musical community described in Ruth Finnegan's book *The Hidden Musicians*,[191] where she charts the plethora and range of musical activity in Milton Keynes, a remarkable and revealing snapshot of British Culture in the heart of England. An important part of her argument which emerges from this study concerns how those who hold to established definitions of what constitutes "real" music might fail to notice the significance of creative composing and improvising which is taking place in more or less hidden spaces of the community, hence the book's title.

---
191 Op. Cit.

music-making, by and large, is perceived as something that happens either in dedicated spaces (concert halls, opera houses), or else as acoustic "cheesecake" which comes to us through speaker cones as ubiquitously distributed through our lives as security cameras.[192] The idea that live music-making could somehow be woven into daily life is alien to most of us. Yet, whilst advocating the use of improvised music in dedicated contexts and at specific times, there is also an argument to be made for harnessing the power of participatory music to serve people in their everyday lives, for example in team building, professional development and management training or simply as a means of enhancing well-being, inducing relaxation, promoting good relationships and reducing stress. If music is to be useful as well as enjoyable it may be necessary to find a way of demonstrating how it can be socially beneficial as well as culturally relevant.

The emergence of what is now generally termed *Community Music* has been charted elsewhere, notably in Anthony Everett's (1997) comprehensive and compelling survey *Joining In* and, more recently in Pete Moser's and George McKay's engaging handbook of Community Music published in 2005. Everett's book in particular demonstrates the sheer diversity of cultural strands which seem to have been distilled into participatory music philosophy and practice. In Chapter 4, where he discusses how communities might be identified, reinforced and even re-created through musical acts, we get a sense both of the fragmentary nature of the contemporary world and of the ability of people to seek out commonalities and express them through musical activities, many of which are workshop-based rather than performance-oriented; in other words, they focus on process rather than product.

And it is not only common identities which motivate some of the many projects and people described and interviewed by Everitt but also the zeal of the social reformer, the need to use music as a transformative tool to enhance well-being, certainly, but also to influence attitudes towards equality, tolerance, social cohesion, inclusion, access and equal opportunity – "because music is part of broad social processes and is both universal and ubiquitous, it can be a metaphor and a mechanism for a comprehensive social and political enterprise."[193] Thus, community music, in its development, has become in many ways politicised, recognising that musical forms and the manner in which music is

---

192 The defnition of music as "cheesecake" comes from Stephen Pinker's 1997 book *How the Mind Works*. "Music is auditory cheesecake, an exquisite confection crafted to tickle the sensitive spots of at least six of our mental faculties" (P. 534).
193 Everitt, Anthony (1997) *Joining In: An Investigation into Participatory Music*. Gulbenkian Foundation. London. P. 88.

produced and mediated is deeply connected to the ways in which people view themselves and articulate their aspirations, hopes, dreams and relationships.

In Chapter 3 of Moser and Mckay's book[194] we find improvisation directly linked to the development of community music in Britain. In a succinct passage subtitled 'from improv to institution' George McKay outlines this link, showing how improvising musicians, pioneers such as John Stevens, Edwin Prevost, Maggie Nichols and Trevor Watts who cut their teeth in the freedom music which grew largely though by no means exclusively from avant-garde jazz in the sixties, became some of the early movers and shakers who brought improvisation to people in diverse places, upstairs rooms in pubs, school classrooms, higher education colleges, where improvisational practice was often marginalised or misunderstood. Initially, there is little doubt that community music was seen as a counter-balance to established culture and attitudes and this became perhaps most acute during the 1980s, the era of Thatcherism. Yet, community music, as it has become more established and people have begun to understand what it has to offer, is beginning to gain a foothold and today, even though the definition is still debated, its advocates are much more widely consulted and taken seriously in the debates surrounding the future of music and cultural renewal.[195]

Yet very little, if any, space is made in these surveys and debates for the archetypal power of music; how it injects soul into life. Pinker's position is, as with most reductive arguments, ultimately risible, though he can be forgiven, as a successful evolutionary psychologist with a fast brain, for missing the point and forgetting that music can, and regularly does, change people's lives. Cheesecake never did this! Underwood draws her portraits with the sociologist's accuracy and with enthusiasm for her subject's creativity; Everitt's overview is convincing, community music as a present and potent phenomenon. But one aspect of Moser and McKay's book which carries some of the depth potential of participatory music and which makes this book such a gem are the poems by Lemn Sissay which are interspersed with the chapters. Here we find the archetypes, the images, the ambiguities and the contradictions which connect people to the dance, to time and to each other. In *Applecart Art*, for example, Sissay plays richly with words, melodies, rhythm and images to create an energetic and iconoclastic call for creative renewal – "*Upset the art. Smash the applecart!*"

---

194 Moser, Pete and McKay George (Eds) (2005) *Community Music, A Handbook*. Lyme Regis.
195 This is due in no small part to the activities of the organisation Sound Sense and the tireless advocacy of its director, Kathryn Deane.

Musical Culture and Musical Function.
There are complex issues involved in determining how cultural renewal is activated. These concern our relationship to the past and the present as well as how we imagine the future. It highlights the tensions between fixity and flux and the often uneasy relationship between the norm and deviations from the norm, a theme explored earlier in relation to improvisation. As argued in Chapter 1, the connection to time is central: without a *feel* for the moment, its meaning and its significance, it is only too easy to neglect the "kairos of transition" and instead to derive a steadily diminishing comfort from the familiar patterns of the past. Music provides a vital canvas of feeling, a backdrop to our lives, but as long as we continue to focus on music as a series of objects, packaged as scores or CDs or non-participatory concerts, rituals encased in procedures and structures which belong to another time and another place, then we may easily fail to meet the challenges of our own time; our own culture is then in danger of becoming no more than a storehouse, a museum of rich but ultimately impotent musical artefacts.

In his discussion of the complex definitions of culture Raymond Williams (1976) suggests three uses of the term: the first points towards a "general process of intellectual, spiritual and aesthetic development"; the second delineates "a particular way of life" whilst the third use "describes practices of intellectual and especially artistic activity".[196] Looking at these definitions we might conclude that, in our contemporary understanding of "culture" we oscillate between that which is fixed and unchanging and therefore clearly identifiable (meaning 2) and that which is fluctuating, changeable and therefore difficult to pin down (meaning 1). Williams' third definition points to the *flowing process* of culture, something lively and creative. If, as discussed in Chapter 1, periods of renewal and transition are characterised by diversity and polarisation, then the contrasting uses of the term serve to underline this: is culture to be understood as a fixed set of precepts or objects which we value according to what we believe in? Or is it an organic process characterised by imaginative experimentation, exploration and transformation? Of course, it is both and it is also the dynamic flow between the two.

The kind of renewal which I am discussing here places emphasis on culture as organic process (meaning 1) finding channels of expression through creative action and fluctuating debate (meaning 3). Life itself is both organic and unstable, if not irrational, so *Life-music* might be

---

196 Williams, Raymond (1976) *Keywords*. Fontana Books. P. 76-82

expected to reflect this condition. Yet, when we view contemporary musical culture what we most often see is the exact opposite of this, with high value being placed upon musics which are fixed in specific genres, easily identified and subsequently labelled as classical, pop, folk, rock, jazz, soul, garage, hip-hop, grunge, heavy metal, progressive, rap, ethnic, world and so on. This creates a cultural paradox: whilst we are busy *particularising* culture (meaning 2 above), fixing music in recognisable idioms, we are simultaneously *diversifying*, demonstrating a need for constant change, flux as opposed to fixity. As music locates itself more in the contemporary flow of culture and less in the traditions of history it appears to fragment. One result of this, which I discussed in more detail earlier in this book, is the typical and very familiar polarisation between "classical and pop" with the former holding very closely to the traditions of European art music, white, middle class and mainly built around tonal systems, whilst the latter, drawing on the generic forms of jazz, rock, blues and soul, preferences modality. Both arenas however are filled with marketable objects; both cling jealously to cultural ownership expressed through copyright laws and performing rights.

When, however, music begins to locate itself more in the localities of community, connecting directly to people and to the time and place in which they work and live, then musical objects might be gradually transformed into musical experiences, living process, improvised as life is improvised, even perhaps avoiding the market entirely, an unfamiliar and radically divergent paradigm. Is it possible to imagine a music which is so purely located in the "here and now" that labelling and individual or corporate ownership becomes impossible since the music simply does not hang around long enough for a label to be attached to it? And what happens to copyright law when music belongs to everybody? The musical texts of the historical tradition begin to lose their sacrosanct qualities and the recording industry might as well pack up and go home. As Brian Eno recently remarked:

> *I think records were just a little bubble through time and those who made a living from them for a while were lucky. There is no reason why anyone should have made so much money from selling records. I always knew it would run out sooner or later.*[197]

So what happens in times such as ours to the musical canon – the

---

[197] Brian Eno interviewed in *The Observer Review* on 17 January 2010.

accepted and often unquestioning support for a body of works regarded as culturally indispensible? This is not to argue against the notion of a canon *per se*, a group of works borne aloft by the cultural tide, recognised as particularly emblematic of the nature, character and will of the populace and subsequently regarded as indispensible. But we might consider that there is also much regarded as canonical which is *artificially* preserved and invested with special status even when this is undeserved or, worse, when its canonical status is maintained in order to preserve the special privileges of an elite group which converges around the cultural status of the music and who therefore benefit at the expense of others. (An example of this would be the vast sum granted to the Royal Opera House from lottery funds raised mainly from people who never go to London and rarely listen to opera.) *The maintenance and preservation of the canon then becomes a political act rather than a cultural imperative.* This is almost certainly why classroom music, which, especially in the early years of curriculum development was built primarily around the classical tradition, remains to this day a problem area and a "turn-off" for many pupils. To relocate music in the hearts and minds of the masses of people who ultimately determine the organic flow of culture we might turn to a phenomenon which *defies* fixed definitions and which stands in many respects at an opposite pole from the canon - *carnival*.

Carnival and the Hilarious

In an earlier chapter, I was arguing that improvisation generates 'liminality', a state of being, or an aspect of mind, which is always in-between, neither one thing nor the other, at the threshold. When improvising music, this liminal state is articulated through time in such a way that, when a piece is in progress, the players' relationship to time becomes uniquely specialised: the regulated and hierarchical or controlling function of time – *timetabling* – is replaced by something felt – *experiential time* – in effect, time itself is being articulated, celebrated but also in some way, transformed. The collective expression of liminality finds a home in carnival and carnival articulates itself through the *mask*.

I want to suggest here that the mask provides both a visual and psychological analogue for improvisation: when we improvise, we are, as it were, trying on alternative identities, playing with them and using the anonymity they bestow not to conceal reality but, paradoxically to open out the multifarious nature of reality, releasing the many-layered aspects, the diverse potentials of the self. In drama improvisation, the mask is a powerful tool through which multiple identities can emerge: it becomes possible to shake off the imposed or enculturated patterns within which we normally function in order to enter a neutral space which is at one and the same time revealing, energising, transformational and potentially healing. This is exactly what happens when improvising music.

In carnival the mask is "connected with the joy of change and reincarnation, with gay relativity and with the merry negation of uniformity and similarity". (Bakhtin, 1984) In carnival we encounter insights into both the human imagination and the social event, the one becoming a reflection of the other.[198] Those aspects of mind which exist in the interstices between meaning and unmeaning, between dark and light, between conscious and unconscious are reflected in the borderline between cultural norms and the individual imagination as well as between political hegemonies and individual liberties. In all of these borderline arenas we find celebration, participation, laughter and ambivalence.

Ambivalence is, most of all perhaps, the key to the structure of carnival. The logic of carnival is not the true or false, quantitative and causal logic of science and seriousness, but the qualitative logic of ambivalence, where the actor is also the spectator, destruction gives rise to creativity, and death is equivalent to rebirth.[199] Ambivalence means, in effect, that any number of realities or meanings can co-exist simultaneously: where fixed meaning has been replaced by ambiguous meaning, the normal social controls over thought and behaviour are temporarily suspended and anything can happen. This is the essence of improvisation. In carnival this state of being is directly associated with the kind of Dionysian ritual activity which I was referring to in Chapter 2. Yet, this does not need to manifest itself in specific festivals since the essence of Carnival suggests a heightened (or deepened) level of consciousness, providing for a fluctuating dance of possibility which temporarily replaces, indeed challenges the fixed and rigid patterns of musical and social norms as well as political control.[200] It is when we suspend our fixed adherence to norms that we enter into a liminal state and in this state of ambiguity renewal, whether social, political, personal or spiritual, becomes possible. Improvisation finds a natural home in carnival. In effect, we enter a 'state of carnival' whenever we suspend, even temporarily, or in small ways, our fixed adherence to given

---

198 See Lechte, John (1994). *Fifty Key Contemporary Thinkers*. P. 8. London, Routledge.
199 Ibid
200 Every dictator, from authoritarian schoolmaster to totalitarian madman, knows this.

principles and, instead, improvise, thereby loosening our ties to social or political norms and giving ourselves the freedom to enter into and identify with the natural flux and eternal ambivalence of life.

Carnival then, means foregrounding the imagination and burying theory, those rule books which all too easily prevent the emergence of new and revitalising creative energy. When people improvise music together, they may be constantly testing the boundaries, inventing new rules and throwing out the old. To introduce carnival into music-making inevitably means disturbing and challenging rule-bound behaviour and this can often lead to seeming chaos. It is at this point that it may become necessary to trust in the process and in the capacity of the imagination to discover structures which lead from chaos into integrative musical and human relationships which emerge from the deep space of subjectivity, strengthening identities and bringing people together with a sense of shared purpose.

This often creates laughter. Laughter occurs when a predictable norm is suddenly replaced by an unpredictable outcome. According to Bakhtin, carnival laughter is "one of the essential forms of truth concerning the world". Unlike some therapy, which tends to focus on the pathology of the client and on the disturbing quality of hidden complexes, the concept I am describing here embraces laughter both as a symbol of wellness and as a tool for creating gateways into precisely those difficult spaces into which we may fear to tread, potentially opening up and venting complexes which perhaps only really become disturbing when repressed. Laughter is the opposite of repression, or rather it is a response to the release of repressed material; perhaps, even, it makes the release of such material possible, somatically, that is, directly from the body. Laughter is not simple. It is a complex form of expression which may be a response to any number of stimuli. But laughter is only part of it, the autonomous response to a shared perception of ambiguity: this is what Bakhtin calls hilarity, "...rather than a spectacle to be observed, carnival is the hilarity lived by everyone".[201]

In carnival then, everyone participates; there is no audience and the music, together with the dance and the spectacle, flows directly from its chthonic (Dionysian) roots into the gathered community. *Lifemusic*, in practice, draws upon this same flow of energy, inviting people to participate in this *hilarity* whilst not attempting to replicate carnival as a spectacular event. There is no separate audience for the improvisation

---

201 Lechte, op.cit.

which underpins the practice, simply groups where people spontaneously interact, performing and listening by turns. When expanded into whole communities, carnival becomes a social tapestry of dance and music, celebration, sexuality and intoxication. But the carnival which informs *Lifemusic* represents that *aspect of mind* which, impatient with fixed and ordained structure, challenges tradition, deviates from norms and ultimately seeks to replace the old and the obsolete with the new and the vital, a means through which people can 'unstick'. Hilarity then becomes a spontaneous celebration, a "transport of delight".

We might introduce hilarity, in this special sense, directly into whole areas of musicking where it is currently only partially apparent or largely absent such as those listed at the start of this chapter. We can also employ it to enhance activities where music is already used as a participatory medium, such as music therapy and community music. But it may even be of special value in contexts where any notion of musicking currently seems entirely alien such as the board room, busy offices, banks, town halls and even amongst civil servants, politicians and the military. This might seem a very strange idea in our literally-minded, concretised world but that is only because we have become so accustomed to narrowly framed cultural patterns and the relegation of music to a purely entertainment function, that we easily ignore or forget its subtle, esoteric, alternative or traditional uses. We do not have to think that far outside of the box to imagine how music might permeate life in radically opposed ways to the currently piped and broadcast varieties: music as active enhancement to life as opposed to passive accompaniment. The remainder of this chapter therefore examines some ideas on how music might be applied in a variety of social contexts but first a short detour into ritual.

Lifemusic as Ritual

When we enter a musical space we are also, potentially, entering a ritual space. Some might think of rituals as those regularly repeated activities which delineate and punctuate the day or the week such as cleaning our teeth, washing the car, taking a coffee break, reading the Sunday papers or doing the shopping on a Friday evening. But of course, this would be to confuse ritual with routine. These examples would be better described as maintenance tasks, so what makes a ritual event different? And what role might improvised music play in ritual activity?

Ritual is characterised by a number of particular qualities:
1) A specific time and place set apart from the normal round;
2) A gathering of people with a shared sense of purpose;
3) A sequence of acts, each of which carries symbolic meaning;
4) The presence of a guide or facilitator who takes responsibility for the ritual and has a depth understanding of its meanings;
5) The expectation of a transformational outcome: a shift in consciousness, mood, energy or understanding, an elevation of spirit;
6) The use of significant artefacts, music and dance uniquely created for or tailored to the ritual event.

In our time and in the developed world, it is not so much that ritual itself has become debased (after all, people still get married and celebrate their birthdays) but that the ritual functions of music have been seriously weakened by being attached to all sorts of routine events or maintenance tasks which do not have any symbolic significance.[202] In order then to restore to music its ritual power it may be necessary to create it afresh, either through creative improvisation, as advocated here or through some other means. The most important consideration might be that the music should be fit for purpose, should match the occasion. It seems no accident that the very term "occasional music" has taken on a meaning which suggests peripheral activity or something insignificant whereas its proper meaning is the reverse of this, music specially suited to the event. When music which originally had great ritual importance, such as the Mozart Requiem, can be heard over breakfast on the radio, it is a clear sign that we have lost a sense of the ritual significance of music generally.

To begin with, making time and space for music and only music is one way to achieve ritual quality. A drum circle which meets regularly on a Friday evening, or an improvisation group which meets every month will automatically develop this sense of significance partly because of its regularity and partly because it is likely to happen in the same space. This then becomes a ritual space and it is useful, if not essential for it to be enclosed, safe, warm and uncluttered, though maybe decorated with symbolic objects: sometimes even a single candle suffices to provide this special sense of the moment, keeping the flame alive.

The time of day is also important, as is the point in the week and the time of the year. It is well known that Indian classical music, for example, employs musical forms, ragas, which are specific to particular moments

---

[202] Of course, it is not only music which has suffered from this kind of devaluation. Eating, sex and Christmas are other instances where inflation and over-exposure has diluted their ritual significance.

in time as well as points in the calendar. This special connection between a musical device and the precise time in which this structure or mode resonates has been largely lost in European music-making. Yet simply to be conscious or aware of the uniqueness of time, the transience of time and the fact that a session, a workshop, is going to take place in a discrete and unique time frame may be sufficient to endow the occasion with the special sense of temporality required. A ritual is not a rehearsal, it is not a preparation for an event, it *is* the event.

The people who attend may be from diverse backgrounds but there will be a sense of shared purpose. Each has made an effort, a journey, a decision to attend and it may be useful therefore to acknowledge this, to frame the journey and the expectations as part of the ritual process. The gathering will sit in a particular formation, the most obvious being a circle since this instantly dissolves hierarchies and allows instant communication with the potential for bonding. A musical improvisation might provide the necessary first steps in this bonding process provided of course that it is something everybody can do or share in. This opening improvisation might also provide the opportunity for people to introduce themselves to each other, sharing their expectations and bringing something of themselves into the space.

In previous times and in different cultures ritual events almost always celebrated the belief system or shared mythology of the group. No-one would argue that we live in a society in which celebrations of the spiritual or symbolic life are, for many, simply absent. This places even more emphasis on the music itself and the way in which the making of the music will itself articulate or engender a sense of unity within the group. The archetypal qualities of music, discussed in chapter 2, allow for almost any image, aspiration or feeling quality to be given musical expression and when such music is being improvised then these two aspects can grow and develop simultaneously – the qualities of the sound patterns reflect the specific collective purpose whilst the purposive character of the group will create specific sound patterns.

The facilitator will ideally allow for this, supporting the exploration but not imposing a system, whether of belief or musical style or structure. Drum circles, for example, are often taught rhythms and techniques which have their roots in African culture, even employing African musicians to run the workshop. Whilst this can result in some very energising, challenging, inspiring and satisfying group music-making it is an inescapable fact that this is the music of another time, another place and another culture, a music which represents very different belief systems. Is it not preferable to encourage original musical patterns to emerge which reflect the special nature and qualities of the group itself? In this case such a ritual might be revelatory as well as celebratory, invoking not some exotic (and inevitably distorted or idealised) image of Africa or India but accurately reflecting the inner aspirations and previously hidden ideals of the gathered community. Whatever the nature of the group, a ritual will always bring with it the potential for some kind of transformation. This might be a simple shift in mood or it might be an epiphany, but music has the capacity to take a group to a threshold of change. Shifts of consciousness and the potential to enter a liminal state are amplified through improvisation in a way that would be nigh impossible if the group was merely practicing to perform an already created work, imitating a foreign style or repeating previously learned material.

This suggests the primacy of musical activity: rather than serving a particular set of ideas or beliefs, music is now called upon to create something afresh, to open up the imaginative potential of a group of people and thus bring unconscious material into some kind of conscious awareness. This is no doubt of enormous therapeutic value, but the process can also work the other way around in that music, when introduced into situations and events, not as ambient sound or to fill in the silent spaces of our lives with noise, but as a guiding force, may endow all kinds of activity with ritual qualities rather in the manner that "work songs" were traditionally used, not necessarily to help people to work more efficiently but to articulate people's underlying relationship to life itself. This is the essence of ritual; it is what distinguishes it from routine and it points towards a valuable role for music-making in contexts where it might otherwise be regarded as insignificant.

The Outcomes of Lifemusic

Lifemusic seeks to engender a sense of individual well-being, collective empathy, ultimately reaching beyond the self, a beacon pointing towards the transpersonal. These are very broad states of feeling and concepts of mind and, as with any process-based activity, it would be impossible and contradictory to aim for precise, behavioural objectives of the kind that are commonly used in the political arena or in conventional teaching and learning, indeed, the difference between the

two approaches could not be greater. In most learning programmes we find precise outcomes dictated by an agreed curriculum or graduated learning structure which are frequently legally binding, a contract between an institution of learning and the student. Typically, in the kind of jargon which has today become an institutional norm, this structure is formulated around a set of culturally (if not politically) determined *bench marks* or, *targets* and outcomes will be stated as behavioural changes which can be observed and assessed once the learning is 'complete'. "At the end of this session, the student will be able to..." do whatever the teacher intended, the programme requires or the government decrees. This kind of prescriptive approach has become common not merely in subject areas which might automatically demand it, for example electrical engineering or fluid mechanics but also in arts and humanities where one might expect to find a less materially based, rationally inspired epistemology. The literal domain demands literal procedures but the imaginal domain surely requires something much more...
well... *imaginative*.

So if we travel to the opposite end of the spectrum we might be tempted not merely to re-phrase the outcomes but to re-design the paradigm. Perhaps here, where the work is largely person-centred and process oriented, it looks more like therapy. Yet, therapy takes place all too often perhaps, within very tightly controlled boundaries whereas the healing power of music, to be truly effective, may need wider and less closely-guarded applications. As suggested in the previous chapter, it is not merely about introducing improvisation into the practice of music, but of introducing music improvisation into areas of social practice where music-making per se, let alone improvised music, is almost certainly absent, a fresh paradigm. As Stephen Nachmanovitch articulates it:

> *...some activity beyond individual creativity, beyond art. Let us call it the Imaginary Liberation Front. Not art for art's sake, but art for life's sake. This means an explosion of creativity into areas of life where it has largely been excluded.* [203]

So what might be the purpose of making music in this way? Previously, I have written about pathways to healing (see Chapter 4), transformative process, well-being and therapeutic relationships as well as social cohesion, carnival, laughter, hilarity and celebration. Music has a major role to play in all of these and it seems important to remain as

---
203 Nachmanovitch, op.cit.

aware as possible of the links between sounds as they are being created, the structure of the music and the meanings they are carrying, the content of the music. This requires deep listening, rare in contemporary forms of mediation and *honest reflection*, requiring time and a space of trust. One of the persistently annoying characteristics of the way that music is currently mediated both in concerts and on the radio is the lack of any reflective pause between the end of the music and the following applause or commentary. Classic FM, in particular, seems to thrive on the way that the announcer dives in at the instant a CD track comes to an end whilst popular music stations sustain a barrage of musical sounds throughout, never allowing for any reflective silence whatsoever. Of course, we might argue that this is merely the result of the editorial decisions of programme makers responding to perceived audience demand, perceptions which often seem to me to be delusional. Maybe we need to gauge more closely what people actually want and simultaneously examine what happens to the experience of music when it is dressed in this kind of clothing, garments which might easily cloak or disguise deeper meanings or restrict movement in such a way that any potential pathways to healing become sealed off.

So if we take the responsibility for access to music away from programme makers, away from producers, from advertisers, from recording companies, from conductors, away even from song writers or composers, and simply give it back to people, what happens? And how can this work? Can we realistically envisage a new way of making music which entails the relocation of the contexts of creation and performance: from concert hall, recording studios and broadcasting venues to workshop spaces, workplaces and ritual spaces?

Re-birthing the Concert

Where does all this discussion leave that sacred emblem of European civilisation, the classical concert and that elegant model of hierarchy and privilege, the symphony orchestra? There is no doubt whatsoever that the orchestra makes an extraordinarily beautiful noise; neither is it in question that the structures of this noise are entertaining, expressive, extraordinary, elaborate and often profoundly moving; or that the composers who create these structures are exceptional human beings with remarkable minds. Since its development in the 18th Century, the symphony in particular, (together with its bed-mates the overture and the concerto), has become, beyond almost any other musical genre, a major symbol of enlightenment, progressive civilisation and cultural health. It is for this reason no doubt that so many non-European countries, whilst emulating the economic development and material well-being of Europe have simultaneously embraced the classical symphonic tradition often at the expense of their indigenous musics. We find this particularly in countries such as Japan, South Korea and, more recently, China. The classical concert is taken very seriously; hilarity seems largely absent even though some of the music is exceptionally witty whilst the formal taboos are so strong that it is even frowned upon to cough let alone to laugh or to dance. The seated audience subscribes therefore to a mode of being which suppresses the physical in favour of the mental, accepting without question the hierarchical and divisive social customs which keeps them in their seats, passive and largely anonymous except during applause.[204]

In Chapter 1, I was arguing that the objectivisation of music had in many ways reduced people's capacity to experience music intimately. Attending a classical concert can be a profoundly moving occasion yet, at the same time, it represents a very specific model of cultural behaviour which is largely confined to a particular strand of society. One only needs to watch the images portrayed by a TV camera roving its lens across a typical 'proms' audience to be reminded that this particular ritual is mostly the preserve of white middle class Europeans whose willingness and capacity to pay for such an event is probably linked also to non-musical motivation such as social status and a set of values which makes it seem worthwhile investing money in such an experience. A symphony concert is a celebration of cultural and economic achievement quite independently from the music that is actually being performed and the classical tradition is built upon a system in which the musicians' paymasters often hold themselves at a distance from the creative act itself. The gap between professional musician and seated audience is therefore well-preserved.

The musicians themselves, upon whose professional expertise and depth of musical understanding the success of the orchestra depends, are also to some degree set apart from the musical event. Partly due to their dependence on notation; partly because the music they are performing is often drawn from an oft-repeated repertoire which loses its sheen after so much repetition; partly because the primary responsibility for the performance rests with the conductor; and partly, if not mostly, because

---

[204] A notable exception would be the El Sistema initiative in Venezuela which has opened up participation in symphonic music to underprivileged young people with remarkable results resulting in performances which engage audiences in novel ways.

the music so often belongs to another time, another place and another culture – dislocated. Their own creative musicality is so often by-passed, a wasted resource and many become disillusioned after only a few years of playing.

Yet, most orchestras are now required as a condition of their funding to develop closer links with their communities through the employment of education officers and in some cases animateurs who facilitate creative projects which bring people together, de-mystifying the specialised domain of the orchestral world. We can see the beginning of this kind of development in the work of pioneers such as Andrew Peggie, Phil Mullen and Richard McNicol, community musicians who have developed an educational and community project in the UK known as the *Open Ear Orchestra*, working alongside the London Philharmonic Orchestra, bringing musicians from a wide range of genres together to create original music often with audience participation. When we see such projects in action we might be witnessing the beginning of the transition towards a very different kind of cultural event, one in which the audience participates and in which professional musicians are able to draw upon their individual creative abilities as well as their interpretative skills, where the conductor becomes also a facilitator, bringing new music to life, music which belongs to the time, place and people who are performing it. Far from being the death of the symphony orchestra this would surely amount to re-birth: the symphony concert as carnival. There is no reason at all why the format and the contexts in which these rich reservoirs of sonic delight currently operate cannot be modified and expanded to embrace a new kind music-making in which the riches are shared out more equitably and with greater relevance to contemporary life.

Healing and Therapy

If the symphony concert can be such a moving event, even where there is palpable gap between audience and musicians, how much greater might the effect be when people are themselves 'in symphony', making music alongside trained musicians, taking ownership? The contemporary practice of music therapy has been exploring and evaluating the benefits of improvised music-making with individuals and groups for five decades. But the use of music as a medium of healing has a deeper and longer history which crosses cultural divides, embracing traditional practices such as shamanism and reaching to the historical roots of our own culture. In past times music was viewed not merely a pastime but as an essential element in the well-being of communities. In the Europe of the Renaissance, the rediscovery of Plato, Hellenism and the cult of Orpheus spearheaded by Ficino (1433-1499), generated a deep interest in the power of music to heal since this was one of the primary functions of the Orphic and Pythagorean traditions. The magical qualities of song and the soothing strains of the lyre were there at the birth of opera in 1600; and it is no accident that Apollo is both the god of music and of medicine as well as the father of the god of healing himself, Asklepius. Thus the link between music and healing has archetypal and mythical roots which have only relatively recently been masked by the Cartesian dualism which separated body and mind, resisting notions of magic and soul, privileging an attitude to the body as a biological machine and relegating musical healing to the margins of history and the academic investigations of ethno-musicologists.

Non-European cultures, having largely escaped this scientific revolution, have never been in any doubt that music is potent and effective medicine. For example, the *ngoma* traditions which permeate Southern Africa across many different communities are based around healing rites in which music and dance play central roles. Janzen (2000) translates *ngoma* as 'drum', 'drum of affliction' or 'rite of affliction' and in his descriptions of *ngoma* practice, emphasises the manner in which the individuals and the community are equally involved in the music and dance around which such healing rituals revolve.[205]

There remains a discernible cultural divide between contemporary music therapy and theory and music as a traditional form of healing. As Janzen (op.cit.) points out, "of the 75 dissertations produced in music therapy between 1989 and 1998, not a single one was devoted to African music therapy". Clearly current models of music therapy, eager to remain grounded in empirical method, encounter similar difficulties with traditional musical healing as conventional medicine does with homeopathy, acupuncture, aromatherapy and other practices classed as complementary to medicine. This might be felt as unnecessarily narrowing and culturally retentive. At the same time, there are not a few contemporary "healers" who make wide-reaching claims about the healing properties of music and sound (and their own practice) with little or no grounded research to support their methods. It is inevitable perhaps, in times such as ours, when people are both hungry for change but often

---

[205] Janzen, John M. in Gouk, Penelope (Ed.) (2000). *Musical Healing in Cultural Contexts*. London.

simultaneously prone to suggestibility that such practitioners often create large and enthusiastic followings.

It is surely possible to acknowledge roots without attempting to emulate ancient traditions, borrow from other cultures or make scientifically unsupported claims about the effectiveness of sound as a healing medium. In Chapter 4, I argue that the healing properties of music might be identified in the structures of the music itself as well as in the interactive process through which these structures emerge: the clues are there perhaps in the pathways which criss-cross the many layers of the psyche as well as in the relationships which give birth to these structures. If we view mind and body as a whole, we begin to see that the same kind of balance and integrity created between conscious and unconscious, foreground and background, light and dark, consonance and dissonance, internal and external, individual voice and collective voice find a counterpart in the balance and functions of the physical body. The imagination is both a physical reality and an aspect of mind, so imaginative musicking can be expected to affect body, mind, soul and spirit as a whole. To bring music into the hospital ward, not through earphones or loudspeakers, but through musical instruments and live music-making is something which currently happens all too rarely. A recent long-term experiment on the Isle of Wight with young mothers and babies was considered a success[206] and current research with neuro-disability and rehabilitation in which the nursing and medical staff themselves have been trained to improvise music with their patients has also proved to be uniquely beneficial.[207]

Lifemusic in the Classroom

A class of nine-year-olds is having an art lesson. A small group clustered around a table in the corner sing as they work. The teacher comes over and admonishes them, "that's enough now, this isn't a music lesson!" Yet, in this instance, the music-making was undoubtedly assisting the creativity. Music in education has for long suffered from not only being restricted to being taught by specialists but also from being separated out as a discrete discipline rather than allowed to permeate the rest of the curriculum, in primary schools, where young children might be given creative free rein.

---

206 The Sound Start and Music Start projects which ran through 2002-2008 are linked to a wider series of projects demonstrating the considerable health benefits of music, particularly choral singing and supported by the Sidney de Haan Research Centre for Arts and Health based at Christ Church University, Canterbury. .
207 The former was funded by the Arts Council and the latter through the South East Coastal Communities programme supported financially by the Higher Education Funding Council for England and the NHS.

Despite this example, creative music is encouraged amongst children and, in the UK and elsewhere, is enshrined in the national curriculum. Yet, since improvisation has been generally neglected in the training of musicians and in music education in general, this primary creative act of music is too often ignored for the riches it offers. Instrumental teachers very often work entirely with notated forms, priming children and young people for the music centres or county orchestras. The general class teacher may often feel inadequate in musical matters, neglecting their own natural creativity, unwilling to experiment. Young musicians, especially if they are learning an orchestral instrument, will almost certainly be taken out of class to have their lesson or else stay behind after school hours. This may be the only way to learn this kind of instrument. Yet this inevitably privileges the "talented" student, or at least those whose particular dispositions, whether innate or nurtured by family background, lend themselves readily to these particular musical practices. The drawbacks are clear in terms of social divisiveness and cultural elitism.

Improvisation, freely created and spontaneous music-making, but inherently structured and integrated, offers a means whereby all can participate on an equal basis. It is not difficult to imagine music permeating classroom activity, directly enhancing other aspects of learning. It is a known fact, well-supported by research, that learning a musical instrument enhances other cognitive faculties. Yet, too often this argument is used to defend and support the maintenance of music services in a way which diminishes the value of music as something of value in itself. Perhaps the most effective use of music in the classroom, therefore, would be to integrate it directly into all kinds of learning, simply by devoting short but regular amounts of time to creative music-making within the classroom with everyone participating. Musical instruments, both the 'instant access' kind and the more specialised sorts, might then be permanently present by the side of desks rather than, as is so often the case, collecting dust in music cupboards, neglected and forgotten because no-one quite knows how to use them.

Lifemusic and Ability

Where music is concerned, we all have varying degrees of ability. Improvisation provides the potential for a *levelling* of competences, making it possible for those with limited technique to play alongside those with more sophisticated skills. The point is not how clever it might be, but how expressively it communicates. People whose specific needs may prevent them from participating in the performance of written down or complex music have an equal investment in expressive communication and improvising allows for this. Those who have received formal musical training for most of their childhood are very often disabled to the point where they are likely to seize up when invited to play freely.

It is sufficient perhaps to be *aware* both of people's abilities and of their natural limitations. Some of these are obvious, others less so. A person with the practical use of only one foot can still use a single foot switch; someone with the use of one hand can still "clap" with a shaker or castanet; a person with hearing difficulties will still be able to sense rhythm through gesture and touch; those with cerebral palsy will be still able to play at a slow tempo and with rhythms free from fixed pulse; those with learning disabilities may not understand verbal instructions but will respond directly to sound, rhythms and facial or eye contact. Other forms of communication, using photos, pictures or signing may also be helpful. During a vocal exercise with a mixed group of disabled and non-disabled adults, I was initially taken aback when a woman with no speech, little hearing and almost total sight impairment, grabbed me by the throat but quickly realised that this was her way of hearing the voice as it was directly vibrating through her fingertips.

With all groups, allowing plenty of time for ideas to be grasped, decisions to be made, things to happen, underlines the connections to time which music articulates. Working with a group with cerebral palsy I encountered a participant who had taught himself to play the theme from the film Exodus on a keyboard, albeit at a pace which seemed at first hearing painstakingly slow. A piece then developed around each note of the melody as it sounded, decorated by the rest of the group improvising on tuned and untuned percussion instruments. The results were unique and not unlike the technique of *cantus firmus*, common to some forms of early music, where a single melody becomes an anchor for the inventions which surround it. Abandoning an authentic performance in favour of an original approach demonstrates just how much may be learned from the limitations imposed by disability.

Lifemusic in Public Places

Imagine a restaurant, where, instead of piped music accompanying the food, musical instruments were available for customers to play, facilitated by staff;[208] imagine a cafe where a music corner was available for people to improvise when waiting to be served; or a coffee house where conversation could be interspersed with musicking; imagine a park where the playground was also a sound centre with robust resonating instruments at the ready for children of all ages to generate rhythms and riffs; or a supermarket where the aisles were occasionally enlivened by a burst of rhythm. Introducing creative music into non-dedicated spaces, integrating music into the life of communities in unusual ways is not such a crazy notion though it might be redolent of a "flash-mob". How might a post office queue be immeasurably enlivened were a group of musicians to suddenly appear, improvise a ten minute burst of creative improvisation and then disappear into the high street!

Sound Company

Generally, apart from the odd whistling or humming, people who work in offices do not make music together though many will either have music piped to them or else will pipe it to themselves via i-pods or similar devices. It is entirely feasible however to create a situation in which the office, the boardroom or the staff club could easily become a musical space. Working teams could be provided with good quality but easily accessible musical instruments – shakers, bells, small drums, simple keyboards, including perhaps i-phones, pads and pods or other digital instruments which would be kept directly in the workstation, alongside the computer and the phone. They could attend an initial group improvisation workshop, learning very quickly how to initiate a group improvisation. They would then be encouraged to devote short amounts of time each week to group improvising either spontaneously in working periods or during coffee or tea breaks.

This might seem like a strange idea yet it is only a brief step away from the work song which, as argued earlier, is not so much designed to support physical labour but to introduce an element of soul into the working day. The benefits would surely include lower stress levels, increased well-being, enhanced communication, less fatigue, enriched relationships, even perhaps more effective and creative work outputs.

Suits, Ties and Uniforms

Furthermore, how might "direct injection" music benefit civil servants, politicians? In what ways might critical decision making be

---

[208] The Missing Sock restaurant in Cambridge is a rare example of an eatery where this kind of thing regularly happens.

influenced were meetings to be preceded by a session of collective improvisation or group drumming? Music shifts the emphasis from left brain rationality towards right brain activity and in the process it allows reason to be informed by imagination. So we might expect the subsequent discussions to be balanced by a greater degree of empathy, invention and creative thinking than is the norm. The team will certainly be more alert and, quite literally attuned to each other. They may also find that problem-solving is more streamlined. It is impossible to judge what the overall effect of this would be, but I cannot imagine that it would be anything but beneficial to the outcomes of high level discussion. Even a few minutes of simple drumming will resonate with the whole person in a way which makes it possible to listen with greater depth, awareness and understanding. It is not simply that music enlivens the mind and awakens the senses, or that it stimulates right brain thinking, but that it engages the soul, transforming otherwise dry and hot proceedings (analytical discussion) with a refreshing coolness and dampness, with a broader sense of the human perspective, connecting to that wider field of understanding which soul awareness inevitably creates.

And if this enhancement of thinking and feeling is important for politicians and civil servants how much more might it be of benefit to policemen and soldiers. "Do not give a man a sword 'til he learns to dance" runs the Welsh proverb and in this dance (and song) we surely find the rhythm and sensibility of the warrior. We know that military music can be stirring and stimulating as it batters its way into our consciousness with drums, trumpets and triangles; such music has been with us no doubt as long as people have been in conflict with each other. But for those who have chosen the path of the warrior there is another kind of music offering something else, a glimpse into the deeper purpose and meaning of conflict, an understanding of its symbolic function. Might this go some way towards reducing the terrifying toll which the literalisation and mechanisation of warfare has had and is taking on people's lives? It is no surprise that fundamentalist regimes, such as existed under the Taliban in Afghanistan, virtually banned music and dance altogether from people's lives whilst other totalitarian states favour strident military music as a staple, streaming from speakers in homes and public places. Conflict is inevitable but a literal response to it is not. To make music together, whether it is the earth power of the drum or the soul music of the voice, could only strengthen the warrior's focus on inner strength. No-one who has chosen to spend or potentially sacrifice their lives in the theatre of war or even on the streets of Reading on a Friday night could fail to benefit from the strength and compassion, the sound judgment which music carries. After all, if music puts the "hum" into human can it not equally put the "soul" into soldier?

No Barriers

Ultimately, participatory music, improvisation, collective musicking, whatever we choose to call it, is available to anyone at any time and in any place. It is only a matter of will and belief: the effort needed to drop other activity in order to devote some time to connecting with others in this way and a belief that this is a worthwhile, life-enhancing process. It is so easy to access music at the flick of a switch or to consider that music-making is out of place anywhere other than a concert hall, club or pub or in the hands of specialists. Yet these are all artificial barriers to the unique and easily forgotten benefits which self-made music can supply.

If we can imagine participatory music taking place in office, board room or barracks then what about in the home, in the family, parents and children improvising together? A recent project with families and children in support centres in West Sussex produced a wave of enthusiasm amongst participants. The support workers who regularly deal with families undergoing challenges or crises reported unequivocally how the group music-making, improvising using a wide variety of "game-plans", brought a sense of joy into the centres and created new bonds of trust between participants. It is only a short step from here to families making music together in their own homes, taking time out from TV to connect up with each other through imaginative sounds, renewing bonds and enhancing relationships which can so easily become neglected in the race to keep up with contemporary living.

I began this chapter by discussing the barriers which exist between musically active groups and those for whom music is not an automatic option. To start with the family, to reinstate living music as an integral element of family life would be a major step towards dismantling the barriers which we place between musical and non-musical communities. In the final two chapters of this book, I focus entirely on some practical ways in which this might be achieved.

CHAPTER 7

GENERAL PRINCIPLES OF GROUP IMPROVISATION

Playing with Apollo

The first part of this book was concerned with the nature of music itself and how the act of improvisation, especially group improvisation, might bring people into direct contact with the elemental properties of sound, the mysteries of time and the soul qualities of life. The social value of improvising rests in how it potentially enables people to experience music instantly, as a living art; how they might create music in forms which precisely and directly resonate with their immediate social context; how this might connect them to time, to place and to each other. Furthermore, the musical expression of this "immediacy" imparts to each moment greater depth, increased significance, a kind of numinosity which can be both revelatory and mysterious, giving rise to the precept that *music turns life into soul.*

But exactly how does an improvisation work? How to start? Where to start? How to set the context, prepare for activity, create the necessary atmosphere, bring the group into a suitable frame of mind, alert and relaxed, purposive and playful? How to maintain the flow of energy and how to balance the variety of skills amongst the participants? Most importantly perhaps, how to draw upon those archetypal qualities of music outlined earlier in this book: at what point to invite Apollo into the workshop space, when to sing with Orpheus, dance with Dionysus, hold hands with Psyche and when to allow the music-making to be led by the mercurial slipperiness of Hermes? This suggests mixing purely pragmatic principles, ground rules of action, with a constant awareness of the flexible and maze-like qualities of creative flow, never allowing attachment to a rule to stand in the way of changes of direction driven by *inner necessity.*

This underlying principle is contained in the *Holding Form* theory discussed in Chapter 4. The HF in practice is, in effect, a hermetic tool; meaning that, though operating as a guiding principle with boundaries and handrails it is also challenging, hazardous, flexible, slippery, ambiguous and surprising (if not amazing). So whilst an improvisation might begin with a simple instruction which can be followed and understood (rationally) by the whole group, an Apollonian position, this is only the *access point* to the HF. Improviser or improvising group needs to be able to *allow the piece to find its inner principle*, the point at which the foreground moves into the background to be replaced by a spontaneously expressed new foreground which, emerging as it does from the group unconscious, is free of individual ego, free of rule attachment, or of anything other than the purposive drive of the music itself. It is always at this point that an improvisation finds its truth, with the participants themselves carried along on a stream of musical consciousness which has its own structure, its own depths and which quite often leaves everyone feeling somewhat stunned. There is often a silence at the point immediately following the end of a successful improvisation during which there is a palpable sense of the need to pause, to wait, to allow the energy to subside and to wait for Apollo and his companions to depart.

In these guidelines, therefore, I am attempting to find a balance between the practical and the magical, between simple rules and signposts which point towards those creative journeys and partially-hidden, mysterious structures and unexpected departures which are in no way obvious, though they are accessible. The guidelines are in some respects aimed principally at music leaders in a variety of guises: community musicians, music therapists, music teachers. But it is my hope that many people who currently lead and work with groups in non-musical ways will also find here points of departure which they can use to greater or lesser degree in their own workplaces. One of the basic aims here is to de-mystify the practice of music-making and therefore it is to be hoped that even those who would not describe themselves as musicians will find something of value in these pages. If everyone is musical, then running a music session need not be restricted to trained musicians. All it needs is to invite Apollo in to the space and to play.

The Art of Facilitating

In defining the role of the facilitator it might be useful to begin by considering the difference between instructing (which could describe traditional styles of music teaching) and facilitating (a slightly awkward term which describes something more akin to therapy or midwifery). In essence, whereas an instructor might be employed to teach skills which are difficult to master, a facilitator, by definition, makes things easy. The teacher is usually working towards a precise outcome which may well be dictated by a curriculum, a fairly precise body of knowledge. This means that there is a well-defined notion of what the desired results are going to look like: a set of *behavioural objectives* as the old-fashioned jargon described them. A teacher can therefore set up a learning route and then put the pupil though a series of graduated hoops until the goal is reached, or the behaviour becomes apparent. Having observed this behaviour, usually in some form of examination, the instructor can then judge, with reasonable precision, whether the student is successful, whether the outcomes match the objectives. This model stems from a well-worn philosophy which assumes that the teacher knows things which the student does not; it places the teacher therefore in a superior or senior relationship to the learner. The skill then rests in how this knowledge is transmitted and an imaginative teacher will devise various ingenious and motivational ways of transferring this knowledge from their brain to the brains of their students. Ultimately, clear instructions, however subtly encased, will deliver the goods.

This model works perfectly well within any musical tradition which can be clearly defined, where there is a fixed genre encased in a recognisable framework around which a consistent theory can be constructed. This applies certainly to the historical music of Europe which has been well-defined in theoretical and historical terms by generations of musical historians and analysts. But it applies equally to any musical idiom which has defined boundaries of style and form. The very act of theorising creates these boundaries and therefore renders the music capable of the "taxonomic" treatment. So today, in the UK at least, this approach is very well-established, with children and young people (and sometimes older folk as well) instructed through a graded process in the arts of instrumental playing according to the precepts and theories of not only classical music but now also jazz and rock, learning scales, arpeggios, tone production, fingering, embouchure and so on, all in service of an already existing and defined style of music.

One of the results of this approach, as I have already touched upon in an earlier chapter, is that it easily creates a fatal dependence on notation which becomes very difficult to shed: in fact, most classically trained musicians find it impossible to imagine improvising once they have been exposed to notated practice for a few years so that the notion of getting together with fellow musicians and simply playing by ear or from scratch seems entirely alien. This approach also creates forms of muscle memory, autonomous, kinaesthetic patterning which ensures that the sounds being made represent faithfully the idiom being learned. This is of course essential for any kind of music-making which wants to remain embedded within a particular genre but the downside is equally obvious, making it much more difficult to step outside of this idiom in order to create something original. What is more, if the particular taught style is presented as "right" and any divergence as "wrong" then fear of failure is built into the learning process. As creativity guru Ken Robinson recently pointed out,[209] fear of failure has become so deeply ingrained into our systems that any kind of divergent experimentation or original exploration is generally avoided. *Schools kill creativity*.

In comparison, facilitating falls within a totally separate paradigm. There is no fixed notion of what the (musical) outcome is going to sound like. Even where the material might be familiar or the style recognizable, the facilitator will allow the piece to have its own life and simply clear the pathway for this to emerge. Old ideas will be revisited as often as new ones are invented. The facilitator thinks on his or her feet, always prepared to abandon something decided upon earlier in order to follow the organic flow of the moment. Instead of preparing a single plan, the facilitator needs to be prepared for anything and everything, drawing upon any previous idea which seems appropriate or abandoning planning altogether in order to respond to the moment, the time, the space and the group they happen to be working with at that point. This may well mean creating a completely new and untested action idea on the spot or at least choosing one from a diverse source, an internalised "toolkit" which fits the moment.

Perhaps we can identify three key faculties to the facilitator's skill – *resonance, communication and participation*. First and foremost the facilitator will be able to gauge the needs, character and ambience of the group. This requires considerable empathic skill, an ability to listen, to pace things sufficiently slowly and to provide an unhindered, non-judgmental, non-threatening space in which the feelings of the individuals

---

[209] See www.ted.com/talks/ken_robinson_says_schools_kill_creativity.html

in the group are able to emerge without anxiety. This is called "resonance" because it is like picking up the vibration which any group of people create when they enter a space. This quality is present in the relationships between the people themselves but it is also affected by the physical properties of the space, the temperature, the time of day, year and weather. Being sensitive, resonating with these critical factors is part of the facilitator's skill. The aim is to improvise from the heart of the community, the spirit of the place and the awareness of time and therefore the facilitator will want to resonate with all of these elements.

The second quality surrounds the skill of communication. Communicating effectively is not simply a case of finding the right words, or creating the appropriate images or even of graduating the information so that each stage is clearly understood. This can be effective enough for an instructor but in contrast to the instructional approach, the facilitator may well spend more time listening than explaining, a reminder that communication is a two-way process. Explanation itself may need to be indirect, a 'wobbly' route which maintains creative alertness, not presenting anything as gospel. The pace will be gentle, seeking always to make space for things to emerge, for a participant's own truth to have voice. Communication as reflection: "What happened there?" "Where did that leave you?" "What did it feel like?" In other words, we are asking either literally or through the senses, whether everyone is aware of process rather than reducing the event to an explanation: staying with the quality of the event instead of analyzing it away. Keeping to the "what" and avoiding the "why".

A facilitator also participates in the process though they would not allow their own skills to mask, intimidate or discourage as this would instantly set them apart, shutting down the possibility of communication. However, this does not mean suppressing their skills but using them with subtlety and awareness and in support of the group. A facilitator shares knowledge but also participates in its creation. During an improvisation, this might mean listening for the core of the emerging piece and subtly underlining it, reinforcing a rhythm perhaps, or complementing a melodic shape or supplying a drone or chord. It means being aware, as far as is possible, of every sound being made and feeling for the musical potential, the piece that wants to emerge.

In the light of all of this, there are some questions which it may be useful for a facilitator to ask themselves when planning to facilitate sessions. How far do I need to predict outcomes and how unsafe do I feel if things do not go according to plan? How do I define structure? How do I cope when trying to achieve an outcome which seems to defy resolution? How comfortable am I when someone else makes an unpredictable decision which moves everything in an unexpected direction? To what degree do I feel the need to be in control of a situation and how far am I able to let go of the reins? Am I leading or following? Can I blur the distinctions between these roles? There are no precise answers to these questions but asking them will raise awareness of the constant flux which attends improvisation and perhaps also of the principles, also time-based, which connect music to life itself. Connection to time is not something that can be methodically constructed; it is a journey through the maze of the imagination in which the facilitator is as much a witness as a route planner.

Setting the context

In purely practical terms, the context for *Lifemusic* has three aspects: first, the nature of the client group; second, the nature of the project and the time period over which it will take place; and third, the physical space. In a nutshell, *people, projects and places*. The first of these will inevitably determine the mental preparation and the kinds of questions to ask about the aims of the session or sessions. The balance between process and product is likely to be a major factor in setting the context: will there be any kind of performance at the end or will the music-making be for its own sake or undertaken principally to generate well-being, reflection, discussion and transformation? Do participants know what to expect and, in the case of a client group which may have special needs or is otherwise challenging, are there safeguards in place to protect the well-being of both facilitators and clients? How long is the project going to last, a single session, a weekly workshop or a weekend intensive?

Who is *Lifemusic* for? What might motivate people to come together to improvise music in this way? In the previous chapter I was suggesting some of the ways in which participatory music could be brought into the lives of a wide variety of people, some of them perhaps surprising. Yet, people might be simply looking for an element of self-fulfilment or seeking to re-discover a musical self which was erased through unhelpful or insensitive schooling; classically trained musicians might be wanting to renew contact with a creative self neglected through a profession which often suppresses individuality; a hospitalised group might need to be accommodated around a schedule of clinical routines; a corporate group might be on a motivational away-day or fitting in a session in a lunch break. In each case the nature of the group will inevitably determine the approach, how the context is set, what kind of exercises or introductions to prepare, what instruments to employ, even perhaps what clothes to wear.

If the session is going to be with a group of people with physical impairments or learning disability then it will be invaluable to have carers or helpers at hand who know the clients and understand their special needs. I feel that it is important that care staff are also willing and prepared to participate fully in the music-making and in some cases this might even form part of their own training in the skills of music leadership. On the other hand, a corporate group can expect to have a fairly clear outline of what to expect, especially in terms of the potential non-musical outcomes, in advance of the session. If the session is in a hospital or care home, then ample discussion will need to take place with the consultant or ward manager beforehand, especially if, as is usually the case in healthcare, the sessions need to be clinically documented. If the session is one of a series or if it is leading to a performance or event then this will also need to be acknowledged and agreed upon.

A session or group of a series of workshops may benefit from having a specific theme linked, for example, to the season or to some other festival and in this case, an introductory letter or email to the participants might focus on this theme, providing some clues as to the kind of music-making which might be expected to come out of the workshop. It will be invaluable to include in any outline a reminder of the basic precepts – "no wrong notes", "every sound has meaning", "freedom to break the rules", and so on. This sets the context and reassures participants who may be nervous about improvising or playing music in front of others. The letter can also suggest that participants bring something with them, physical or otherwise: an instrument, an object of significance, a poem, a photograph, a candle or just an idea. This helps to create a sense of ownership.

The physical space, or venue for the workshop is critical to the success or otherwise of the session. Ideally, the space will be uncluttered, carpeted, warm and light. It is worthwhile checking whether light bulbs or heating systems are noisy. Fluorescent lighting is harsh and can often hum an annoying g sharp and heating fans are no better. Needless to say, the space will also benefit from some kind of privacy and isolation, certainly in terms of sound. More than a few workshops have suffered from intrusive traffic noise, aircraft, anonymous drilling, even, on one occasion, workmen walking across the roof. It is worth seeking out venues in wooded settings or near a lake or the sea since the proximity of elements of wood and water will inevitably have a positive influence on the playing. The musical space is a ritual space and this means creating an atmosphere which has inner focus as well as outer containment. A single burning candle can be a subtle reminder of the connection to time.

Introductions

The start of a workshop has such a strong influence on its subsequent development that it is worth giving it plenty of thought. It is important for the group to feel a sense of autonomy and this can be achieved in a number of ways. It may be useful to ask, in a variety of ways, what their expectations are, what they feel about making music together and what previous experience they might have had. Three useful questions: "What is your earliest musical experience?" "What was your most powerful or most moving musical experience?" "Have you ever had a negative or personally challenging musical experience?" It may be best simply to ask these questions and then leave them "hanging" for a while. There is no reason why they should be answered at once (or at all) since simply asking them will set a reflective tone. All the same, many participants will be more than ready to identify themselves musically through their memories, their musical history, their connections to time past.

It might be useful to leave formal introductions until after the first improvisation. Starting almost wordlessly with something everyone can do, or simply allowing people's natural tendency to "noodle" to become the initiating point of the first improvisation, can be surprisingly productive. An improvisation game such as "Dropouts" (see Chapter 8) can be used as an introduction game, the person who is left playing on their own invited to say a few words about themselves. This particular exercise also allows people to self-select the order in which they introduce themselves which may be preferable to going around the circle one at a time or doing it by age (youngest to oldest) or birthdays (earliest in year to latest). Ultimately, however, the facilitator will need to make their own judgments as to the most appropriate method of introducing group members to each other.

Talking and playing

It is now generally accepted that talking rationally, explaining things, is a left brain activity whereas improvising, making music spontaneously is a creative activity and thus a function of the right hemisphere. Left brain activity also seems to be more dominant, more controlling and therefore there may be a tendency to talk through the opening of a session in some detail since this feels safer, more controlled. Yet this can also be counterproductive since the longer the talking goes on the more difficult it becomes to leap across the divide and start improvising. So, keep it right brain, get into the playing as quickly as possible. Do not be daunted by the shift, the motto might be – *more percussion less discussion*.

Once an improvisation ends, there may be a need for silence. Let this continue for as long as it needs to. In fact there may be a similar reluctance to get back into words as there was to abandon them in the first place.[210] When talking does resume, it may well be of an entirely different quality to the kind of discussion or explanation which preceded the improvisation. It may be more hesitant and reflective. Try to maintain this quality of reflection even when, as often happens, someone in the group may want to refer to another time, another place, other people, another experience or even an entirely different type of event. By staying in the "here and now", or, since this is music, the "hear" and now, the group will both maintain connection with time and understand something about how the music worked, how it began and ended, who did what and what happened in the middle. This understanding then inevitably feeds into the next piece.

As with any group work, the relationships which are being formed at this point will benefit from people's capacity to own their own feelings. Gentle encouragement may be needed to speak in the first person and to avoid attributing personal reflections or feelings to others or to the group as a whole. Some of the discussion will highlight the different roles people take on during an improvisation: some may have consciously led, changing the direction of the piece, whilst others may have been happy to follow or to simply stop and listen. These are always significant pointers to how the relationships within the group are forming and developing. There may be feelings of impatience or even annoyance that the piece went in one direction rather than another, or that someone else in the group continued playing when others wanted it to stop, or on the other hand, someone might have wished to continue but felt left high and

---

210 In one session, the silence lasted for many minutes at which point someone remarked "I can't do silence", to which the obvious answer was "but you just did!"

dry when the piece ended. Let as much of this surface as possible and then choose an appropriate moment to introduce another improvisation and bring the talking to an end. It is often in the course of these reflections that a clue to the next idea for an improvisation starter will emerge.

Beginnings and Endings

So what actually happens when the talking stops? Every piece has its beginning, the moment of decision when to start and how to start. Whatever happens in the opening seconds determines the rest of the piece. Sometimes an opening will emerge from people simply fiddling around until some rhythm or texture is identified as the one. Sometimes the facilitator will suggest an access point. Sometimes a member of the group will decide that they want it thus and the rest are happy to follow. But all improvisations begin with silence and out of this silence the piece is born.

Initiating the improvisation may then require some kind of access point, an invitation to play. These seem to me to fall into three related and overlapping categories: 1) *structural* - a purely musical idea which generates development; 2) *relational* - an interactive game or pattern which focuses on the relationships between participants; 3) *thematic* - an extra-musical theme, image, pattern or narrative. The suggestions in the final Chapter of this book generally fall into one or other of these categories, each of which seems to call upon the energies and qualities of particular archetypes: structural ideas favour Apollo – the relational puts us in contact with Psyche whilst Orpheus presides over themes and narratives.

Balance is the key. Relational openings emphasise relationships but leave structure entirely to the collective imagination and therefore it may be useful to follow such a starting point with something purely structural such as counting and clapping. Narrative forms or thematically-based improvisations are often useful later in a session once the group is comfortable with playing spontaneously.

Endings often create themselves and may be influenced by unconscious factors or because the time has run out. A musical structure will find its own ending and the improvising group will almost always be aware of this: a feeling that everything which needed to be expressed has now been played out. Sometimes a piece will end suddenly and take everyone by surprise, or else a single player will create an (artificial) ending with a loud bang or a sounding bell. Other endings may be drawn out with a sense of anticipation. Whilst everyone will sense the ending, will feel its inevitability, sometimes a player or players will keep going for other reasons not directly related to the music itself, keeping the piece alive, not wanting to let go or even perhaps feeling more comfortable with sound than with silence. Music therapists are familiar with the "perseverative" playing which is common with clients diagnosed with autistic tendencies, but all participants are likely at times to feel this need to keep the piece going. Often in an improvisation which has been very busy or chaotic, with everyone playing, the ending might well be the most satisfying part, a moment when the inner structures and sense of the piece become most audible. This clarity is important and can be allowed to influence the development of the musical awareness in the group.

Free Play and Idiomatic Play, Chaos and Structure

No one is free from cultural influences and musical conditioning. This means, in effect, that totally "free" improvisation is virtually impossible since even the least tutored participant will be influenced by what he or she has experienced through their lifetime. In fact, it is surely impossible for any sounds to be created purely at random since the (musical) mind naturally structures its environment. Free improvisation is not genre specific in any sense but, at the same time it allows for people's capacity to recreate sounds which they are familiar with. The division between free play and idiomatic play is a spectrum, a wide arc across which people improvising music might roam freely even in the course of a single improvised piece. Freedom means being allowed to play in whatever way one wishes; yet in group improvisations, if one player decides to introduce a specific idiom, a chord progression for example, or a series of blues "licks" the effect of this on the rest of the group is going to be impossible to ignore. Free play might be expected to result in seeming "chaos" and yet the attempt to play idiomatically or recreate already existing material will be more likely to produce chaotic results as some struggle to engage with the idiom. It is surely possible to accommodate this spectrum, allowing people to make music without fear of entering chaos, knowing that structures will sooner or later emerge.

But what happens when a participant suddenly decides to start playing, for the sake of argument, a blues progression on the guitar? In itself, this is neither right nor wrong but the effect on the rest of the group will be controlling, even perhaps intimidating, if not downright irritating. The blues idiom carries extremely powerful musical, social, cultural and emotional *fingerprints* which becomes impossible to ignore and which will therefore exert a potentially dominating influence on the developing piece. It may be necessary to open this up as an issue for discussion, raising the level of awareness both in the group as a whole and in the would-be bluesman. It might leave some participants stranded, unable or unwilling to join in. Idiomatic playing is not in any sense taboo (I will be including some examples in the following chapter) but it is "cultural baggage" which carries enormous weight. A player might be motivated to play idiomatically either because they feel uncomfortable with the unknown, needing to remain inside their comfort zone or simply because they want to show off. Both attitudes are ego-bound. Yet all too often, this means isolation since others might be technically unable or unwilling to access this particular idiomatic zone. Who is then left stranded? A facilitator will need to confront the issue sensitively, perhaps asking the group whether they want to turn the session, or this part of it, into a "blues workshop" maybe even set up a "follow me" exercise in which the blues player leads. But whatever happens it will be necessary to bring the whole situation into awareness so that the group can work with the process.

A similar issue arises with the use of the piano. The piano represents European music with all of its hierarchical, equally tempered, rationality mapped out in black and white and placed at arm's length. Merely sitting down at a piano is a major cultural gesture – it places the player in the spotlight, it confers status, it says "I am in charge." In the improvising group a player might decide to sit at the piano or keyboard and play a chord progression, instantly determining the character of the improvisation, forcing the whole piece in a precise channel which other players will then choose to follow, or not. The facilitator is then faced with a similar dilemma as with the bluesman, either to let the chords determine the outcome or to gently suggest a less determining approach. "There are no wrong notes" but sometimes the "right" ones may feel too exclusive.

In each of these cases the principle of *limitation* may be one way of avoiding the "fingerprinting". Cage developed the concept of the "prepared piano" where only certain notes, those that had been "doctored" with muting rubbers or jangling screws, were permitted to be used. A guitar can be similarly limited, tuned so that only open strings or single notes are advised. This principle of limitation is fundamental to any creative work and a competent flautist or violinist will find that group improvising is curiously liberating when they are encouraged to improvise initially only with two or three pitched notes. For identical reasons a xylophone tuned to the pentatonic mode is an ideal improvising instrument and will often blend in effortlessly with almost any other sounds people care to make.

Formations

Musical choices and musical structures are heavily influenced by how people are positioned. The classical orchestra is understandably formed in 'ranks' and 'desks', all players facing in one direction and this inevitably colours the relationship to those sitting behind them, establishing a hierarchy. In the practice of participatory music the default formation is the circle, ensuring that everyone can make eye contact with everyone else and establishing the principle of equality. Furthermore, the circle itself creates its own potential for musical structures not only because of the ease with which players can communicate but as a prompt for various permutations, grouping and order of play which in themselves will generate musical ideas.

Improvisations might begin with sending sounds around the circle in either direction or playing in pairs or trios. Sometimes it can be equally useful to spread out around the space, moving together as the piece progresses, creating a flexible and shifting series of musical textures and a variety of interactions. Two opposing lines facing each other may prompt call and response or even symbolic conflict, two tribes facing each other or calling to each other across the valley. Sitting back to back creates another kind of relationship altogether and eliciting more sensitive listening, feeling, sensing and greater intimacy.

Magical Objects – The Lifemusician's Toolkit

To hold a musical instrument in one's hands is to become a god. The archetypal musical instrument, the lyre, was invented by Hermes and Apollo was taught to play it by the muses. Therefore, simply to be in the presence of musical instruments may be awe-inspiring and the vast range of instruments available to us is an extraordinary testament to the inventiveness and ingenuity of the musical mind. Even the simplest of them, such as a pair of claves, or a seed pod shaker, can instantly transform a mundane space into a musical space whilst the most technically complex, such as the orchestral horn, cathedral organ or full drum kit may take years of dedication to master. However simple or complex, there is always an element of magic about sounding an instrument. Striking a bell, for example, seems to purify the acoustic, preparing for a moment which is special, unique, ritualized, clearing the sonic space for the event; shaking a rattle feels like an invocation, a calling up of the spirits; beating a drum takes the body into a heightened or deepened sense of awareness; blowing a horn is dynamic, life-affirming; coaxing a string to vibrate, whether a guitar held close to the body, a violin nestling beneath the chin or a cello lying between the legs will always feel intimate, sensual, even erotic; flutes are channels for the breath of life whilst the xylophone or balafon celebrates the dance of the spirit.

In open improvisation, all available instruments can be brought together in any combination. Fixed traditions inevitably use instruments in fairly standard formats: this is as true of a Klezmer band or Irish fiddle group as it is of a brass band or symphony orchestra; the integrity of such traditions depends upon an accepted and consistent format. But the alternative to these traditions has less to do with the tried and tested combinations of texture and tone in support of a specific musical style and more to do with people coming together to communicate, uniquely and spontaneously and this allows for all sorts of combinations of instruments. All that is required is to listen, to invent, to experiment and to explore. This actually makes musical life much simpler since success does not depend upon gathering together the "right" players with their instruments all together at the same time in the same place; rather, anyone, playing anything to whatever level of technical competence can communicate musically with anyone else. The challenge of the music in this case then becomes not so much technical as relational, so that the instrument, whatever it sounds like, however potentially loud or soft and whatever levels of technical skill might be available, becomes primarily a tool for opening up channels of trust, improvised forms which map the mutual, shifting feelings and interactions of the players.

If a player has been learning an instrument formally within a specific genre, they will already have developed technical skills which may tend to lead the music in pre-ordained directions. This does not mean abandoning learned techniques, but it could mean extending, adapting and experimenting; the journey into the new territory will then create a fresh perspective when returning to the home pastures. However, it may be necessary to remember that previously learned patterns can easily become a barrier to communication and the experimentation is also therefore a means of keeping channels to other players open: a skilled pianist can so easily swamp the rest of the group and, as noted earlier, a guitarist strumming conventional chord progressions will inevitably lead the music in a single direction which may not take account of other players' wishes. This is not to place a ban on anything since the improvisation may naturally lead in this direction but it may mean encouraging players to avoid at first fixed and previously learned idiomatic patterns.

Musicians who have not received any previous formal instrumental training (including those with disabilities) will probably be using "instant access" instruments, mainly tuned and untuned percussion and also perhaps simple flutes, such as the penny whistle, ocarina or similar. These are more widely available today than ever before and it might be useful to think of them as falling into three elemental categories:

o *wood*, containing the qualities of earth, resonance, flexibility & strength;
o *skin*, with the qualities of water, soul, depth and feeling;
o *metal* with the qualities of fire, brightness, passion and velocity;
o *flutes* with the qualities of air, lightness, spirit and song.

These qualities are physical, symbolic and of course *timbral*. The sound of wood carries with it whole forests, air, rain, sap, photosynthesis, slow growth. The sound of skin puts us in touch with the heartbeats and living tissue of animals, literally sacrificed (whether or not ritually) in order to make the instruments, something which is not always considered by those playing them. The sound of metal carries the intense heat of the fire used to smelt the ore from the rock. Flutes channel the breath of life and the song of the spirit. Such qualities and the images they carry may not need to be discussed in any detail but they underline the need for a respect which is often absent, especially in schools where these wonderful instruments are so often and so easily taken for granted, discarded, collecting dust in forgotten cupboards, skins broken, metal glazed over, wood dried out and cracking, unused, misunderstood and under-valued.

Generally, wooden instruments provide the most precisely delineated rhythmic sounds – the click of the claves for example providing a bright, vital sound, clearly audible within even the most complex cacophony, hence their ubiquitous presence within samba bands. Tulip blocks, guiros, woodblocks, log drums, even chop sticks on table tops provide instant, precise, rhythmic textures. Wooden instruments also tend to be the most portable.

Skin means drums of all shapes and sizes. The wide popularity of the djembe in recent years is due in part, no doubt, to the power and depth of its sound but the widest possible variety of drums including frame drums, darabukas, bongos, congas, shamanic drums, gathering drums, doumbeks, ocean drums, buffalo drums to name a few, provide a rich base for inventive improvisation.

All the metal instruments, from the not-so-humble triangle, across to the mighty gong provide an incredibly dense range of harmonics – white noise – so care will need to be taken that this quality is respected and appreciated. The fire that produced them can easily consume both wood and skin. Experiment with a variety of beaters and explore the different effects created by striking different areas of the instruments. The most commonly used tuned instruments, xylophones, glockenspiels and metallophones will also yield very divergent tone qualities from the use of a variety of beaters: wood, hard and soft rubber, woven thread, soft and fluffy heads will all create distinctive varieties of tone colour. Whole improvisations can be built around the simple exploration of these colours.

The main point about the use of tuned percussion has already been made (see the paragraph on Rhythm and Pitch, above) but is worth reiterating here. Since it would be normally inappropriate to use these instruments for the re-creation of classical, tonal forms, tuning them diatonically to the common c major scale seems rather pointless, although this is the form in which they are often manufactured.[211] So it can be useful to 'de-tune' them by removing bars or by replacing diatonic bars with chromatic additions, thereby producing an original variety of modes which will prompt equally original improvising. These may be of the simple five-note pentatonic variety, or entirely original inventions but however a group chooses to shuffle the bars, the guiding principle can be summed up in three words – *explore, experiment, express*.

Energy Flow – letting the music lead

"If it feels boring, keep doing it" says John Cage. Repetition is the essence of change, I want to add. In building energy in an improvisation, it may be necessary to allow a simple rhythm or riff to have lots of space

---

[211] A remarkable exception to this is the South African township version of Mozart's Magic Flute directed by Mark Dornford-May in 2008 which was (heroically) recreated entirely for xylophones which had to be specially constructed and tuned for the purpose.

to develop and this inevitably means repetition. The change will happen in its own time but meanwhile the group has got used to the idea of energy flow. One of the suggested forms in the following chapter simply involves everyone playing exactly the same pulse together for as long as possible "until the music wants to change". This is one way of creating energy flow: repeating.

A second kind of energy flow comes from passing individual sounds between players, each sounding within their own space. This idea dissipates the energy, as divergent as the previous exercise is convergent. At an extreme from this is the "scribbling" technique where players play as fast as possible and as randomly as possible for as long as possible. Yet, in this case, the energy soon finds its own dynamic, slowing down the playing, creating a need for reflection and greater sensitivity of listening.

In each of these examples, it can be sensed that the flow of energy is dependent both on the general condition of the players, their physical, mental and emotional states and on the structures suggested as soon as the sounds begin. Perhaps the most important aspect rests in allowing the energy to have its own dynamic through which the structure of the music is linked to the volition of the players. There is nothing as frustrating as the drum circle tutor who constantly intervenes just as the group is getting into a groove simply in order to correct a "wayward rhythm" or a rogue pulse. This adherence to 'perfection' can so easily disrupt a deeper principle, the musical truth which is wanting to emerge.

Music has its own life and its own forms, often developing and expanding in surprisingly autonomous ways. In Chapter 4, I was exploring a theory of improvisation which suggests a pathway between unconscious and conscious process. The nearer we are to the unconscious part of this dynamic, the more autonomy the piece will take on. Many times in an improvisation session I have been struck by the extraordinary nature of synchronous musical events – players suddenly plucking exactly the same pitch out of the air, or creating a little flourish at exactly the same time or singing a melodic phrase in perfect unison or harmony. The laws of music are universal so it is therefore unsurprising that when the liminal quality of an event draws us closer to the collective voice, closer to the archetypal source, then events and structures coincide and crystallize.

The group can promote this quality by letting go of conscious control, not being over-concerned about the original game-plan or the correct way of doing it, focussing on listening to each other and to the piece, even in this way allowing their conscious focus to stray from their own playing. If the music itself is to be allowed to lead, this means letting go of ego, understanding that the musical event has a life of its own, a structure with its roots in the autonomous laws of nature, the archetypal source of expression.

Breaking the rules, celebrating error

When a rule is being followed it provides a sense of safety and structure. The concept of a rule in music represents the Apollonian gifts of grace and order: sometimes the muses lead and sometimes they follow but Apollo's instinct is towards strength, balance, continuity and therefore beauty. The rule then becomes a recognisable norm which sits in the conscious aspect and pleases us with its coherence and predictability. Yet this predictability can also easily atrophy into a rule-bound rigidity which runs contrary to the underlying principle of life, which is flux. As Keller puts it (see Chapter 4) "art arises where the arbitrary and the predictable are superseded by unpredictable inevitability".

In the wider sphere of things, breaking the rule is thus akin to the overthrow of the old king (the ruler) whose Saturnian, outmoded behaviour may be standing in the way of inevitable and necessary renewal. In the history of classical music we can see this process very clearly at work through centuries of changes from Byzantine hymns, through to medieval modality, renaissance polyphony, equal temperament, counterpoint, harmony, tonality, chromatic expressionism and so on. The history of jazz provides a condensed pattern of similar development and changes. When rock music exploded into life in the early 1960s, jazz itself seemed to be temporarily toppled and when punk rock emerged in the mid 1970s it seemed in part to be pricking the pretensions of glam and progressive rock which had become too clever and self-observing. In group improvisation, this whole process might be re-enacted on a microcosmic scale, but the same principle applies: a rule is set up, a norm is established and, at a certain point this rule is then broken, or rather, it is quashed only to be instantly replaced by a fresh rule. This kind of transformative process puts us back in the domain of Dionysus.

When it first appears, this new principle, diverging from the norm which has been established and which is now familiar, may be experienced initially as an "error". (Traditionalists frequently bay at new music, non-authentic or non-traditional practice.) But in the theory of the holding form this fresh rule would be latent in the unconscious, appearing at exactly the right moment, just as in those fairy tales where magical animals arrive at critical points in the narrative creating significant transformations. Furthermore, far from being a product of the imagination of a single composer, these new principles are born out of the group unconscious, the whole process taking place in the instant. There is no delay - the moment the new rule pops up it instantly comes into play. We might conclude then that the group is truly connecting to time and the "error" can be celebrated.

Intention and Attention

These two guiding principles, two qualities of presence, are crucial in developing within the improvising group cohesiveness, coherence, identity and creativity. Each exists on a spectrum. Intention describes the degree to which the playing is purposive: at one end of the scale, an individual may simply be coasting, strumming, idling or "noodling"; at the opposite end, they will be deeply embedded in or focussed on the creative improvisation. It is an attitude, a frame of mind and the musical outcome will reflect this as accurately as a barometer reads air pressure. Giving full attention to what is happening means becoming absorbed in the totality of the piece as it emerges. This is not only about listening to others, though that is of course essential; but it is also about listening with the heart as well as the ears. Giving full attention means paying respect to the sounds others are making but also being curious about the emerging structure, conscious of the staging posts in the musical journey. Playing with intention is to make sure everyone else in the group can hear what you are playing. Playing with attention means that you can hear what everyone else is playing. The ideal is for everyone to be able to hear everyone else at the same time.

Entraining, Anchoring, Interacting and Reflecting

However hard one might try, it is virtually impossible to improvise with others and not find coherent structures emerging. In *Search and Reflect*, John Stevens (1987) includes an exercise called "Scribbling" in which small groups are encouraged to improvise freely as fast as possible until one of them stops. I have used this exercise many times with different groups and within a very short space of time the scribbling becomes defined, either by a fixed pulse and a group rhythm or by a quieter, reflective form of playing. Allowing music to have a free rein inevitably creates structure out of chaos. One player starts and this instantly feels like an invitation for others to join in, sometimes playing in identical fashion, at other times complementing. We might think of an improvisation like a conversation in which everyone can talk at once, interacting simultaneously.

Anchoring techniques are an essential part of improvisation. A musical anchor might be a single rhythm or a melodic fragment and it will certainly involve repetition. But the repetitions will naturally produce a need for variation, for change. Anchors are about convergence, variation and divergence and there will be a balance between these in any improvisation. Some pieces begin to run away as soon as they begin, the anchor is raised almost at once and with the wind in the sails the vessels may spin off in different directions. At other times, the group will want to cling to the same pulse, rhythm or melodic phrase for much longer, staying in port or in a safe haven. The way that a group anchors (or not), and the interactive process involved can be extraordinarily revealing and this is very useful in any kind of team building work where the creative decisions may shed significant light on the inner conflicts and decision-making qualities of the team.

Interactions within an improvisation are not simply imitations but *responses* to others' playing and this may at times be realised as a challenging or contrasting idea and at other times as a simple reflection. Sometimes it feels good to be joined on the same notes and rhythms; at other times it is equally satisfying to be in contrast or counterpoint with other players.

Why did you do that?

As players contribute to the group improvising, they may feel that the particular sounds, motives or rhythms they are playing demand a specific response. If this response is not forthcoming or even worse, if they feel that other players are responding in an inappropriate way, cutting across their imaginative horizon, scribbling over their drawing, chopping down their tree, they may feel disappointed, annoyed or angry.

When a piece does not go according to an individual's expectations this may be because the collective will is stronger or it may be that someone else in the group is attempting to control the outcome. Or it might be because the music itself, the initial content, is *autonomously flowing* into certain channels, rather in the way in which a piece of wood or granite will to some extent follow its own laws in the hands of a sculptor. Sometimes, an individual player will chance upon exactly the motive or phrase which the piece is calling out for at that precise moment and then it is likely that others will follow the same path. At other times, a single player will be frustrated because this creative direction is missed by the others. A player whose ego is in control may well want to dominate the piece and this will potentially frustrate the intentions of the rest of them. This kind of dynamic is one of the most valuable aspects of group improvisation and it will be familiar to anyone with experience of group process. The facilitator may need to be skilful in holding the group, allowing for honest reflection and the development of trust.

The Feeling States

Ultimately music is a language of feeling. The feeling states – joy, grief, fear, anger and love are all involved in the way that we make music. As Bach demonstrated frequently, the tightest musical structures may also be carrying the strongest, most contained forms of any of these five generic feelings. Furthermore, music is not one-dimensional: the blues, for example, often wringing joy and compassion out of grief, mixing fear and anger with love. Neither are there any fixed rules. Despite conventional wisdom, minor modes do not automatically carry sadness, any more than major modes are exclusively joyful. Anger may well find a cathartic outlet in drumming and yet will be as easily transformed into joy.

Whatever the exact nature of the feelings which music stimulates, two things seem certain: first, that nothing is fixed; music, moving through time, may chart a whole gamut of emotional expression within a single movement, work or session. Secondly, those creating the music will be changed, they will come out of the process with greater and deeper understanding (even though abstract and wordless) of how emotions work. Music makes us all more emotionally literate.

In Chapter 2, in discussing the presence of Psyche as a musical archetype, I was wanting to emphasise that the one constant in making music, whether improvised or not, is the power it has to make us feel, not necessarily this way or that way, but simply that it raises our capacity to feel. Psyche, as her name tells us, is the soulbird whose wings carry us through time, and through the articulation of time which is music. So the ideas for musical improvisations which follow are all ultimately designed to stimulate, broaden and work with feelings. Whilst some may seem purely structural, others humorous or thematic, or narrative, the purpose is always to allow the inner voice to surface, create space for the inventive genie of the imagination to spark into life and carry the improvisation forwards, downwards, upwards, sideways, around the corner, always surprising, never predictable but ultimately, surely, joyfully.

CHAPTER 8

PATTERNS, PROJECTS AND PIECES

The exercises, games and pieces contained in this final section of the book are designed as *access points* to the Holding Forms which lie, partially hidden, in the musical imagination. The imagination itself is (as Jung observed) the primary resource of the human psyche and its scope and power far exceeds the localised boundaries represented by any of the external forms described here. Therefore it is important to use them simply as keys which open the doors to the playground of the imagination.

The music-making which will hopefully develop spontaneously from these generative starters may in some cases stay close to the original access points; or it may stray far, developing in surprising ways, exploring unpredictable regions of adventure and mystery which could not possibly be predicted at the outset. This will depend on the nature of the group, the relationships between the players, the different levels of confidence and skill, the purpose of the gathering, the context, the spirit of the place, the physical space, the time of day, the day of the week, the season and even perhaps the temperature and the weather. It will also depend to some degree upon the skill of the facilitator in subtly guiding the improvisation, always remaining creatively alert, listening for the piece which *wants to emerge* semi-autonomously from the improvising and providing appropriate musical support whilst not determining too closely the detail. But what cannot be overstated is the importance of not taking any of these generative starters literally. So many hidden factors determine the *unforeseeable outcomes* of an improvisation and therefore, these access points can be thought of as almost arbitrary, a convenience for launching the holding form, which, as described earlier, is more of a shifting sand, an unpredictable dance choreographed by a shape-shifting, mercurial trickster.

In short, they are tools, not rules!

Generally, each generative idea falls into one of three possible types though they are not grouped together as such: type 1 (e.g. "Pulse") is *structural*, a purely musical idea, an abstract musical game or pattern of sounds; type 2 (e.g. "Dropouts") is *relational*, growing out of the game-like interactions between players; and type 3 is *thematic* (e.g. "Bowl of Fruit"), the music emerging from an extra-musical idea or narrative which is then translated into musical form.

Instant Access
30 Improvisation Starters

Time Holes
- Sit in a circle in silence.
- Create time holes by saying "click" and then, after a moment, "stop".
- Anyone in the group can do this but no-one starts a new time hole until the previous one has ended.
- Time holes will vary in length from very short to quite long.
- Each is responsible for the length of their own time hole and how this may impact the rest of the group.
- There is no need do anything within a time hole other than listen.
- End when it feels appropriate and no-one decides to start a new time hole.

Extensions:
- each player makes a single short sound in each time hole.
- (if you do not get your sound in before "stop", simply wait for the next time hole to start).
- each player makes long or short sounds in each hole.
- each player makes a pattern of sounds in each hole.
- fill each time hole with as much sound as possible.
- make each time hole into a mini-composition.

Sound and Silence
- Sit in a circle.
- Everyone plays together drumming on laps.
- At random, any player raises their hands and says "stop".
- After a pause someone restarts.
- When one plays all play...when one stops all stop.

Extensions:
- Acknowledge the player who says "stop" with wiggling fingers (silent applause).
- Use the "stops" to allow players to introduce themselves.
- Do the same exercise in smaller groups – 3 or 4.
- Vary the durations of sound and silence.
- Use instruments instead of lap drumming.

Points in Space
- Sit with instruments in a circle
- Each player attempts to make a single short sound when no-one else in the group is making theirs.
- Wait for a space and place your point (make your sound) in it.
- If you make your sound (by chance) at the same time as someone else give them a nod and a smile.

Extensions:
- Listen out for or intentionally create repeated sequences, the sounds appearing in the same order.
- Try to make as many sounds as possible without colliding.
- Make your sounds longer so that the points begin to join up.
- Create a sense of pulse.
- Make some sounds soft and some loud.

Pulse
- o Using any instruments, all play together at a uniform pulse.
- o Choose a tempo which is about twice the normal pulse rate.
- o Simply sound the pulse together at first without any rhythmic variety.
- o Keep going until changes occur either accidentally or by design. e.g.
    - ...extra sounds in between the pulse...
    - ...doubling tempo...
    - ...creating patterns by leaving silences between the pulses...
    - ...changing the pitch...
    - ...adding vocal sounds...
    - ...making the sounds longer...
- o Follow the patterns as they develop and allow an improvisation to freely emerge.

Beep Beep
- o Sit in a circle and set up a 2+2 pattern with hands (L-L R-R L-L R-R etc.)
- o Add voices (Beep-beep Bap-bap Beep-beep Bap-bap etc.)
- o Make "Beep" low and "Bap" higher.
- o Elongate some of the sounds at random.
- o Add "Billy billy billy billy" (double the tempo) at random.
- o Add silent spaces at random.
- o Introduce instruments gradually.
- o Develop into a free improvisation.

Extensions:
- o Introduce movement – "Beep-beep Bap – bap" jigging from one foot to the other and moving forwards.
- o "Baaaa" opening out the arms in a wide arc.
- o "Billy-billy billy-billy" rotating on the spot.

Circles
- Sit in a circle with instruments.
- Send single sounds around the circle three times.
- Continue sending sounds but in random order.
- Allow this to develop into an interactive improvisation.

Extensions:
- Send single sounds around the circle as fast as possible
- When someone plays two sounds reverse the direction
- "Toss" your sound to someone sitting opposite
- "Toss" the sounds back and forth in pairs

Big Wheel
- Working in pairs, build up the texture by adding one pair at a time, working around the circle until everyone is playing
- Every so often a pair will decide to get off the wheel, i.e. stop playing
- Allow this to create a variety of texture
- Think also about ascending and descending

Rhythmsearch
- Everyone begins playing together.
- Keep playing until everyone comes together on exactly the same rhythm.
- Allow this rhythm to dissolve as players individually follow their own paths.
- Then move together again until all are playing an identical rhythm.
- Repeat this process a number of times.
- Allow the piece to develop into an original improvisation.

Invitations
- One player starts improvising.
- This player then gestures to a second player inviting him or her to join in.
- This new player now invites a third to join in.
- Keep this process going until all are playing together.

Extensions:
- Any player can invite any other player to join in.
- Once an invited player has joined in, the player who made the invitation falls silent until invited back in by another.

Follow me
- Set up a piece so that at any moment, everyone is following a single player.
- Ensure that this player is audible to all, all of the time.

Extensions:
- Follow two or more players.
- Divide into two or more groups with each group following a chosen player in each – all groups play together.

Passing Wave
- Sit in a circle with percussion instruments at the ready.
- One at a time, players raise a hand, making contact with another in the circle.
- With the other hand, they play a short motive.
- The player who receives the wave then passes the wave (and the motive) on to another player.
- Gradually build this idea into an improvisation.

Extensions:
- Develop a free-for-all in which more than one player at a time passes the wave.
- Instead of a wave, make a shape with the hand which the receiver turns into a motive.
- Turn the shape into a movement which uses the whole body.

Dropouts
- Everyone begins playing (randomly) together.
- Gradually, in any order, players fall silent until only one is left playing.
- everyone listens intently to what the "soloist" is playing and then joins in – supporting but not directly imitating.
- Build up the improvisation and then begin the dropouts again.
- Repeat this process until the "piece" come to a natural ending.

Four-three-two-one
- Each player chooses a number between one and four.
- Set a fixed pulse for everyone can follow.
- Each player then improvises using their chosen number to form a pattern of between 1 and 4 sounds, i.e. either 1 or 1-2 or 1-2-3 or 1-2-3-4, each sounding their patterns anywhere within the framework of the pulse.
- Keep this idea going, developing dialogues as players become more aware of each other's patterns.
- Once the flow has been established players begin to change their chosen patterns at will, adding or subtracting sounds.
- The improvisation may end when all converge onto one of the patterns, or when everyone is playing 4s, or whenever it feels appropriate.

Three-four-five
- Divide the group into three: A – B - C
- Group A counts to 3, clapping on 1
- Group B counts to 4, clapping on 1
- Group C counts to 5, clapping on 1
- Now all begin together at the same speed so that, theoretically the claps fall together every 60 beats.
- Try this a few times – it's fun when it works out and everyone stops at 60.
- Repeat this a few times and then allow the piece to continue, developing into a full improvisation.

Extensions:
- o replace the claps with instrumental sounds, pitched and unpitched.
- o count silently.
- o Keep going until the original form dissolves naturally and the piece develops its own structure.
- o Use different counting sets (e.g. combine 5 – 6 – 7 where the claps will fall together after 210 beats!).

Sixes and sevens
- o All count to six over and over.
- o All clap on 1 (or 2 or 3 etc.).
- o Now choose any two consecutive counts and clap on these.
- o Every so often, at random, move forward a count (e.g. if you are clapping on 3-4 move to 4-5).

Extensions:
- o Make a vocal version – instead of 1-2-3-4-5-6 sing doo-da-dee-doo-dee-da using any tones (or perhaps on a dominant seventh arpeggio).
- o Make different harmonies by holding on to some of the tones.
- o Use instruments in place of voices.
- o Divide group into two halves. The first half claps (or plays) on 1 / 3 / 5 / and the second claps (or plays) on 1 / / 4 / /.
- o Let this develop into a free improvisation.

Tuk - Tuk Bobo
- o Divide into two groups.
- o All count to seven over and over.
- o Group 1 chants tuk – tuk on beats 1 and 3.
- o Group 2 chants "bo bo" on beats 5 and 6.
- o Repeat until secure then swap over.
- o Now without pausing move the chants to instruments simultaneously allowing the groups to merge.
- o Improvise with greater and greater freedom.
- o Every so often return to the group chants before allowing them to dissolve again.
- o The improvisation might end with everyone calling out "tuk –tuk bobo!"

Sound Swaps
- Sit in a circle and choose a partner who sits opposite.
- Player one improvises a simple riff or repeated phrase.
- After a short moment, the partner attempts to imitate this.
- Player one then starts a new riff, again passing it to their partners.
- Players three and four join in similar fashion.
- Develop freely.

Add-ons
- Player 1 begins by improvising a simple riff.
- Player 2 responds with the same riff plus an 'add-on'.
- Player 3 responds by adding another extension.
- Players continue to join in until the idea becomes too long to remember at which point whoever is playing starts a new riff.

(N.B. Do not allow the pursuit of accuracy to get in the way of the improvising. Work with the idea but celebrate any 'errors' by ignoring or emphasising them.)

Extensions:
- Players keep going so that all the riffs and 'add-ons' develop and grow on top of each other.
- Work simultaneously in pairs or in threes, adding on to each other's riffs.
- Improvise freely with the idea of 'add-ons' with any player at any time either creating a new riff or responding to another's motive by adding on to it.

Anchors
Anchor 1:
- Everyone plays together an identical motive – this is the anchor.
- One by one, at random, players drift away from the anchor, improvising freely.
- Every so often, all converge back onto the original anchor.

Anchor 2:
- One player creates an anchor (a fixed repeated rhythm or riff).
- The other players improvise freely around this anchor.
- Every so often, the anchoring player abandons their anchor which is then taken up by another player.

Paraphrasing
- o Divide into two or more groups.
- o Group 1 develops an improvisation using add-ons or anchors or another access point.
- o Individual players in group 2 focus on the playing of someone in group 1, recreating what they are playing in their own way.
- o As soon as players in group 1 become aware that group 2 players have taken over, they slowly fade out.
- o Group 3 then responds to group 3 in exactly the same way, gradually taking over.
- o When the final group is playing, all the other groups join in, developing the piece into a full improvisation.

Duos Trios and Quartets
- o Sit in a circle.
- o Player one starts improvising.
- o Player two joins in.
- o When player three enters, player one stops.
- o Continue around the circle in similar fashion playing in duos.
- o Next time around play in trios (i.e. when player four joins in, player one stops etc.).
- o Then in quartets.
- o Continue in quartets or simply allow the piece to develop into an open improvisation.

Duologues
- o Begin with two players having a musical conversation.
- o Question and answer.
- o Then overlapping.
- o Other players listen carefully then add responses to the responses.
- o Build into a full improvisation.
- o Either end with everyone playing or reduce back to the original duo.

Quintets
- All start playing together.
- Reduce the texture so that only five players are sounding together at any given moment.
- If less than five seem to be playing, there is room to join in; if more than five seem to be playing, then drop out.
- Work with the idea of this without allowing need for accuracy to inhibit the improvising.

Drip and Flow
- Players sit in a circle.
- Send a single short sound slowly around the circle.
- Second time around, each play two sounds, then three, then four and so on until the sounds are all overlapping, flowing into each other.

Extensions:
- Begin as before.
- Gradually increase the tempo until all the sounds flow into each other.
- Sit or stand randomly spaced in the room and drip and flow in any order.

River of Sound
This improvisation develops around two concepts – 1) widely spaced or sustained sounds/rhythms and 2) closely spaced or faster moving sounds/rhythms
- Begin by using tones pitched very closely together.
- Enter one at a time playing at a steady pace with fixed pulse.
- Keep the piece flowing.
- Gradually widen the spaces between the pitches and broaden the lengths of the notes or the silences between the notes.
- Keep the tempo even.
- Gradually mix the two sound concepts together so that each player chooses to play either sustained sounds or faster moving sounds.
- Widen the spacing between tones more and more towards an ending of stillness and silence.

Extensions:
- o Divide into two groups facing each other, one group sustaining and the other moving.
- o All start playing together but when one player from either group decides to swap from sustaining to moving or vice versa then everyone swaps.
- o Allow this swapping to develop into a freely improvised piece.

Soundbath

Method
- o One participant sits or lies down in the middle of the circle while the others improvise.
- o The improvisers may stop every so often to enquire how the music is impacting whoever is in the centre. It may be too loud, too soft, too fast or too slow, too hot or too cold and so on.
- o The "soundbather" may request modifications to the playing.

Extensions:
- o Improvisers try to judge or intuit the effect the music might be having on the bather.
- o The bather chooses someone in the circle, either in the middle of a piece or between improvisations, to take their place in the centre.
- o More than one sit in the centre.

Clock and Clouds

- o Begin with clocks – mechanical, interlocking "tick-tock" rhythms.
- o Maintain a strict pulse.
- o Leave plenty of spaces so that the rhythms follow and overlap.
- o One at a time, players begin to fill in the spaces with more sounds.
- o Keep this process going until the pulse dissolves and the whole sound becomes "cloudy".
- o Return slowly to the clocks mode.

Extensions:
- o Divide the group into two.
- o One half plays clocks, the other clouds.
- o Every so often swap around.

Conduction

(This idea is based on the work of American improvising musician, Butch Morris, who dissolves the hierarchical approach to music-making by conflating the roles of composer, conductor and musician. Performers become composers, conductors become performers, performers become conductors, all taking an equal share in the process of creating musical forms, responding, rather than directing.)

- o Choose a conductor.
- o Players sit in a semi-circle.
- o The "conductor" stands in front of the group and responds to what they are improvising with a wide variety of gestures.
- o The improvisation then becomes a co-creation between conductor (who follows the lead of the players) and the players who cue the conductor.
- o Always try to follow the direction in which the music wants to go.
- o Should the conductor display symptoms of control freakery, the players can become rebellious!
- o At any point, a player may stand up and replace the conductor who then sits down and becomes a player.

Waterfalls

Method
- o You can either BE the waterfall – playing notes which cascade downwards.
- o or stand beneath the waterfall – playing rapid notes which repeat at the same pitch.
- o whichever you choose to be, make the sounds continuous and relentless.

Extensions:
- o make small waterfalls using very quiet sounds.
- o make large waterfalls using loud and deep tones.
- o make "cataracts", all using tones very close together in pitch.
- o make "niagaras" using tones which are widely spaced in pitch.

Forest and Plain

Method
- o All play together as quickly as possible, trying to create a dense carpet of sound (forest).
- o Now play very slowly, long sustained or slowly repeated tones using voices or instruments (plain).
- o Create an improvisation which moves freely and spontaneously between these two poles.

Extensions:
- o Divide the group into two halves, one half 'forest' and the other 'plain'. Then alternate freely between the two.
- o Each player decides for him/herself whether to be 'forest' or 'plain'.

Voicework

We all possess voices which can function in many different ways, employing a rich variety of expressive tones and textures, each of which carries its own individual and collective meaning. One of the pioneers of the human voice in the 20th Century was Alfred Wolfsohn whose own journey into voice was a form of self-healing. Having suffered deep trauma in the trenches of World War 1 during which time he was exposed to sound of the human voice *in extremis* Wolfsohn re-visited these cries and calls for mercy, uncovering the full range of pitch and texture of which the human voice is capable. His disciples included actors such as Roy Hart whose theatre company pioneered the extended use of voice. His legacy has also been a significant influence on the development of voice therapy, particularly through the work of Paul Newham. These pioneers take account both of the extraordinary untapped expressive potential of the voice and its capacity to open up the individual and heal the psyche.

The expansion of interest in World Music in recent decades has opened people's ears to styles of singing which were either totally unfamiliar or regarded as exotic or even "wrong". The standard form of singing in Europe, which is still generally taught to students of voice, is the "bel canto" or operatic style. Whilst a powerful and rich style in its own right, it is however only one way of using the voice and largely inappropriate for any style of music other than the operas, oratorios, cantatas and art songs for which it was designed. More recently, organisations such as the Natural Voice Practitioners Network[212] have been actively promoting a much wider and more eclectic approach to singing. Many people who might have been put off singing when they were young are gradually coming back to it through community choirs which do not focus solely on the oratorio tradition or else replace it entirely with styles which derive from all parts of the globe and a wide range of styles and genres.

So the approach here advocates an open approach, not rejecting anything but, above all, taking account of the individuality of each person's vocal texture. The natural voice is like a sonic fingerprint, unique to each one of us and revealing the depth of soul of which each of us is capable.

Warm-ups – Stretching, Breathing and Toning

- Gather energy from the ground as if scooping it up with your arms. Breathe IN
- Reach upwards with both arms stretched as if holding up the sky. Breathe OUT
- Gather energy again. Breathe IN
- Now stretch to the side – right arm outstretched, left arm pulled back. Breathe OUT
- Same in reverse.
- Scoop up the energy. Breathe IN
- One arm stretched to the sky, the other to the ground. Breathe OUT
- Same in reverse.
- Scoop up the energy. Breathe IN
- Stretch both arms upwards, outwards and behind the body to the right. Breathe OUT
- Same to the left.
- Now repeat all or any of the above but allow the voice to sound on any tone or pitch each time you exhale. Sustain tones all the way to the end of the out breath if possible.
- Create an improvisation with everyone stretching and toning in their own way but mindful of what everyone else is doing.

---

212 www.naturalvoice.net.

Intoning

After warming up, work up through the vowels with long tones on each vowel in the following order

>...ooo (as in pool)
>...oh (as in song)
>...aah (as in far)
>...ah (as in clan)
>...eh (as in wed)
>...i (as in tea)

- Improvise for ten minutes with these vowel tones, using full outbreaths.
- If possible move around the space slowly, listening and attuning with each other.
- Come to rest on a single chord before starting the attuning process again.

Attuning

- Freely sound long tones together.
- Listen to each other and allow harmonies to appear spontaneously.
- Experiment with different vowel sounds.
- Try different positions, e.g. back to back, lying on the floor.
- With closed eyes or blindfolds.
- In the dark.

Communing

(this works best in a large resonant space such as a chapel or large hall)

- Each finds their own space at the perimeters of the hall or chapel
- Each sounds their own note in their own way – long tones, each tone taking a full outbreath: use any vowel, any pitch
- Everyone now slowly moves from the perimeter to the centre gradually converging onto a single pitch or harmony and a single vowel (ah)
- Move gradually back towards the perimeter sounding a different tone with each step.
- End with everyone sounding their own tones.

Humming and Babbling
- All sound together on any note - keeping lips slightly parted.
- Each breathing at their own pace, change pitch with each new breath (when changing pitch begin the tone with a consonant such as 'd' or 'b' or 'm' or 'l').
- At a given signal change to a new pitch in the middle of each breath.
- Then three pitches per breath, then four and so on until everyone is "babbling".
- Reverse the process, slowing down the changes until everyone is again humming together.

Me-you
- Sustain the sound of "me" over a whole outbreath.
- Sustain the sound of "you" in the same way.
- Now move very gradually from the sound of "me" to the sound of "you" using a whole outbreath.
- Listen for the harmonics (overtones) which cascade downwards during the transition from "me" to "you". These will become stronger with each repetition.

Hoo He
- Stand in a circle and create a group pulse by gently stamping the feet in time with each other or by tapping with two fingers on palms (around two per second or 120 bpm)
- Sound "hoo" on each stamp/tap, creating a pulsating and regular "hoo hoo hoo hoo hoo"
- Individually and randomly add "hes" in the spaces between the "hoos", e.g. hoo hoo hoo hoo-he hoo hoo hoo hoo hoo-he hoo etc.
- Make the he a high note and the hoo a middle pitched note
- Gradually add instruments and develop into a free improvisation

Chanting

- Begin by chanting any of the chants or texts offered below (or make up your own).
- All begin together, starting softly and slowly.
- Experiment with different rhythms around the same vowels or texts.
- Allow pitches to appear naturally then emphasise them.
- Add a drone perhaps, using singing bowl or voices.
- Add a beat from a frame drum and perhaps a bell.
- Keep time if necessary with both hands together gently on laps.

Naio naio / naio naio / naio - nai / aaaa (in 2)
Dooway dooway - - / dooway dooway - - (in 3)
Sala sala saio sala / sala sala saio sala (in 4)
Ma mana-mana maa - - / ma mana-mana maa - - (in 6)
Dum – dum – dumbara / dum – dum – dumbara (in 7)
Kyrie Eleison
Amor vincit omnia
B was a bat
who slept all day
And fluttered about
when the sun went away
Brown little bat...brown little bat etc.
(Edward Lear)

Stepping Tones

- Divide the group into two halves.
- Stand facing each other about 15 feet apart.
- All begin toning together, each allowing a full breath for each long tone.
- Slowly move towards each other and with each footstep, change to another pitch.
- Cross in the middle until the two lines have exchanged places completely.
- Then move back again in the same fashion.
- Move in any direction, freely changing pitches.
- Build to a climax before returning to the original formation or simply allow a freely improvised vocal piece to find its own route and its own destination.

Yoiking

This is a style of singing from northern Europe which is characterised by pentatonic melody, rhythmic vitality and singing from the back of the throat. Use the syllables "lo" "lay" and "la" sometimes interspersed with breathing sounds (huh).

A single voice can set up the basic phrase and then all join in. Develop improvisations around the original yoik by overlapping, holding on to some notes, repeating parts of the yoik, developing drones, adding drums and woodblocks etc. Here are some suggested starters:

Yoik 1

Yoik 2

Yoik 3

Yoik 4

Billy-doo-dap

- o Set a pulse by clapping or stamping
- o Vocalise with scat rhythms
- o Improvise freely
- o Here are some starters:

Billy doo dap - / Billy doo dap - / Billy doo dap doo / dap doo daa - / etc.

Billy doo dap doo da / billy doo dap doo - /
Billy doo dap doo da / billy doo dap doo - /

Bap dodap dap bap dodap - / bap dodap dap bap dodap -/ etc.

Bap – dap – / billy billy doo dap / Bap – dap – / billy billy doo - / etc.

- o Chant these together to start with, simply repeating over and over.
- o Then begin to play with the vocal sounds, repeating some, sustaining others.
- o Add more harmonies and new melodic riffs, building up a chorus of chanting rhythms.
- o Slowly introduce instruments if desired and open up into a free improvisation.

Hum-drum
- Each chooses a drum or non-pitched percussion instrument.
- Set a pulse and improvise freely together.
- Gradually each begins to hum softly without stopping playing.
- Develop the hum into a rhythmic chant.
- As the chanting gets louder the drumming fades out until all are chanting together.
- After a few moments, bring the drums back in and the process starts over again.

Water water
- Divide the group into three.
- Allocate to each group one of the following phrases:

You never miss the water 'til the well runs dry
All the rivers run into the sea
Water water everywhere nor any drop to drink

- Disperse randomly around the workshop space.
- All begin chanting together the given phrases.
- Gradually form into groups around each phrase and continue chanting.
- Develop improvisations by playing with the words in a multitude of different ways – repetitions, elongations, slow motion, fast motion, on a monotone, using lots of tones etc.
- Using "paraphrasing" (see above), where one group at a time leads the improvising around one of the phrases and the others gradually join in.

Extensions:
- Develop one long improvisation with all four phrases simultaneously.
- Introduce instruments to accompany or replace the vocal improvisations.

Seven Tones
- o All begin together by toning on their own individual pitches.
- o At the sound of a bell, or similar, all converge onto a single pitch.
- o Then at the next signal, diverge onto a consonant harmony.
- o Then to a dissonant harmony.
- o Back to consonance.
- o To single pitch.
- o Finally return to individual pitches.

Themed Approaches

Translating concrete ideas and images into music will be unsatisfactory if interpretation is too literal. Music is abstract and although concrete images can be enriched by musical expression, pure musical description will lead to at best a kind of cartoon music and at worst, sound effects. So begin by talking through the qualities or attributes of the image or narrative and then follow this up by discussing the feeling states which attach to these qualities, whether happy or sad, fearful or angry or loving. Then think about the purely musical qualities which attach to these feeling states: fast or slow, high or low, loud or soft and so on. Then begin improvising without any specific preparation. Once the music starts, focus as closely as possible on the music itself, the rhythms and tones, tempi and textures and allow the images or narratives to float to the back of the mind.

Bowl of Fruit
Attributes: variety of colours and shapes – various sizes - different tastes and smells.
Feeling states: happiness – sensuality.
Sounds:
- o Contrasts of pitch and tempo.
- o A mix of light and heavy, loud and soft.
- o Brisk tempo and jaunty rhythms.
- o Playful interactions.

The Sea and the Sky
Attributes: wide open spaces – wind and waves – sun and clouds
Feeling states: sense of wonder – physical energy
Sounds:
- o Long sustained tones.
- o Slowly moving.
- o Gradual crescendo and diminuendo.
- o Rising and falling melody.

Poppy Fields
Attributes: single colour – thousands of heads – waving in wind
Feeling states: fragility – lightness – sadness
Sounds:
- o Lots of small melodic cells.
- o Fast tempo.
- o Rhythmic repetitions.
- o Slower melody emerging below or beneath.
- o Perhaps add long vocal harmonies.

Conflict and Resolution
Attributes: opposing states of feeling – a narrative which moves from tension and difference to calm and peace.
Feeling states: anxiety and calm
- o Work with the two feeling states – anxiety and calm.
- o Each player decides individually (without saying) which feeling state they will work with.
- o All begin improvising together.
- o As soon as any player notices someone playing from the opposite feeling state they move to this mode of playing.
- o Maintain this process for some time.
- o Then slowly, all move towards the state of calm.

The Descent of Orpheus

Create a musical narrative which moves through the full range of the feeling states which colour the Orpheus myth.

    The wedding - Joy...happiness...sun...warmth.
    The death of Eurydice - Grief...sadness...rain...cold.
    The journey to Hades – fear...danger...weariness.
    The supplication – pleading...humility.
    The return – hope...
    The fateful glance – loss...pain.
    The epilogue – reflection...love...the final song.

Idiomatic starters

These projects are based on specific idioms. Although some titles might appear tongue-in-cheek, each also has behind it a serious intention. The idea is not to create a faithful replica or authentic reproduction of the compositions, styles or genres suggested by the source but rather, by entering into the *spirit* of the original to create a springboard for lively and original improvisation, to *improvise with the idea of* Bach or Blues or Boogie.

Bach in the bath

Bach was incurably creative and music poured out of him like water from a tap. He was certainly capable of composing whilst lying in the bath (if he had one) as he was also very domestic, fathering twenty children. People came from far and wide to hear him improvise on the organ, though his improvisations were of course based upon the rules of harmony and counterpoint over which he had complete mastery. This project does not demand any precise knowledge of harmony though it will inevitably produce a free counterpoint and some form of harmony will inevitably result from this.

Method
    o Begin with voices but have instruments available.
    o One person begins by "scatting" vigorously using dynamic,

repeated rhythmic/melodic motifs descending or ascending in sequences.

e.g. Doo dooby dooby dooby / dup dup daa /
Doo dooby dooby dooby / dup dup daa (a tone lower).
- o Others join in a similar vein, concentrating on keeping the energy flowing and the rhythm steady.
- o Once the vocal improvising is in full swing, add instruments (pitched or unpitched) one at a time until all are playing freely together.
- o Without interrupting the flow, try different combinations – duets, trios, quartets and so on.

Extensions:
- o Try improvising over a "ground bass" or repeated bass riff.
- o One player "solos" whilst the rest keep up a simple pulse.

Beethoven in the oven

What characterises Beethoven's music? Seriousness of purpose? Dynamic forward movement? Lyrical depth? Teutonic formality? We could take any one of these, or all of them and improvise with the idea, the sense of the man. Beethoven challenged conventions. He was also a great improviser, capable of moving people to tears with his instant compositions. He was also an obsessive who worked at his ideas until the essence, the prime reality was achieved. He literally cooked them! (Well, not literally.)

Method

In this improvisation, participants are encouraged to find a motive or a riff to play with – choose one from the group. When going through this process of choice, you might consider deciding which one gets the most votes and then abandon this in favour of the one that gets the least. (It's just a thought...often it is the least significant motive in a Beethoven composition which becomes the guiding force.)

Whatever your choice of material, work this idea "into the ground": stay with it, play with it, repeat it, even until it feels boring and then repeat it again, allowing the transformations to appear spontaneously (as they certainly will) and, when the piece feels as if it ready to end, emphasise the finality.

Mozart in the bedroom

Mozart's music can be highly sensuous and erotically playful. The string quintets, for example, and the operas *Cosi fan Tutti* and *Marriage of Figaro* contain some of the most sensually charged music ever created.
Method
- o Divide the group into pairs.
- o Each pair sits back to back.
- o One partner from each pair begins playing, inviting the other to join them.
- o Everyone then plays together for some minutes allowing the improvisation to grow and develop.
- o At a given signal (e.g. bell or horn) one half of each pair moves up one so that new couples are formed.
- o Repeat this process until the original couples are re-united.

What Did William Tell?

How many of us became familiar with the music of Rossini as children watching "The Lone Ranger" in black and white? Anyone who, inspired by the gallop of the opening titles, went out to buy the LP might have been (pleasantly) surprised to discover that, well before the masked rider mounted his steed, we could hear a ravishing cello melody, a thoroughly bracing storm and a melody on the cor anglais to rival the newest of new world symphonies!

The game-plan for this improvisation is to choose any musical theme recalled from childhood (TV, film or otherwise) and to use whatever rhythms, melodies or motives which might remain lodged in the memory as the basic material for an improvisation.
- o Choose any piece (it does not have to be the Lone Ranger) which everyone in the group can recall hearing.
- o Either all begin together, improvising with confidence, or
- o Allow fragments and motives from this piece to emerge tentatively,
- o Play freely with the sounds in whatever order they come out.

(Remember that the idea is not to produce a replica of the music itself but to use the recalled material purely as creative starters for entirely original music.)
- o Do not reject ANYTHING. Honour EVERYTHING. Re-enter your childhood.

Boogie

'Boogie-woogie' as most will know is a specific style of piano playing characterised by a relentlessly repeated "jogging" rhythm in the left hand and repeated swinging melodies or syncopated chords in the right. Apparently the style was invented by a barrel house pianist called "Pinetop Smith" who used to pepper his playing with invitations for people to dance with reckless abandon. Some say that on the night before he was stabbed to death in a pub brawl he drew his room-mate, Albert Ayler, to his side and whispered in his ear, "Albert, you have to learn my boogie-woogie!"

Method
- o Start with drums, wood-blocks and shakers. Set up a basic boogie rhythm, "slow and mean" – choo-ka choo-ka choo-ka choo-ka and keep this going throughout as an anchor.
- o Other instruments now improvise over this anchor, maybe trying (unsuccessfully) to disrupt its progress.
- o Every so often everyone stops to allow one player to interject a brief solo.
- o Then the rhythm starts up again.

Remember, as previously, that the aim is not to recreate the "boogie-woogie" idiom but to use the *idea* of boogie to generate improvisation.

Minimode

Minimalism appeared in contemporary classical music during the nineteen sixties as a welcome antidote to the strict serialism and hyper-modernism of the post war avant-garde, crossing boundaries between styles and appealing equally to rock, jazz and classical audiences. It provides a useful platform for improvisation.

- o Everyone starts playing together on a single, moderately fast but comfortable pulse – pitched instruments using only one note to start with.
- o Make spaces in the pulse wherever and whenever it feels necessary or comfortable – this will create natural rhythm.
- o One at a time or in pairs get louder, emerging from the texture, and then softer again, retreating back into the overall sound.
- o Expand the range of pitches being played, but gradually, like taking cautious steps out and then back again.
- o Imitate instrumental sounds with vocal additions.

- o Allow the texture to dwindle to single players or singers before filling out again.
- o Continue making small alterations or developments to the repeated rhythms.
- o Add chords on keyboard or guitar using any combinations of pitches already being used.
- o Develop into a freely improvised piece.

Lifemusic Through the Seasons

6 projects for seasonal use

The underlying, archetypal patterns of time: the deep, rumbling rhythms of the cycles which come to us from the moving spheres, provide a natural canvas for *Lifemusic* improvising. Each stage of the annual cycle has its own potential music. The projects outlined here do not draw directly on existing festivals, whether Christian or pagan, although there may be hints of both. Rather, the themes are based upon what, for most people, will be a natural cycle of feelings connected to the weather, the changing quality of light and heat as the sun draws its arcs and the almost hidden traces of how we once responded to these before central heating and all year round strawberries caused us to forget!

Once the improvising group has worked through some of the earlier exercises and games, a few simple descriptive ideas should be sufficient to generate pieces which may last up to an hour. The following forms are only suggestions. The aim is simply to create freshly-minted music out of the spirit of time.

Returning (January/February)

Myths of returning abound – Orpheus from the dark, Ulysses from the great adventure of life and Jason, triumphant with the fleece. My favourite is of the little boy who disliked eating bread. He leaves home to seek his fortune in distant lands, becoming rich and successful, eating his fill of meat until, one day, he wakes with an unquenchable longing for bread and travels back home where he receives a rapturous welcome.

This particular return, the beginning of the calendar, is from point zero (the week of the winter solstice when time seems to stop altogether)

towards new light and new resolve. If we care to become time-wise and sound-wise, the music here might be expected to take on qualities of stillness followed by a gradual opening outwards.
- o Slow steady pulsating rhythm...
- o long connecting tones...
- o sustained vocal harmonies...
- o space and stillness...
- o vocal and instrumental togetherness...
- o footsteps...
- o a gradual crescendo...

Renewal (March/April)

At the Spring equinox the considerable drama of change, transformation and rebirth is often played out in the weather: light and dark, sunshine and showers, a chill breeze but a warm sun, when it appears. There is a sense of things breaking open (ice, eggs, blossom) sometimes suddenly.

The theme of renewal goes to the very core of musical mythology, with Dionysus more in attendance now perhaps than at any other time of the year. In his narratives we find themes of transformation, a bursting forth of primal energy but also death and resurrection, making Dionysus a prototype of the Christ figure and early Spring the moment when this dramatic theme harmonises with nature. Orpheus is also present as the prototypical musician in nature –

> *"'Tis Nature's voice. We hear, and straight we grieve, rejoice and love".*   *(according to Nahum Tate)*[213]

Renewal means a resurgence of life energy, bursting with creative ideas,
- o New growth - a gradual unfolding of melodic and rhythmic ideas gradually piled one upon the other.
- o Contrasts – high and low, loud and soft, solo and tutti, slow and fast.
- o A ritual process – a relentless pulse, the whole "tribe" sounding together.
- o Raw energy – a wild dance full of rushing and gushing tones and rhythms.
- o A moment of silence – followed by long vocal chords.
- o A blessing - bell and rattle.
- o Another wild dance with drums, chanting, calling and "yoiking".

---

213 From the text for Purcell's *Ode on St. Cecilia's Day* (1692). Number 4.

Garlanding (May/June)

In earlier times, garlanding was a festival of flowers which celebrated the high point of Spring and the beginning of Summer. Garlands were exchanged between lovers and appeared as crowns. Public spaces were festooned with blossom and petals were freely strewn on paths and lawns.

A time for enjoyment and enjoinment...garlanding suggests also (re)connecting to each other.

- o The circle ritual, an image of bonding and togetherness, sounds passed around the circle, building up a group rhythm and an interweaving of melody.
- o A garland is also an offering from one to another – a simple way of honouring someone by offering a ring of flowers. Shared sounds, tone and echo, call and response.
- o A circle dance. A dance of life. Two circles moving in opposite directions, the inner circle using voice, the outer circle using hand held instruments – shakers, rattles, small drums, flutes, ocarinas, even horns or trumpets. Allow the movements to generate the improvising – do not forget to look at each other.
- o Spiralling – pass sounds and motifs in this order around the circle – 1-3-2-4-3-5-4-6 etc.
- o Spinning - make processions of sound...one begins and others join in one at a time until there is a glorious cascade.
- o Improvise with the rhythms and melodies which grow from these words:

Spring, the sweet sweet spring,
When all is blossoming
then let's go garlanding.

Summer Revels (July/August)

High summer provides a kind of plateau in our connection to time. In contrast to the winter solstice, when time seems to stop altogether, the summer solstice broadens out our sense of time to the point where, for a moment, we might sense eternity. Even when the weather is not ideal, the longer days seem to encourage us to move at a slower pace (though busy people with deadlines to meet will inevitably ignore this). In the north of Europe, where night and day blend into each other, we might stay present with the whole passage of time through midnight when the sun still hovers on the horizon and the light seems endless. As the solstice passes, we enter a period of rest so it is no accident that, in Europe at least, this has become a time for vacations.

- o Slowly moving vocal or instrumental motives, moving by step.
- o Improvise separate musical ideas which then join up to form a slow, single, long trail of sound.
- o Use voices and instruments to form slowly changing harmonies – use the full range of vowels and overtones.
- o A steady drum beat builds up the energy.
- o Keep building and rising until the whole improvisation turns into a midsummer dance of the sun.

Perhaps incorporate this chant for midsummer which can be accompanied by drones using just the black notes of a keyboard or piano:

Feel the heat of the midsummer sun
(Gently warming)
Feel the heat of the midsummer sun
(Through the night)

Hear the song of the midsummer wind
(Gently blowing)
Hear the song of the midsummer wind
(Blow wind blow)

Follow the track of the midsummer sun
(Gently glowing)
Follow the track of the midsummer sun
(Warm and slow)

Feel the strength of the midsummer wind
(Gently holding)
Feel the strength of the midsummer wind
(Blow wind blow)

Gathering In (September/October)

As daylight begins to dwindle we slowly become once again aware of the inexorable movement of time. The evenings also become cooler and, even in the cities, we begin to smell the closing in and the decay of natural growth. Thus, three primary senses – sight, feeling, smell – work on our moods reminding us that it is time to gather in. Rural communities, even today, will be harvesting. Urban communities will be re-gathering after vacations and looking towards new plans, new curricula, new timetables. People come together with purpose.

o   Improvise with steady, purposeful rhythms.
o   Allow melodic riffs to grow from the rhythms, forward moving but not wild.
o   Reduce the texture so that only 2 or 3 are playing together at any time.
o   Then gather in again so that all are playing similar rhythms and riffs.
o   Perhaps allow a single vocal chant to emerge from the improvising – eventually converging onto a single long tone or chord.

Sacrifice (November/December)

Why "Sacrifice"? In my understanding of the idea of sacrifice there is always an element of deepening our relationship to life and to our own understanding of ourselves: making things sacred. This can only be achieved, according to many traditions, including contemporary thinking, through some kind of descent. Transformations take place in the deepest recesses of the self and of the imagination, the places perhaps where our own music vibrates in resonance with the archetypes.

In the myths surrounding Orpheus, he descends to Hades in order to retrieve his lost soul, the image of his deepest Self. This journey is only made possible through music. It is a journey of grief, but also of joy; of despair, but also of hope; of rage, of fear but, in the end, of love. It is a journey we all make, I believe, when our hearts are in need, when we suffer loss, when we hope for the fulfilment of our dreams, when we seek truth and when we summon up our inner resources to overcome adversity, or our own demons.

This is perhaps, what Orpheus tells us.
o Improvise with the voice, the drum, the shaman's rattle and with guitar or lyre or piano.
o A slow deep beat, like the heart.
o Long, soft vocal tones.
o Allow for a single tone on each breath, then two tones, then three, until an interweaving of vocal melody, anchored by the drumbeat, emerges from the deep space of the heart.
o Slowly add rattles, bells and perhaps slowly changing modal chords on piano.
o Allow the music to breathe and open up spaces.
o Let it flow where it will.

Turning Point - celebration, community and the mystery of the carol

As we approach the turning point of the calendar it is natural to celebrate the year which is about to end, condensing experience into a single, symbolic event. Celebration may be as much about reflecting on the meaning of things as it is about partying. In this process we may be balancing those aspects of life which have been enriching with those which have been challenging. Music carries within its structures a natural balancing order and this will be reflected in improvisation.

More importantly, perhaps, the turning of the year finally brings our relationship with *time* into sharp focus. The winter solstice, with its long night, reduces our sense of time to zero. We have a heightened sense of past and future, often saying things such as "I'll catch up with you in the new year", or, we'll try and get it done before Christmas."

This moment when time seems to stop and then restart is usually nowadays extended to a week, as if we cannot bear to let it go. The mystery of the carol rests in the quality of this liminal period - those special songs which feel totally inappropriate should we hear them sung at any other time of the year – the last true remaining example of musical taboo in our all-too-rational culture? I return now to my own definition of music as "intentional time". Let us embrace this sense of purposeful sounding energy which emerges spontaneously and, I hope, finally, joyfully, through *Lifemusic*.

- o Sing together through any remembered carol.
- o Between each verse keep the pulse of the melody alive on a drum, woodblock or bell.
- o Decorate the pulse with vocal and instrumental improvising, rather like the musical equivalent of decorating a tree.
- o After the final verse, sustain the notes and rhythms and allow the improvisation to continue until the energy is spent.

```
L    Let
I      Intuitive
F        Feeling
E          Enfold
M            My
U              Unique
S                Soul
I                  In
C                     Communitas
```

POSTLUDE

Lifemusic in Action (CD)

The accompanying CD provides a glimpse into a *Lifemusic* session through 14 tracks, recorded as a single session without any rehearsal or prior preparation. The group is made up of a mix of trained musicians and untrained musicians some of whom have attended the *Lifemusic* training programme. With one exception (track 6) the starting points used on the day of the recording were chosen from those described in Chapter 8 and are therefore intended to provide an authentic flavour of what kind of results can be achieved by musicians playing together in this manner though no session is ever typical. During the lunch break two of the group began "noodling" freely with instruments and voices and the others joined in. Half way through, we turned on the recording equipment in order to capture what became one of the most spontaneous and affecting pieces of the day. Some players used their own (specialised) instruments, such as oboe, piano, bassoon and horn and all had the use of a large range of "instant access" instruments, tuned and untuned percussion from all corners of the world. Many of the pieces were too long to be included in their entirety so each track has been edited in order to demonstrate as far as possible how the initial idea for each improvisation develops and expands in such a way that, whilst never disappearing altogether, it recedes into the background to be replaced by the piece which "wants to emerge".

List of Participants

Alison Woodward – bassoon and voice
Alison Mawdsley – percussion and voice
Anna Clarke – drums, Vietnamese bamboo xylophone and voice
Chris North – conga drums, tuned percussion and voice
Mike Fry – keyboard, percussion and voice
Petra Klimesova – tuned and untuned percussion and voice
Suzie Shrubb – oboe, piano, voice
Vita Fojtu – tuned and untuned percussion, violin and voice

Tracks

1.	Points in Space	5:10
2.	Pulse	4:08
3.	Circles	2.57
4.	Big Wheel	3:27
5.	Dropouts	5:35
6.	Free Improvisation	5:51
7.	3-4-5	6:12
8.	Anchors	3:59
9.	Attuning	3:02
10.	Me-You & Hoo-Hee	4:20
11.	Yoik 1	3:10
12.	'B' Was a Bat	7:24
13.	Bach in the Bath	5:04
14.	Summer Revels	11:57

BIBLIOGRAPHY

Achterberg, Jean (1987), The Shaman: Master Healer in the Imaginary Realm. In *Shamanism* (ed. Nicholson). Quest Books, Wheaton, Illinois.
Alvin, Juliet (1975), *Music Therapy*. Hutchinson, London.
Ansdell, Gary (1995), *Music for Life*. 1995. Jessica Kingsley, London.
Attali, Jacques (1988), *Noise – the political economy of music*. Manchester University Press, Manchester.
Bailey, Derek (1992), *Improvisation: its nature and practice in music*. British Library National Sound Archive, London.
Bartal Leah and Ne'eman Nira (1993), *The Metaphoric Body*. Jessica Kingsley, London.
Bentley, Arnold (1966), *Musical Ability in Children and its Testing*. Novello, London.
Berendt, J. E, (1993), *Nada Brahma. The World is Sound*. Element Books, Dorset.
Bergson, Henri (1994), *Matter and Memory*, tr., N.M. Paul and W.S. Palmer. Zone Books, New York.
Blanning, T.C.W. (2002), *The Culture of Power and the Power of Culture*. Oxford University Press, Oxford.
Blanning, Tim (2008), *The Triumph of Music*. Penguin Books, London.
Bruscia, K. (1987), *Improvisational Models of Music Therapy*. Springfield, Illinois.
Bullfinch, Thomas (1913), *The Age of Fable*. Ed. Bryan Holme (1995), Penguin Books, London and New York. Online http://www.bartleby.com
Chernoff, John Miller (1979), *African Rhythm African Sensibility: Aesthetics amd Social Action in African Musical Idioms*. Chicago University Press.
Cooper, Lyz (2009), *Sounding the Mind of God*. O Books, Ropley.
Copper, Bob (1971), *A Song for Every Season: 100 years in the Life of a Sussex Farming Family*. Heinemann, London.
Cox, Murray and Theilgaard, Alice (1987/1997), *Mutative Metaphors in Psychotherapy*. Tavistock Publications, Jessica Kingsley, London.
Davie, Alan (1997) *Towards a Philosophy of Creativity*. University of Brighton.

Dean, Roger (1989), *Creative Improvisation*. Open University Press, Milton Keynes.
Durant, Alan (1989), *Conditions of Music*. Albany Books, State University, New York.
Evan Eisenberg (1987), *The Recording Angel*. Picador Books, London.
Everitt, Anthony (1997), *Joining In, An Investigation into Participatory Music*. Gulbenkian Foundation. London.
Finnegan, Ruth (1989), *The Hidden Musicians. Music-making in an English Town*. Revised edition c 2007 by Wesleyan University Press.
Geelhaar, Christian (1974), *Paul Klee, Leben und Werk*. M. DuMont Schauberg, Koln.
Hamel, Peter Michael (1978), *Through Music to the Self*. Element Books, Dorset.
Harner, Michael (1980/1990), *The Way of the Shaman*. Harper and Row, New York.
Hegi, Fritz (1986), *Improvisation und Musiktherapie*. Junferman Verlag, Paderborn.
Hillman, J. (1981), *Alchemical Blue and the Unio Mentalis*. Spring Publications, Dallas.
Hillman, James (1975), *Re-Visioning Psychology*. Harper and Row, New York.
Hillman, James (1993), *We've had a Hundred Years of Psychotherapy and the World's Getting Worse*. Harper Collins, New York
Hillman, James (Ed.) (1979), *Puer Papers*. Spring Publications, Dallas.
Hoad, T.F. (1986), *The Concise Oxford Dictionary of Etymology*. Oxford University Press.
Hobson, Robert, F. (1985), *Forms of Feeling*. Tavistock Publications, London.
Hoppin, Richard H. (1978), *Medieval Music*. Norton and Company, New York.
Janzen, John M. in Gouk, Penelope (Ed.) (2000), *Musical Healing in Cultural Context*. Ashgate Publishing Company, Aldershot.
Jung, C.G. (1933), *Modern Man in Search of a Soul*. Trans. W.S. Dell and Cary F. Baynes, Routledge, London.
Jung, C.G. (1944/53), *Psychology and Alchemy*. CW Vol. 12, Trans. R. F. C. Hull, Routledge, London.
Jung, C.G. (1959), *The Archetypes of the Collective Unconscious*. CW Vol. 9 Part 1, Trans. R. F. C. Hull. Routledge, London.

Kandinsky, Wassily (1912), Concerning the Spritual in Art. In *Documents of Modern Art*, Volume 5 (1947) Wittenborn, New York.
Keller, Hans (1986), *Music, Closed Societies and Football*. Toccata Press, London.
Keller, Hans (2005), *Essays on Music*. Edited by C. Wintle and B. Northcott. Cambridge University Press, Cambridge.
Kenny, Caroline (1995), *Listening, Playing, Creating. Essays on the Power of Sound*. Suny Press, New York.
Khan, Hazrat Inayat (1921/1996), *Music*. Shambhala Publications, Boston and London.
Langer, Suzanne (1953), *Feeling and Form*. Routledge, London.
Langer, Suzanne. (1947), *Philosophy in a New Key*. Routledge, London.
Lechte, John (1994), *Fifty Key Contemporary Thinkers*. Routledge, London
Lewis, Penny (1993), *Creative Transformation*. Wilmette, Chiron Publications, Illinois.
Mellers, Wilfred (1968), *Caliban Reborn. Renewal in Twentieth-Century Music*. Victor Gollancz, London.
Moser, Pete and McKay George (Eds) (2005), *Community Music, A Handbook*. Russell House, Lyme Regis.
Nachmanovitch, Stephen (1990), *Free Play – Improvisation in Life and Art*. Penguin Books, J.P. Tarcher, Inc. New York.
Nachmanovitch, Stephen (2007), *The Discipline of Improvisation*. www.freeplay.com
Nietzsche, Friedrich (1871), *The Birth of Tragedy*. Trans. Ian C. Johnston (2000) Nanaimo.
Nordoff, P. And Robbins, C. (1977), *Creative Music Therapy*. John Day, New York.
Paton, R. (1996), *The Process of Renewal in Music*. D.Phil Thesis, Sussex University
Paton, R. (2000), *Living Music*. WSCC, Chichester, West Sussex.
Pavlicevic, M. (1995), Interpersonal Processes in Clinical Improvisation. In Wigram et. Al. (eds) *The Art and Science of Music Therapy: A Handbook*. Harwood Academic Publishers, Chur.
Pavlicevic, M. and Ansdell G. (2004), *Community Music Therapy*. Jessica Kingsley, London.
Payne, Anthony (1979), *Schoenberg*. Oxford University Press, Oxford.
Paynter, J and Aston, P. (1970), *Sound and Silence*. Cambridge University Press, Cambridge.

Paynter, J., Howell, T., Orton, R., Seymour, P. (Eds) (1992), *Companion to Contemporary Musical Thought*. Vol. II. Routledge, London.

Paynter, J., Mellers, W. and Swanwick, K. (Eds.) (1990), *Companion to Contemporary Musical Thought*. Vol. I. Routledge, London

Pinker, Steven (1997), *How the Mind Works*. Norton and Company, New York

Pirsig, Robert (1976), *Zen and the Art of Motorcycle Maintenance*. Corgi Books, London.

Pressing, Jeff (1988), Improvisation: Methods and Models in Sloboda, J. (Ed.) *Generative Processes in Music*. Oxford University Press, Oxford.

Prevost, Edwin (1995), *No Sound is Innocent*. Copula, Matching Tye.

Priestley, Mary (1994), *Essays on Analytical Music Therapy*. Barcelona Publishers, Phoenixville.

Proctor, S. (1999), *The Therapeutic Musical Relationship: A Two-sided Affair?* British Journal of Music Therapy 13:1

Ross, Malcolm (1978), *The Creative Arts*. Heinemann Educational, London.

Ross, Malcolm (1984), *The Aesthetic Impulse*. Pergamon Press, London.

Rowan, John (2001), *Ordinary Ecstasy*. Routledge, London.

Rudhyar, Dane (1982), *The Magic of Tone and the Art of Music*. Shambhala, Boulder.

Ruud, Even (1995), Improvisation in Kenny, Caroline Bereznak, *Listening, Playing, Creating – Essays in the Power of Sound*. Suny Press, New York.

Schopenhauer, Arthur (1818) *The World as Will and Representation*. Translated by E.F.J. Payne, Dover Publications, New York (1969).

Shepherd, John (1990), Music as Cultural Text. In *Companion to Contemporary Musical Thought*. Ed. Paynter, Mellers and Swanwick. Routledge, London.

Shepherd, John (1991), *Music as Social Text*. Cambridge University Press, Cambridge.

Skewes, K. (2002), *A Review of Current Practice in Group Music Therapy Improvisation*. British Journal of Music Therapy, Vol. 16.

Small, Chris (2004), *Musicking: The Meanings of Performing and Listening*. Wesleyan University Press, Hanover, New Hampshire.

Small, Christopher (1987), *Music of the Common Tongue*. John Calder, London

Sorensen, N (1988), *Understanding Improvisation*. Unpublished MA Dissertation. University of Sussex.

Sorrell, Neil (1992), Improvisation in Paynter, J., Howell, T., Orton, R., Seymour, P. *Companion to Contemporary Musical Thought*. Routledge, London.
Steiner, Rudolf (1983), *The Inner Nature of Music and the Experience of Tone*. Anthroposophic Press, New York.
Stern, Daniel (1985), *The Interpersonal World of the Infant*. Basic Books, New York.
Stevens, John (1987/2009), *Search and Reflect*. Rodk School, London.
Storr, Anthony (1992), *Music and the Mind*. Harper Collins, London.
Stravinsky, Igor and Craft, Robert (1981), *Memories and Commentaries*. University of California Press.
Swanwick, Keith, (1988), *Music, Mind, Imagination*. Oxford University Press, Oxford.
Tucker, Michael (1992), *Dreaming with Open Eyes, the Shamanic Spirit in Twentieth Century Art and Culture*. Harper Collins, London.
Tucker, Michael (1998), *Deep Song, the Music of Jan Garbarek*. Eastnote, Hull.
Turner, Victor (1977), *The Ritual Process*. Routledge, London.
Von Franz, Marie-Louise (1978), *Projection and Re-collection in Jungian Psychology, Reflections of the Soul*. Kreuz Verlag, Stuttgart.
Von Franz, Marie-Louise (1978), *Time - Rhythm and Repose*. Thames and Hudson. London.
Von Franz, Marie-Louise (1995), *Shadow and Evil in Fairy Tales*. Shambhala Books, London.
Von Rilke, Rainer Maria (1999), *The Selected Poetry of Rainer Maria von Rilke*. Translated by Stephen Mitchell, Picador.
Wigram, A. (2004), *Improvisation. Methods and Techniques for Music Therapists*. Jessica Kingsley, London.
Williams, Raymond (1976), *Keywords*. Fontana Books, London.
Winnicott, D.W. (1971), *Playing and Reality*. Tavistock Publications, London.
Witkin, Robert (1974), *The Intelligence of Feeling*. Heinemann Educational, London.
Zappa, Frank with Occhiogrosso, Peter (1989), *The Real Frank Zappa Book*, New York: Poseidon Press.

INDEX

Abba 46, 74
Achterberg, Jean 165
Adorno, Theodore 49, 50
Aebersold, Jamie 135, 175-177
Agrell, Jeffery 135
All Angels 57
Alvin, Juliet 131
Amador, Raimundo 103
AMM 130, 131, 174
Anderson, Cat 126
Angelo, Marie 15
Ansdell, Gerry 136, 138
Aphrodite 100
Apollo 30, 63, 71, 72-82, 107, 127, 156, 212, 219, 220, 228, 231, 236
Apollonian spirit 182
Ariadne 107
Ariel 180
Armstrong 125
Armstrong, Frankie 105
Armstrong, Thomas 72, 73
Asklepius 212
Associated Board 53, 123, 176
Aston, Peter 135, 173
Attali, Jacques 44, 45, 129
Ayler, Albert 267
B minor Mass 159
Bach 118, 34, 53, 66, 73, 74, 83, 84, 92, 96, 148, 172, 188, 239, 264
Back Door Man 128
Bailey, Derek 111, 135, 174
Bakhtin 202-203
Ballet Russes 41
Band, The 103
Barrett, Syd 71

Bartok 83, 128
BBC 43, 76
Beatles, The 46, 78, 87, 140, 178
Beauty and the Beast 99
Beecham, Thomas 192
Beethoven 34, 38, 48, 77, 81, 83, 84, 92, 93, 96, 157, 184, 265
Beethoven's 'Eroica' Symphony 116
Beethoven's Fifth 159
Beiderbecke, Bix 125
Bentley, Arnold 170
Berendt, Joachim 25, 65, 137, 167
Berg, Violin Concerto 104
Bergson, Henri 62, 86, 153
Berio 127
Berklee School of Music 55
Berlioz 63
Birth of Tragedy 63
Bitches' Brew 127
Bjork 103
Blacking, John 135
Blakey, Art 126
Blanning, Tim 51, 57, 58, 75
Blues 39, 40, 41, 42, 43, 51, 78, 128
Blues for Alice 129
Borodin 93
Boulez 178
Bowie, David 87
Brahms 75, 81, 93
Breuker, Willem 130
Britten 178
Brown, Clifford 126
Brubeck, Dave 126
Bruch, Max 104, 105
Bruscia, Kenneth 135

Burnard, Pamela 16
Burrow, Laurence 18
Cage 23, 24, 130, 178, 230, 234
Caliban 178-180, 182
Calliope 90
Cardew, Cornelius 130, 174
Carmen 92
Cartesian dualism 212
Cerberus 90
Chernoff, John Miller 40
Chopin 63, 81, 125, 184
Chuck Berry 46
Cinderella 99, 102
Clement, Catherine 92
Coker, Jerry 135
Cole, Bruce 16
Coleman, Ornette 89, 93, 127, 178
Coltrane, John 89, 93, 127, 181
Community Music London 175
Contemporary Music Review 14
Copland 128
Copper, Bob 88
Cox and Theilgaard 155, 156
Credence Clearwater Revival 87
Creole music 128
Crosby, Stills and Nash 87
Cupid 72, 76
D'Arezzo, Guido 121
D'Inverno, Ray 19
Darling, David 130
Darwin 92
Davie, Alan 179
Davis, Miles 89, 127, 116, 157, 182
Dean, Roger 135, 154
Deane, Kathryn 16
Debussy 93
Deep Purple 87
Delphi 73

Diana Ross 46
Die Schöne Müllerin 95
Dionysian freedom 182
Dionysian ritual 202
Dionysus 30, 39, 41, 63, 64, 71, 74, 82-89, 90, 95 127, 148, 156, 219, 269
Disneyland 164
Dixieland 128
Doherty, Pete 71
Dolphy, Eric 89, 127
Donnelly, Hugo 19
Durant, Alan 112, 135
Dury, Ian 71
Dvorak 93
Dylan, Bob 178
Einstein 26, 92
Eisenberg, Evan 129
El Sistema 210
Elgar 93
Elgar violin concerto 104
Ellington 125/6, 129
Elvis Presley 46
Eno, Brian 155, 200
Enya 103
Euripides 86
Eurydice 71, 90, 94, 98, 161
Evans, Bill 61, 81
Everett, Anthony 197
Feldman, Morton 130
Ficino 212
Finnegan, Ruth 172, 196
First Viennese School 38
Five Pieces for Orchestra Op. 16 38, 40, 82
Florentine Camerati 92
Franz Ferdinand 46
Frayn, Michael 39

Frederick the Great 51, 75
Freud 39, 92, 144, 159
Gall, Alison 18
Garbarek, Jan 47, 101
Gare, Lou 174
Gary Glitter 46
Gerhard, Roberto 38
Gershwin 55, 80, 93, 126
Gillespie, Dizzy 126
Gnosticism 186
Godwin, Joscelyn 91
Goofy the Dog 164
Gordon, Dexter 126
Grateful Dead 87, 181
Gregorian Chant 51
Grieg 81, 84
Gurrelieder 83
Hades 71, 90, 94, 96, 100
Hamel, Peter Michael 25, 167
Handy, W. C. 125
Harmony of the Spheres 25, 67, 92
Harris, Steve 18
Harvey, Jonathan 15, 77
Haydn 38, 58, 92
Hayley Mills 46
Heifetz 104
Hendrix, Jimi 87
Heraclitus 109
Hermes 73, 80, 106, 167, 184, 219, 231
Higgins, Lee 16
Hilliard Ensemble 47
Hillman, James 29, 34, 35, 113, 114, 160-162, 167, 180, 184
Hobo Blues 39
Hodges, Andrew 19
Holiday, Billy 103
Hooker, John Lee 39

Hoppin, Richard 121
Horsley, Imogene 121
Howlin' Wolf 128
I Will be Released 103
Icarus 97
Iggy Pop 46
Instant composers' Pool 130
Jagger, Mick 86
James, Jamie 92
Janet Jackson 46
Janzen, John 212
Jason 268
Jefferson Airplane 87
Jewitt, Clement 15
Johnson, Robert 39
Joplin, Janis 71, 87, 103
Joplin, Scott 125
Jung, C. G. 33, 37, 44, 62, 64, 106, 110, 144, 153, 163, 241
Jungian 147, 157
Jungian psychology 178
Jungians 97, 184
Kagel, Maurizio 93
Kairos 21, 33, 29, 34, 42, 59, 106, 183, 199
Kandinsky 37, 38, 40, 42, 116, 162
Kant 65
Kata Kabanova 92
Katy Perry 46
Keats 184
Keller, Hans 50, 54, 69, 141, 142, 144, 149, 151, 152, 157, 236
Kepler 22, 110
Khan, Nusrat Fateh Ali 121
Khan, Hazrat Inayat 167
Kind of Blue 116, 182
Klee, Paul 163
Kreisler 104

Kremer 104
Krishnamurti 118
Kronos 21, 22, 106, 183
Lacy, Steve 109
Lady Gaga 46
Langer, Suzanne 23, 62, 167
Lewis, John 126
Lewis, Penny 133, 137, 159, 167
Liszt 63, 81, 83, 122
Lloyd Webber, Andrew 74, 95
Luhrmann, Baz 94
Lulu 92
Maenads 84
Mahler 22, 85, 92
Mallarme 83
Marriage of Figaro 92
Mash, John 25
Mawdsley, Alison 19
Mayall, John 129
McGavin, Bruce 19
McKay, George 197-198
McNicol, Richard 16, 135, 211
Me and the Devil Blues 39
Mellers, Wilfred 178-179
Mendelssohn 125
Menhuin 104
Mghee, Brownie 129
Mike Oldfield 46
Milburn, Philip 19
Mingus, Charles 127
Miraculous Mandarin 83
Mitchell, Joni 87, 103
Mnemosyne 79
Monk, Thelonius 81
Morike 102, 103
Morisette, Alanis 103
Morris, Butch 130
Morton, Jelly Roll 125

Moser, Pete 16, 197
Motorhead 46
Mozart – Prague Symphony 159
Mozart 34, 38, 52, 53, 55, 81, 92, 110, 118, 188, 266
Mozart Requiem 205
Mullen, Phil 16, 211
Moulin Rouge 94
Music & Psyche 14, 15
Music and Mysticism 15
Music industry 14
Music Leader 16
Musical learning 36
Mussorgsky 93
Myth of Er 67
Nachmanovitch, Stephen 109 130, 133, 135, 187, 208
Namchylak, Sainkho 47
Napoleon 77
Nares, Susan 15
Natural Voice Practitioners' Network 105, 255
Newham, Paul 254
Nicholas, Julian 19
Nichols, Maggie 198
Nielson 93
Nietzsche 63, 64, 67, 86, 158
Nijinsky 83
Noddy Holder 46
Nono 93
Nordoff, Carl 131
North, Chris 19
Oliveros, Pauline 130
Orpheus 30, 71, 86, 89-99, 106, 161, 168, 184, 219, 228, 264, 268, 273
Orpheus, Cult of 212
Orphic myth 37
Orton, Richard 135, 154

Oxley, Tony 174
Paganini 122
Pandora's Box 99
Papert, Seymour 66
Parker, Charlie 126
Parker, Charlie 129
Parker, Evan 109, 110, 174
Parry 93
Pavlicevic, Mercedes 135
Payne, Anthony 38, 117
Paynter, John 135, 173, 175
Peggie, Andrew 36, 211
Pentangle 46
Perlmann 104
Perry, Frank 15
Persephone 90, 94, 100
Phoebus 84
Pierrot Lunaire 38, 82, 93
Pinker, Stephen 197-198
Pinetop Smith 267
Pink Floyd 71, 87
Pirsig, Robert 153, 172, 178
Plato 65, 66, 67, 80, 91, 212
Platonic philosophy 52
Platonic theory 68
Powell, Dora 104
Prélude a L'Après Midi d'un Faune 83
Presley, Elvis 86
Pressing, Jeff 135, 144
Prevost, Eddie 124, 135, 174, 198
Priestley, Mary 131, 136
Proctor, Simon 139
Prometheus 78
Prospero 178
Psyche 30, 71, 99-107, 128, 161, 168, 184, 219, 228, 239, 240
Puer 34

Purcell 71, 72
Pythagoras 25, 65-67, 91, 166
Pythagorean tradition 212
Pythagoreans 67
Queen 46
Radio Caroline 43
Radio Luxembourg 43
Ravel 93
Regelski, Thomas 135
Reich, Steve 110, 127
Reynolds, Nick 18
Rilke 184
Rippon, Nigel 18
Rite of Spring 39, 40, 41, 83, 181
Robbins, Clive 131
Robertson, Paul 15
Robinson, Ken 222
Roditi, Jenny 15
Rolling Stones 46, 69, 86
Rollins, Sonny 126
Ross, Edmundo 185
Ross, Malcolm 162
Rossini 266
Rowan, John 140
Rowe, Keith 130, 174
Rudhyar, Dane 157, 167
Ruud, Even 136, 165, 167, 183
Sanders, Pharoah 89, 127
Santana 46
Saunders, John 19
Sax Appeal 57
Schenker, Heinrich 141
Schmidt, Peter 155
Schoenberg 24, 41, 117 37, 38, 41, 43, 82, 83, 84, 92, 93, 143
Schopenhauer 61, 62, 65, 86, 110, 144
Schubert 95, 125

Schumann 81, 122
Search and Reflect 175, 176
Senex 34
Shakespeare 44, 80, 107, 126, 178
Shankar, Ravi 87
Shepherd, John 181
Shrubb, Suzie 18
Sibelius 93
Sissay, Lemn 198
Skvorecky, Josef 112
Sleeping Beauty 99
Sloboda, John 46, 53, 135
Small, Chris 16, 29, 123-4, 111, 135, 174-175
Smetana 93
Smith, Bessie 129
So Broken 103
Sorensen, Nicholas 19, 115
Sorrell, Neil 113-4
Sound Sense 16
Sound Travels 19
Spector, Nancy 38
Spontaneous Music Ensemble 130
St. Augustine 21
Stardust, Ziggy 87
Steer, Maxwell 14, 77
Steiner, Rudolf 158
Stern, Daniel 136, 182
Stevens, John 16, 130, 135, 174-175, 198, 130
Stimmung 130
Stockhausen 93, 130, 178
Storr, Anthony 153
Strauss family 41
Stravinsky 22, 26, 39, 40, 41, 43, 82-84, 87, 128, 178, 181
Strayhorn, Billy 126
Such Sweet Thunder 126

Sun Ra 89
Swanwick, Keith 118
Talking Heads 46
Tavener, John 15
Tchaikovsky 81
Terry, Sonny 129
The Band 87
The Real Book 55, 56
The Republic 67
The Tempest 178
The Who 87
Theseus 107
Thomas, Dylan 61
Tilbury, John 174
Tippett 93, 128
Tosca 92
Transblucency 129
Transfigured Night 93
Trevarthen 136
Tucker, Michael 15, 47, 77
Turner prize 34
Turner, Victor 163-165, 167, 183
U2 46
Ulysses 268
University of Chichester 15, 18
Usher, Julia 154
Vanyskova, Jitka 20
Varese, Edgard 22
Vella, Richard 135
Verney-Caird, Sarah 15
Von Franz, Marie-Louise 21, 33, 61, 110
Wachsmann, Phil 174
Wagner 63
Wagner's Ring 122
Walton 93
Watts, Trevor 198
Wellins, Bobby 115

Wiegold, Peter 15
Wigram, Tony 135
Williams, Cootie 126
Williams, John 93
Williams, Raymond 199
Winehouse, Amy 71
Winnicott, Donald 159, 163, 167
Witkin, Robert 139, 151, 167
Wizzard 46
Wolf, Hugo 102
Wolff, Christian 130
Wolfsohn, Alfred 254
World Music 46, 47
Wozzeck 92
Wright, Richard 34
Wright, Ronald 124
Xiu Xiu 46
Yardbirds 46
Ylem 130
Youth Music 16
Zappa, Frank 22, 26, 46, 54, 61
Zeus 71, 73, 100
Zwerin, Mike 128